To Krist—

Warm regards,

Sid

14 Juillet 2022

Learning to Dance with French

A Memoir

Sidney J.P. Hollister

Learning to Dance with French -- A Memoir

Copyright © 2022 Sidney J.P. Hollister

ISBN: 9798414209911

menfiche746@gmail.com

"Slumbering in every human being lies an infinity of possibilities, which one must not arouse in vain. For it is terrible when the whole man resonates with echoes and echoes, none becoming a real voice."
— Elias Canetti, *Notes from Hampstead*

"There's no education like discovering who you are, whatever you are."
— Janet Flanner

Remembrance

To my parents, who did their best with what they had been given.

Contents

Prologue

London, a World without Birkenstocks

In the Autumn of 1973, I was living in Berkeley, California, in a simple three-room rented apartment. It was in a four-unit building with a vegetable garden in back and had been my home for several years. I lived modestly and had a good inexpensive car and work I liked. I even had a girlfriend, though our relationship at that point was iffy. Most importantly, for the first time in my life I had saved enough money either to buy a house or take the trip to France I had been dreaming about for a long time. Both choices meant confronting bedeviling anxieties. If I bought a house, I would be assuming a public identity appropriate to the sensible adult my father kept hoping I would become someday. For those who shared his point of view, taking a trip to France was running away from the socially approved role of getting married and having a family, in other words, some would say, from growing up. For me, an adventurous trip to France was a different version of growing up. It was a continuation of my flight from Connecticut to San Francisco more than ten years earlier, even though that move had not helped me shed my indecisiveness and an undermining sense of not being as fully adult as other men my age seemed to be. Going to France would do the trick, I hoped, but on my terms. I was 37, so I knew that whichever choice I made was sure to change my life, the thought of which had me shaking in my velour bell-bottoms.

I had grown up near Hartford, Connecticut, a world dominated by big insurance companies, a world where a man in a Speedo bathing suit at a beach on Long Island Sound brought tut-tutting people to their lace-curtained windows. In that security-conscious and socially conservative world, you did not take risks unless first getting an actuary to vet your decision. Life, however, has a way of sending us signals that disregard actuarial calculations. I was getting some of those signals. My enjoyable job as a book editor, which gave me some potential work connections in Paris, came to an end just as the woman in my life tired of my dilly-

dallying about commitment and went on a spiritual quest.   She was
enthralled, so far as I could find out, by one of the flimflamming gurus as
common then in Berkeley as asinine window-breaking demonstrators
against the "establishment," which inexplicably included small
shopkeepers.   Also, the disastrous and murderously violent 1969 Rolling
Stones concert in Altamont's sun-blasted hills south of Berkeley, signaled
that a major change had occurred in the laid-back world I knew: hard
drugs had become prevalent and more crime had come along with them.
By 1974, I was not sure I wanted to stay--married or not--in the town that
had been my home for twelve years, which further complicated matters.

Deciding why I liked a movie (I had just received my MA in
cinema), what kind of bread to bake (I am a good cook), what kind of glaze
to use on one of my hand-built pots, (I was invited to join the ceramic staff
of the UC Berkeley Student Union) or what was wrong with a manuscript
I was editing (my profession)--no problem.   Marriage or France?   Big
problem.   If I chose France, in addition to passing up a chance to buy my
first house--whether in Berkeley or elsewhere--I would be putting an end
to my relationship with a woman who wanted to get married and have a
family, which most men I knew had done by my age.   I decided to go to
France.

Much to my surprise, my father finally accepted that I was not
going to change my mind about the trip and wrote that maybe it would be
good for me.   For once, he did not say, "Be careful."   His letter was a
pleasant surprise, but it was too late to offset the years of overprotection
that had given deep roots to my fear of the unfamiliar. The woman who
wanted to marry me, had mocked me for it the first time we took a
backpacking trip.   Other women had added their scornful voices to the
chorus, and a few men as well, for one reason or another.   Accepting their
judgements, I never knew how to respond. I had all kinds of therapy: the
lie-on-the-couch Freudian analysis thing, the group hug thing, the
bioenergetic naked-on-the-bed thing, and the Primal Scream thrashing-
around-on-the-floor thing, but I could not get a handle on that fear, that
lack of confidence that I could deal with life.   Those feelings were a
festering source of confused shame that usually transformed into torture
when I had to make decisions about my life, decisions that men of few
words, strong jaws, and no love handles seemed to make with galling ease.
I, too, wanted to be quick with a riposte, to stop hiding my aggressive
feelings--especially my sexual feelings--and to go after what I wanted
with confidence, whether I succeeded or not.   No more guilt over deciding

which women I simply wanted to enjoy in bed — a mutual pleasure I hoped — and which ones might offer more than that, whatever that meant. Most of all, I wanted to stop being nice, especially with women. I wanted not to give a damn, as Clark Gable famously said in *Gone with the Wind*. My trip to France would be the start of casting off that diffident self, of becoming forceful and self-assured. And not "nice." *Quel naïf!*

When I bought my airline ticket––open-ended to escape my decision at any time––my Berkeley friends cheered. "You can always buy a house when you get back," one said. "You'll meet a rich, sexy French woman and bring her back to California," another said. Still others who had lived in France added: "You speak French like a Parisian. Well, maybe like a Belgian." I believed them all.

My nasal New England accent helped me get a handle on the differences between "*en, an, un,*" and "*on.*" To master them, along with the twenty or so other French sounds not found in English––e.g., *caille, fauteuil, seuil*––meant hours of practicing in front of a mirror until my facial muscles ached. My friends' encouragement bolstered my confidence. Nonetheless, after I bought my ticket I continued to second-guess myself, even looking at a few houses with a realtor. Zigzagging between being "sensible" and going on an adventure made me feel crazy at times. Some nights, I would wake up shouting "A Belgian?"

What finally got me on that plane was a determination to defy my stomach-clenching fear. I felt like a thirteen-year-old making a head-down, eyes-closed charge at a bully. The trip would start off right if fate gave me a beautiful French woman as a seatmate, a Mademoiselle returning to Paris after studying film at Berkeley and free of any Freudian, Jungian or Primal Screaming baggage. Alas, when an avuncular, white-haired gentleman indicated that he had the window seat next to me, it was obvious even to this fallen-away Catholic that divine intervention was at work. My smiling neighbor turned out to be a talkative Irish-American priest. After an hour or so in the air, we each bought a glass of wine and started to chat. I told the good father that after a few days in London, I planned to go either to Ireland, where my mother's father had been born, or to France, and maybe even to Lapland. "Marvelous!" he said. "You won't find a friendlier people than the Irish. I have relatives there, too. They're a lovely people, just lovely. And it's a grand country, though you won't see much sun there," he said. "I don't know that you'll see much sun in Lapland, either. But France! Well now, stay there as long as you can." He had a sip of wine. "It's a wonderful place. Just marvelous! The

French, you see, know how to live, how to enjoy life." Then, smiling, he said, "But you'll discover that for yourself. That's part of the adventure." Raising his glass to me, he said, "To France!" "To France!" I said, touching my glass to his. Then he added, "Once you've been to France, you won't be able to stay away. You'll go back over and over. Every time, it gets better." The padre's words––and the wine––took the edge off my anxiety. We had our dinner as we flew deeper into the night, then I followed the good father's example and fell asleep.

❆

Stepping off the train from Heathrow into the morning rush hour at London's Victoria Station snapped me out of my jet-lagged stupor. Like New York's Grand Central Station, the station's enormous main hall was filled with people rushing in tidal surges toward the many exits as trains pulled into and left the station and loudspeakers made the usual incomprehensible announcements. Dark-suited men with briefcases were much like their American counterparts, though their jackets were double-breasted and their pants flared into conservatively cut bell-bottoms. The women, though, were a different matter. A stunning redhead would draw my eye, then a blonde, then a brunette, all of them seeming not so much to walk as to prance, their suits stylishly form fitting, their hair bobbed, swirled, or free, heels alarmingly high, skirts deliciously short. Not a pair of Birkenstocks in sight.

With my bright orange backpack, which doubled my girth, I side-stepped through the flow of commuters until an eddy allowed me to move out of the swirling stream and park myself next to a newsstand. Then, as a properly agog tourist, I looked up at the station's glass and steel-framed roof marveling at the morning sunlight that dramatically slanted into its vast space. Hearing "Love," "Gov'ner," and "Sorry" all around me made it clear that though I was not yet in France I certainly was no longer in California.

I managed to use the tube, the city's underground system, to find Tottenham Square and located my small bed-and-breakfast hotel in a block-long row of identical buildings that formed a tidy white wall along one side of a square, in the center of which was a fenced garden. The garden gate was always locked, I was told when I checked in, as were many similar city gardens. Owned by landed gentry who usually did not live in London, these patches of green were open only to their gardeners and to the public on special holidays. After paying for a week's stay, I was taken to my room, which, since March is not peak tourist season, was large enough to accommodate several steel-framed beds, all with eight-inch-thick mattresses that sagged down to the tan linoleum floor like hammocks. I sloughed off my backpack, wrapped myself in a couple of sheet-thin gray blankets, and nestled into the embrace of one of the swayback beds. My aching back woke me up in late afternoon.

To work out the kinks, physical and emotional, I walked around the neighborhood looking for a recognizably "English" restaurant where I could eat dinner. I found mostly Pakistani, Indian, and Italian ones, but there was a French bistrot on a side street off my square so I decided to get a head start on my trip across the Channel. A fine meal of Dover sole ended with a small trifle, that wonderful English concoction of pound cake marinated in port, covered with fresh fruit, and topped off by double cream as thick and rich as ice cream. It was still early, so I walked to nearby Trafalgar Square where the raucous fans of some team or other, all wearing red and white scarves and watch caps, were celebrating what seemed to be an important victory (the Welsh rugby team, whose colors are red and white, had vanquished the English, I later found out), climbing light poles, dancing with anyone who would accept a joyous and tipsy invitation, and invariably saying "Sorry" if they jostled me, no matter their state of inebriation. Remarkable! A couple of beers in a pub and I was back at my B&B where I dragged my mattress onto the floor and crawled into my sleeping bag, blissfully out of this world until wakened by the sun streaming in my windows early the next morning.

*

All I can remember now from my first days in London is that I felt acute anxiety, like a novice swimmer suddenly finding himself in water so deep that his wildly churning legs cannot touch bottom. Some of that, of course, came from jet lag, but the city's sprawling size overwhelmed me, the other-side-of-the-road business kept me off balance, and the tube, especially the stations several stories down (used as bomb shelters in World War II) gave me claustrophobia. My friends in Berkeley said stopping in England would clear my head and make my entry into France somewhat easier. What in fact it did do was trigger my second-guessing habit of wondering why I had taken this trip at all. Not knowing what could happen next is one reason people travel, but I kept feeling that I should know what to do and where to go, unable to trust my instincts and let the city itself reveal itself to me: not unlike getting to know a woman.

Growing up I had heard nothing but that worried, "Be careful" whenever I left the house, never "Have a good time!" Those nettlesome send-offs, even when I was just going to a local movie theater, undoubtedly gave birth to my extraordinary ability to convert even the slightest pleasurable excitement into anxiety. They also contributed to my eagerness to get as far away as I could from Connecticut. In the Autumn of 1959, I moved to San Francisco, home to Beatniks and other serious writers, though as a prep school and Yale graduate, I knew nothing about them. In fact, I knew nothing about San Francisco, except what a neighbor told me of its European character and remarkable light. France is where I wanted to go, I told him one evening as we walked along our tree-lined street, but I had little money. I had a car, however, so when this well-traveled neighbor said: "Go to San Francisco. It's as close to Europe as you can get in this country," I set my course west. It was a decision not enthusiastically received by my parents--my father, in fact, never spoke to that neighbor again.

My parents had rarely ventured outside of Connecticut and, having lived through the Depression, believed first and foremost in security and stability. At my father's urging, I tried law school, but dropped out after a few months. There was always the insurance business, my father then said, right in Hartford. Also, banking and Wall Street opportunities in New York were surely plentiful for a Yale graduate like me and it was only a hundred miles away. He even enlisted a few of his friends to help me realize the error of my West Coast yearning ways. I was unconvinced. Wanting to work with words, I had applied to several publishing houses in New York as I fulfilled my six-month National Guard obligation at Ft. Dix, New Jersey. I might have been offered a job had I done my homework for the interviews. In truth, though, my heart was not in that either. My goal was to get away from the rigidly ethnocentric world of the East Coast--the world of WASPS (White Anglo-Saxon Protestants), and "those other people": Wops (Italians), Hunkies (Slavic Europeans), Polacks (Poles), Canucks (French-Canadians), Kikes (Jews), and Harps (Irish).

In that socially conservative world, knowing someone's ethnic background, religion, and where they went to college was, and still is, critical. Only then can people put you in your proper place--and keep you there. My name challenged such pigeonholing. Though not to the

WASP-manner born, as a preppy and an Ivy Leaguer I learned how to act the part. Moreover, I carried an English name (my father's father came from Ontario, Canada). On the other hand, with the first name of Sidney, I could be Jewish. *Oy vey!* What kind of jokes could be told in front of me? That I was Catholic and primarily of Irish ancestry (my other grandfather came from Cork; both grandmothers were first-generation Irish Americans), came as a surprise to many––to the Ryans and O'Briens as well as to the Griswolds and Smithsons. This confusion allowed me a measure of social flexibility, but it also made me an outsider. I did not quite belong to any group. San Francisco was attractive to many people like me.

Ironically, the street my family moved to from Hartford when I was six did not quite belong to West Hartford either. The town was one of the country's wealthiest during my life there, with covenants or "gentlemen's agreements" more or less separating the Anglo-Saxon insurance executives from the Jews and Catholics and other unacceptable types, many of whom filled the lower-level jobs in the companies those executives ran. It was no surprise, then, that I did not often hear the words Polak, Harp, Wop, Dago, Hunky, or Kike — disparaging references to the rich mix of people who lived more or less together in Hartford's heavily ethnic south end, nor see at the grocery store women in babushkas and sturdy boots. Nonetheless, my unique street still offered me a rich mix of of ethnic personalities with several Italian-American families, Connecticut Yankees, a Jewish dentist, Sicilians who could not speak English and filled their yard with fruit trees, and, most importantly for this tale, two French-Canadian families who, except for the fathers, also could not speak English. From the age of six, as a result, I heard French, or at least the twangy Québécois version. Even then, I liked the way it sounded, especially when I heard it spoken by a young black-haired priest who gave a dramatic sermon at the Québécois church where we went with our neighbors once for Sunday mass. I did not understand a single word, but I was spellbound by the rhythmic music of his French and the dramatic gestures he used in speaking it, a far cry from the soporific sermons I heard most Sundays.

In prep school, I slogged through three years of French with generally uninspired teachers––except for a single one-hour class when my regular teacher was unexpectedly taken ill and the head of the school's French department took his place. French-born, with a high forehead and curly blonde hair, Joseph Savoie Stookins was over six feet tall, ramrod straight, and famous at the school for his biting sarcasm and brilliance as a teacher. What he exposed me to that one hour I had never experienced before: a teacher with a passion for what he taught––in this case the beauty, subtlety, and strength of French. Unlike my other French teachers, who rarely got up from their desks, he never sat down. Instead, he strode back and forth in front of the class, throwing a correct pronunciation at this student, a demanding question at another. By the end of class, the blackboard was covered with French idioms. I never had Joe Stookins as a teacher again, but I have never forgotten how he gave life to what he loved, to how it transformed him, and, most importantly for this book, to how knowing French could open an entirely new world to me.

✷

In spite of my feelings of disorientation, London introduced me to European life.   At my first B&B breakfast of bangers and eggs, cold toast and really, really black tea, I shared a table with a man from Northern Ireland who came to London to escape the harassing searches, horrific bombings, and murderous sectarian brutality in his hometown of Derry. Four years of violence had turned him against both sides, but especially against the English. Sadly, he could see no end to it. There had been political upheaval and demonstrations in Berkeley, where I lived, and elsewhere in the States, but nothing came close to the violence and hatred this man had experienced.

After a day or two aimlessly wandering about London, and still anxious, I telephoned Frank, an old friend from the Bay Area, hoping that he was still there. Luckily, he was. When he heard I was headed to France, he quickly offered me a chance to meet a *"très belle cousine"* of his French girlfriend, Mélanie. "Come on over for an Indian dinner," he said, "and you can *parlez français* with Solange." The Indian food part worked out just fine; the "parlezing" *français* not so well. *La belle* Solange spoke almost no English, so Frank thought I could practice my French by taking a walk with her in a nearby park while he and Mélanie went to buy Indian take-out. What Frank had not noticed, however, was that from the moment the lovely red-haired Solange laid her green eyes on me, I could feel from her a sharp hostility that needed no translation. As was my habit, I took her chilly reaction as a challenge, saying to myself––in English–– "I will use my French and my charm to win her over." But even if I had spoken a French as smooth as a *crème brulée*, it would not have mattered. Solange had made up her mind about me *à première vue,* on first sight, and that was that. On our walk, she made an obligatory effort to start a conversation, making me instantly aware that my friends in Berkeley had overdone their praise of my French. By a long shot. I could *répétez* anything said by a recorded *Madame* or *Monsieur,* but those vinyl French people were not standing in front of me waiting for an answer to their questions. Solange was. Solange repeated. Solange spoke more slowly. Solange got bored to death. I could not pull a single word out of her swift-flowing stream of sensuous French, responding to every one of her questions with the same silly smile of total incomprehension. After a few strained minutes, to Solange's relief and mine, we headed back to Frank and Mélanie's, my spirits as sodden as a Cornish pasty on a pub steam table. How would I manage in Paris?

At the end of my first week in London, Arnaud, a French friend of Mélanie's came from Paris on business and at dinner one night with Frank and the French demoiselles, invited me to share his Paris apartment for as long as I needed it. The place belonged to a cousin who was working in Cuba for a couple of years and there was a couch in the living room where I was welcome to camp out. I would have to speak French, Arnaud said, as he spoke almost no English. We could trade language lessons, I said. Maybe, he said, in a French that was almost as incomprehensible to me as Solange's. I accepted his generous offer for lodging and wrote down directions on how to reach his place in the northern part of Paris. Things were looking up.

❄

I spent another week or so in London, going to museums, wandering through the parks, slowly adjusting to a world that was not full of long-haired men, braless women, and daily demonstrations. Knowing I was not happy with my B & B, Frank told me of a friend who spent most of the time in the country but kept a house in London with several extra bedrooms that he rented out to people he knew. One had just been vacated and it was mine if I wanted it. I accepted. My only expenses would be to share food and heating costs with the other two people who lived there, a German banker in his thirties who was almost never there and a young woman who worked as manager of a bookstore and was interested in art. Frank's friend said they were easy to get along with. Geographically, it was not far from Tottenham Court and my B&B, but it was on another planet as far as my bed was concerned. No more sleeping on the floor. Instead, I had a double bed with a horsehair mattress, a thoroughbred compared to the swaybacks of the B&B. I moved into the vacant second floor bedroom on a Friday.

When I entered the kitchen on Saturday morning, I met the young woman who worked at the bookstore. As she was making herself a morning coffee, we introduced ourselves and she asked if I also wanted one. Almost my six-foot height, with the broad shoulders of a swimmer, and a strong almost Scandinavian face, she had thick swirling light blonde hair that kept her busy trying to put it where it had not stayed since she was fourteen and realized trying to keep it in place drew male attention. She was wearing bib overalls over a white cotton jersey whose dark blue horizontal stripes, like ocean swells, rose and fell over full breasts not even overalls could hide.

"Charlie?" I said as I joined her at the small table. "That's an unusual name for a woman."

"Like Sidney for a man," she said with a smile and a voice full and mellow. "My father wanted a son, and when I came along he just kept the male name, Charlie, that he had already picked. How about Sidney? That's often a girl's name, at least in England."

"It's my father's name, though after my older brother was born, my mother wanted a girl so maybe that figured in the naming decision. "

My name has created a few problems for me," Charlie said, "and given a surprise to some people when they met me. You must have had a few mix-ups with Sidney?"

"Sometimes. Almost everyone spells it with a y instead of an i and people who speak French or Italian can't get saying 'ney' like knee, so they just call me 'Seed.' Did your parents ever have that boy your dad wanted?"

"They did. His name is the unmistakably male Derek. How about you?"

"Nope, just me and that older brother, but my mother never stopped wanting a daughter."

After we talked a bit more about the house and the neighborhood around it, she said she had to go but enjoyed meeting me and hoped to see me soon. I asked her if she wanted to take in a Sunday night movie and some Indian food, maybe at a place she liked nearby. She would and she did.

Sunday night we walked to a nearby theater to see an early show of

"Performance" with Mick Jagger.   Wildly violent, sensual, and unpredictable, the film gave us lots to talk about over another of those delicious Indian or Pakistani meals you could find all over London. Later, in front of her bedroom door, she asked me to go with her to an art gallery opening on Wednesday night. It would be early, right after she got off work at the bookstore she helped manage.   I said I would be delighted, though that word did not express the full range of my feelings.

"Sweet dreams," she said, smiling, as she oh so slowly closed her door.

"The same to you," I said, and walked to my room at the end of the hall just a few yards away. Within moments, embraced by the yielding horsehair mattress, I slipped into fantasies about Wednesday night.

My days were full of visits to the Tate Gallery and the British Museum, strolls along the Thames, and walks through some of London's many parks, their trees now in full leaf, their lawns lushly green. Several times, I rented a lawn chair the parks make available for a dollar, and took an afternoon nap in the warmth of the Spring sun. I still felt lost and wanted a connection to something, to someone. I felt the people around me belonged to a different world, which, of course, they did. A street game of Three-Card Monte was part of it, so I stopped to watch one for a while, attracted by the rapid-fire spiel of the dealer and the small crowd around him.

I'll just watch for a few minutes, I said to myself, and I did, until the man next to me, dressed in a fancy gray wool topcoat with a black velour collar and a dandy suit, leaned toward me and said, in a conspiratorial tone:

"This is not hard to figure out, gov'ner. I don't know how that guy makes a quid.   Right then, you see the card?"

"Not really," I said.

"Get closer," he said, "so you can put your money down quick before he does the switch," and we moved up.   The cards flew like darting swallows.

"See. You can pick up a tenner like that. It's that one there," he said.

I believed him––more or less––and dropped my ten pounds on the card I chose. The dealer flipped the cards to reveal that, friendly advice or no, I had picked the wrong one and my note went into his pocket with half a dozen others.

"Next time," my friendly counselor said, as a sharp whistle pierced the air. In one swift move, the dealer tucked the cards into his pocket, leapt to his feet, kicked aside the cardboard box on which he had been doing his shuffling skullduggery, and walked off briskly but without a hint of telltale panic. He was joined by several colleagues, one of them, to my surprise, was my dapper, top-coated advisor. I'd been had, but it was worth the tenner.

Frank had told me not to miss Covent Garden. Like the historic Les Halles in Paris, which had already closed and moved to the Parisian suburbs, it was scheduled to close later that year and would be moved out of central London. The City's principal fruit and vegetable market, the Garden was a raucous and colorful place, the pubs and restaurants surrounding it catering to buyers, sellers, and others whose work ended during the early morning hours. To get there when it was open meant catching the first tube at five a.m., as the market closed by 7. So I took Charlie's advice and had a late dinner at one of London's best restaurants in a hotel in Mayfair the night before my Garden visit. She assured me that if there were such a thing as fine English food, I would find it in one of Mayfair's hotels.

She was wrong, except for one spectacular dish. After dinner, I walked back to my new shared home near Russell Square, cutting through a deserted Soho. Not a wise decision, I was bluntly told. My informant was a man who, having ended work in one of the seedy area's dives, walked his bicycle to block my path and, calling me "gov'ner," said to get the hell out of there. I could be robbed or worse in that neighborhood at that time of the morning. Once home, I knew that if I went to sleep I would never wake up in time for that 5 a.m train. I forced myself to stay awake by doing pushups and walking up and down the hallway as quietly as I could. I got to the tube station a bit early. The only other person on the platform was a younger black-haired man who was wearing a beautiful, white woolen sweater. We smiled at each other and said good morning.

"That's a beautiful sweater," I said.

"Thanks," he said, telling me by his brogue that he was Irish. "You can only get good ones like this at home," he said. "Knit by hand. You American?"

"I am," I said. "My mother's father was born in Cork." He told me he was from a small town near that port city and that I should go there and ask anyone where Mrs. Browne lived.

"She's my mum," he said. "Her house is on the main street, you know, so she's easy to find. Everyone knows her. Tell her you met me and she'll put you up for sure––bed and food and all. She's a sweetheart."

When I asked him how he liked working in London, his face changed like a sunny hillside darkened by a passing cloud.

"I can't stand the lot of 'em," he said. "There isn't one who'll be straight with you, the bastards. They smile and say one thing, and when you turn your back, they put a knife in it. I'd go home in a minute if I could find work there."

His anger, brought to an instant boil, reminded me of how my otherwise quiet grandfather would get so worked up if someone started talking about the English, that he would take the ever-present pipe out of his mouth so he could curse them with appropriate vigor. With the kind of irony that seems to be universal, both his daughters, of course, married men of English ancestry.

"Go to Ireland," the son of Mrs. Browne said. "It's a different world from this place. You'll have a great time." Though I had planned to make Ireland a part of this trip, I have such bad feelings about my parochial school experience and the sexually repressed, narrow-minded Irish-American world I grew up in that a visit to Ireland was no longer high on my list. Even now, though, whenever I read about how the English brutalized the Irish for centuries, I feel an instant boil of anger against them
––my grandfather's wrath rising from the grave.

After a short ride on the tube, I climbed from the nearly empty station into the middle of Covent Garden's commercial commotion, a world of deep shadows and the bright lights from streetlamps and the bare-bulb sellers' sheds. Buyers in y tailored suits dickered with sellers in thick sweaters and aprons, jokes and wise cracks peppering their chatter. Around them, men in woolen caps pushed and pulled in and out of the shadows carts loaded with carrots, potatoes, cauliflower and other spring vegetables, hurling curses and jibes at each other in an incomprehensible Cockney. I ducked into a noisy, high-ceilinged pub packed to the smoke-filled rafters with buyers and sellers and cart men and, making for an odd combination, a dozen or so tuxedoed croupiers from the Playboy Club and Mayfair's other casinos. Waitresses hipped and shouldered through the crowd to deliver pints, hot toddies, and black tea drawn from shining 10-foot-high vats. The croupiers came for breakfast and to play snookers after the casinos closed at 6 a.m., as Covent Garden was the only place in London you could eat and drink that early in the morning.

On Wednesday evening, I was eager to see Charlie and tell her of my encounters with the crooked gamblers and the angry Irishman. Mostly I was eager to see as much of her as I could.

I met her at the art gallery, but have no recollection whatever of the art I was supposed to appreciate there. I do remember, however, the superbly created Charlie, whose every sensuous curve was brought to my attention by a short flared jacket over a conservative maroon dress that exposed a generous bit of her lovely neck and reached midway down her strong thighs. In the Indian restaurant near our flat where we had dinner, I told her of being fleeced by the Three-Card Monte gang––"Just like every tourist," she laughed––and of my trip to the fancy English restaurant in a Mayfair hotel, where I had been the only diner in the deeply carpeted and brightly chandeliered dining room. A regiment of servers, male and female, all in formal black and white attire, tended to my needs: one seated me, another took my order, another shook open my napkin, another brought my water, another took my wine order, another brought the wine, yet another brought my salad.

"There were so many of them, I had to laugh," I said. "But I was the only person there and they had to do something."

"What about the dinner?" Charlie asked.

"I had roast beef," I said, "but I only remember the trifle."

Almost fifty years later, I can still see that layered creation of sherry-soaked pound cake, topped with fresh fruit and double cream and served in a large crystal goblet, brought to my table by two waitresses, one carrying the goblet as if it were a kingly crown, the other a dessert spoon and napkin. I ate it as slowly as possible, savoring each luscious bite, the cream as thick and rich as ice cream. While I was describing my adventures, Charlie's silvery pendant earrings and silver loop necklace did their job of drawing my attention to her ears and unruly hair, to the curve of her neck, to her flawless skin, and, finally to that tantalizing down-slope to her full breasts, which moved slightly every time she laughed or took a swallow of beer.

A decisive moment had arrived, though not the kind the photographer Cartier-Bresson had in mind. My excitement, like the feeling I had boarding the plane in San Francisco, did its usual backflip into anxiety. On the one hand, I felt like leaping across the Chicken Tikka Masala onto Charlie's lovely bones; on the other, I struggled with anxiety whenever I felt such excitement about a woman. The surge of lust made me feel powerfully alive but also stirred deep apprehensions: How would Charlie feel about my randy self? If I let my energy lead me, I knew it would pull me through, one way or the other. It did, but not exactly the way I expected.

❄

My father was convinced that he had inadequate sexual organs and passed that notion on to my brother and me by uttering at critical moments--as we were about to go on a date, for example: "You will be very lucky to find a woman who will have you." He never went into detail, but we understood what he meant. Insecure fathers often find devious--and conflicted--ways to undermine sons they feel might surpass them, even as they encourage them to do exactly that, and my father certainly had found a good technique, unconscious as it probably was. The social context of these encouraging remarks was the 1950s and early 60s in Connecticut, when it was illegal to sell contraceptives of any kind, *Playboy* was sold in a brown paper wrapper, and women were not supposed to be lustful. It did not help that I went to an all-male prep school and university. Most of my college classmates, not surprisingly, married women they met at the all-female colleges of the Northeast soon after they graduated. Until my senior year at Yale, all I knew about my own sexuality was that it was "sinful," which basically meant that I should either repress it or pretend it did not exist. Women were distant, almost sacred, creatures whose bodies I idolized but knew absolutely nothing about. That they might have wanted me sexually as much as I wanted them was to me impossible. They certainly could not have had the conflicts about their bodies that I had. So when jokes about dating a woman named "Hymen Clitoris" were told by my college roommates, I laughed right along with the guys as if I knew what was funny. I probably was not the only one. I also did not have any sisters, or close female cousins, or even close female neighbors I might get to know as people, and I had no close male friends who were willing to admit they were as ignorant as I was. Though my college senior year girlfriend seemed more than willing to teach me what she knew--and she acted, at least, as though she knew plenty--a fear of both my own sexuality and an unwanted pregnancy made me a lousy student.

Satisfying the needs and pleasures of the body were unknown to me. Of my entire family, I can remember only my dad's sister, Bea, giving me

warm and loving hugs. Neither my mother nor father were
comfortable showing physical affection, not even, so far as I can
remember, to my brother and I when we were small. I later realized that
they had never received such affection themselves so had little to give,
needing it as much as my brother and I did.

To fill this need, no doubt, my mother persisted in taking naps with
me until I was 13, when my father finally put a stop to it--way too late.
By then, even I had begun to feel weird about them. I knew instinctively
that I could only stay on that couch if I were not sexual, that is, did not get
erections, but, of course, I got them and felt they were both exciting and
sinful, in spite of my normal curiosity about that part of me. As a result, I
felt I had to be sneaky about my burgeoning sexuality, hiding it from both
my mother--who withdrew emotionally, but not physically, when she
sensed it--and my father, whom I needed as an ally but who had become
my arch-rival.   (The Greek tragedians nailed this Oedipal scenario
centuries ago.)   Thus started my training to become "nice," which meant
hiding my sexual aggression as being "bad" and unwelcome; a lusty
enjoyment of sex was forbidden. Not until my early thirties did I begin to
overcome this malignant attitude, my conflicted sexual needs making it
almost impossible for me to see the entire woman, to consider whether we
could even be friends, let alone a good match.   It caused much grief--to
me and to women who became my lovers, inasmuch as I could give them
love.   It also partly explains why prostitutes attracted me, offering their
bodies for my sensual pleasure, but, like my mother, not being present
emotionally.

❊

If Charlie had any inkling of my turmoil, she did not reveal it,
though she was a bit puzzled when I told her that this was my first trip
out of the States. She assumed, as did others in France,
That someone of my age and background would be an accomplished
cosmopolitan. My Ivy League education certainly schooled me in the
restrained gesture, modulated tone of voice, and composed indifference
essential to playing that role and even a decade out from college I still
could slip into the "cool Yalie," persona like a Brooks Brothers sport coat.
Women, especially on the East Coast, were willingly bamboozled by the
act. For them, a Yalie was a desirable catch. That role did not, of course,
get me what I wanted: a genuine connection with a woman who might be
interested in ideas that excited me and — unlike my college roommates and

that senior year girlfriend — might share my enthusiasm for Bix Beiderbecke, Gerry Mulligan and, just to mix things up, Franz Schubert. In those days, a young man or woman nearing the end of college usually thought primarily of marriage and often pretended to be whatever her "targeted" husband-to-be wanted her to be. I, too, was young, however, and just discovering who I was. I knew instinctively, however, that I did not want to be a "Yalie," and completely lacked any idea of how I could use that persona to help me reach my goals.

Being in Charlie's warm, voluptuous presence, I had no interest in playing the role of a "cool" Yalie or any other kind of "cool" dude. Walking back to our house just a few blocks from the restaurant, she took my arm, a gesture that always gives me a transforming pleasure and I felt with a strange and pleasant suddenness that I was a 37-year-old, not the 13-year-old me I seemed reluctant to leave behind. Charlie quickly skipped up the stairs ahead of me and stopped at the door of her bedroom, a few steps from mine. When I approached her, she turned, gave me a good night kiss, leaning into me so I felt the full strong warmth of her body, and then, with a beguiling smile, slid into her room and closed the door. I stood there, in no state of mind or body to go to bed, at least not alone. In my room down the hall, I tossed my coat on the bed, kicked off my shoes, then, as tense as a randy tomcat, went downstairs to the living room to listen to some quiet music. An hour or so later, the high tide of my lust had slackened enough for me to think about sleep so I turned off the hi-fi and went upstairs. When I passed Charlie's door, I noticed it was partly open. Odd, I thought, as she usually kept it closed, but I kept on walking the last few paces to my room. Then I heard Charlie call my name. I turned back to her door and, saying "Charlie," pushed it fully open.

"Come in," she said, in her alluringly mellow voice. She was standing next to the window facing the street, wearing, I could just make out, a partly-buttoned man's long-sleeve shirt that covered her, more or less, down to mid-thigh.

"Everything OK?" I asked.

"That streetlight is driving me crazy," she said, not sounding at all distressed.

"What's the problem?" I asked, following her lead in the proverbial mating dance.

"It's the cord. It's all knotted. Up there, I think," she said, "where I can't reach it."

She turned on a bedside lamp as I walked over to the window to assess the situation. As I stretched up to disentangle the cord, she moved closer, pressing herself against me, and put an arm around my waist.

"I'll steady you," she said softly, knowing that she was doing nothing of the kind. In seconds, the knot came undone. So did I. I turned away from the window and into Charlie's smiling embrace, my hands sliding with exploring pleasure under her loose shirt, feeling her back muscles tense and ease, savoring her scent and her softness––skin softness, breast softness, sweet-smelling genital softness. Entwining my fingers in that troublesome hair, I bent to kiss the curve of her neck, then her mouth, its moist pressure opening to mine, tongue-teasing me, then pulling my head down to her lovely breasts.

"I left my door open for you," she said, smiling, as I shed my clothes and she finished unbuttoning her almost unbuttoned shirt, "but you walked right by."

"I noticed," I said, noticing all of her lovely body. "Maybe that Three-Card Monte made me wary."

"Foolish man," she said, kissing me down with her onto her bed, her open thighs inviting me into her warm wetness.

Charlie worked Tuesday through Saturday, which left me lots of time to visit museums, stroll through springtime parks, and be at home for her on Saturday, when she got off work early. That I was there waiting for her many evenings, surprised her a bit, though she wasn't disappointed.

"You don't have to hang out here waiting for me," she said. I shrugged in response. Then I undressed her in the living room and we made love sitting on the floor like sweating, lustful yogis. At that moment, Charlie was all I wanted to see, need and pleasure driving me to make love to her, fuck her, do whatever else it is called, whether in the living room, or on the kitchen table or on her horsehair bed. Making love to Charlie was all I imagined when I first met her, reminding me how intoxicating the sweet smell and smooth skin of a woman could be. Moving my hands over all of her round and sinuous parts was intoxicating. She murmured with delight more than once about how much she liked the way I touched her, her pleasure at my touch, something other women had felt as well. After the first week of passionate nights––and mornings and afternoons––I felt in my need for the lovely lady a kind of desperation, exactly what I felt before I broke up with my girlfriend in Berkeley. I wanted something I could not seem to get with Charlie, no matter how many times we made love. Something was missing, something I could not name. I wanted to feel how I felt when she took my arm, but that "me" had slipped away; I was no longer fully there.

Partly, it was because vast London, with its version of English, was not where I wanted to be. The first time I met Charlie, I had told her I wanted to go to France, though the more time I spent with that intelligent and voluptuous woman almost convinced me that my journey had gone far enough, that leaving her would be more of a failure than not going to France. It would be another example of refusing "to grow up," whatever that meant. Nonetheless, after two weeks of lust, and some love as well, I said a difficult goodbye to Mademoiselle Huddleston and crossed the Channel to the continent. The day before I left she had to go home to see her ailing grandmother, who had raised her after her mother's death when Charlie was thirteen. Her leaving made it easier for us both — or at least for me. France was waiting.

Chapter 1

Un Sandwich Jambon (A Ham Sandwich) and A "Slow" Dance

Although it seemed to take forever, the cheapest way to get from England to France in 1974 was by taking the midnight train from London to Folkestone, crossing the Channel in a lumbering ferry, then getting on a French train at Boulogne-sur-Mer that went to the Gare du Nord in Paris. The trip took eight hours, if all went well, but it was usually longer because of delays during the changes from train to boat and boat to train, each of which was supposed to take an hour but often took much longer. Neither the wave-thumping boat nor the swaying train offered much comfort to second-class travelers such as myself, but I was on my way to France and the chimerical search for the real Sid. And I was young, sort of.

While stowing my backpack in the rack above my seat, I seemed to become a subject of interest to a striking, black-haired young woman who was sitting a dozen rows in front of me. Standing at her window seat, she scanned the car as if looking for someone, let her gaze rest on me for several seconds, which was quite enough to spark my interest, then, with a flip of her lustrous hair disappeared into her seat. Maybe during a changeover I would get my chance to find out if I were the one she was seeking, a hope she encouraged by standing several times during the trip and sending looks in my direction that were quick with a searching interest. Did she notice that I returned those looks?

As we left the train at Folkestone, the mysterious raven-haired beauty turned several times to locate me in the crowd behind her, or at least that is what I told myself. Once outside, she found a place a bit apart from the other passengers at the railing of the open shed where we waited to board the ferry. She was smoking and staring down at the dark rhythmic swells as I walked over to stand beside her. When she turned toward me, I introduced myself in my clumsy French. Unsmiling, she answered in French-accented English, saying in an offhand yet uneasy way that she was from Bordeaux and that her name was Adrienne. She learned English, she said, when she was younger and worked as a nanny in England. She still went there often to visit friends.

She was a few inches short of my six-foot height, her thick shoulder-length hair framing a face with high cheek bones, fair coloring, and a sensuous mouth that was almost too large and as quick to change expression as her dark brown restless eyes. Now that we were side by side, her eye make-up, which I could not see clearly in the train, startled me. Her eyebrows had been completely plucked and replaced by half-moons of orchid-colored eye shadow that swept up onto her forehead an inch or so above her brow line. Two thick-penciled eyebrows replaced the natural ones, tapering to thin tails as they arced up into the orchid eyeshadow, then out, and downward toward her temples. In the coming months, I saw several women in Paris with this makeup--all of them, like Adrienne, naturally beautiful. Happily, the often misogynistic panjandrums of fashion had convinced very few women to adopt this disfiguring mask, a grotesque cross between a wide-eyed clown and a brassy streetwalker.

That Adrienne chose such a style of makeup should have set off in me some kind of alarm. It did, but my intimacy with Charlie had intensified instead of dampening my need for a woman--and Adrienne was surely a woman. So I ignored the persistent alarm bell and welcomed her arousing interest, especially when she leaned against me--and stayed there so I could feel the fullness of her breasts. That kind of body language, like Solange's hostility, needed no translation, or so I thought.

The erotic dance between men and women is fundamentally the same in France and California. The nuances and unexpected moves, however, are as different as a California nude beach is different from a *"village naturiste,"* or naturist center, in the French countryside, as I was to discover. Besides, what man in his right mind--although the mind is rarely involved in such matters--would pass up the chance for what the beautiful and voluptuous Adrienne seemed to offer? *Pas moi!*

When the boarding whistle blew, the more experienced Adrienne rushed inside to grab a double seat that allowed us to sit side-by-side during the Channel crossing. I wanted a beer and offered to buy her one, which I accomplished by climbing over travelers who had stretched out in the aisles to sleep. *"Voilà,"* I said, sliding into my seat and placing Adrienne's beer on the fold-down table she had put in place. *"Merci,"* she said indifferently, looking around as if still searching for someone as she had when I first saw her on the train. For an hour or so, I asked her questions about French, and answered her one or two about English, writing out words on newspapers and napkins. Finally, as we drifted into sleep, her head slowly came to rest against my shoulder, until a sudden jolt of the ferry awakened her with a start. She pulled away as if I had committed an unpardonable intimacy. I assured her that her head on my shoulder had in no way disturbed me, which was not true, exactly, for the smell of her hair and perfume disturbed me quite a bit. Nonetheless, she pulled away from me and, composing herself, leaned toward the window, a more proper position for a lady when next to a stranger. She did not shift her body enough, however, and a minute or two later, as I began feeling sleepy myself, her head once again came to rest against my shoulder. She did not move this time.

Once at Boulogne, a short quick walk––the more experienced passengers sprinted––got us to the train in time to grab the last two-seat space in the dining car. The seats faced each other across a small fixed table that was set, of course, at a height for dining not for sleeping. Only by piling up our coats could we make a single pillow high enough to rest our heads. We tried to doze, but without much success. Again, she stood several times to scan the car in her edgy search for a mysterious someone, rearranging every time her thick, satiny black hair. After a while, we held hands and she noticed that some of the hair on my fingers was gray, like the hair at my temples. She liked that, she said, and my long fingers, too. She said little else, perhaps because of sleepiness. Who I was and why I was taking this trip did not seem to interest her at all. Even when, to appear more fearlessly masculine, I said my final destination was Lapland, she did not raise one of her outrageous eyebrows. Moreover, she answered the questions I asked her about her own life mostly with *Oui* or *Non*. I was perplexed, especially after the hand-holding, the head on the shoulder (finally), and words occasionally said close to the ear, all, to me intimations of intimacy.

The frosty Solange had already made clear that my *"Répétez après moi"* French was not going to get me very far. But my lustful interest in this alluring *Française* helped me push aside any apprehensions. I was swimming in choppy waters, fully submerged for one stroke then half out of the water the next––but I was swimming.

As I pulled my backpack down from the overhead rack, Adrienne told me she lived in the northeast corner of Paris, which I knew from my reading was a working-class neighborhood heavily populated for many decades by immigrants. So how did she come to be so fashionably dressed, the outlandish makeup excepted? When the train pulled into Gare du Nord, I asked for her phone number.

She scribbled her address on her boat-train ticket, "So you won't forget where you met me. I have no phone. It takes years to get one in Paris."

"I will come and see you then," I said.

"No you won't," she said, like a challenge, as she kissed me on both cheeks—*grosses bises* or simply *bises*, the French call them—and pressed all of her voluptuous self against me. Then she quickly turned and walked away, as if afraid someone might see us embracing.

After taking a few steps down the platform, she waved to a man who waved back as he came through the crowd to meet her. They hugged and exchanged *bises,* then, as Adrienne took his arm, they moved away from me into the crowd. The man's camel-hair topcoat and dark suit were an unmistakable indicator of his class, a uniform of established wealth common on New York's upper East Side and Wall Street and seen weekly in *The New Yorker* Brooks Brothers ads. Almost unchanged since my 1950s prep school days, it was also common in Paris--and over forty years later still is. I did not know that in the Spring of 1974, nor for some time afterward.

❄

It did not, however, take me long to find out exactly what a burgundy down jacket and a backpack meant to most Parisians: *Alors, un autre Américain!* Yet another American! I exchanged some dollars for francs at the train station and, as Mélanie suggested, bought at a newsstand the indispensable *Plan de Paris* so I could find my way to Arnaud's apartment. This pocket-sized book of a hundred pages contains street maps of the city's twenty Arrondissements, or districts--each with its own mayor--and a wealth of other information: route maps for bus and Metro lines, museum locations, and where public swimming pools and libraries are located, and, this being Paris, the location also of such *"cabarets artistiques"* as Le Moulin Rouge and Le Crazy Horse. I also bought something I could read without a French-English dictionary, the *International Herald Tribune.* Finding an empty bench out of the crush of harried commuters, I used my new *Plan* to trace a walking route to a small nearby park. At a station coffee bar, I gulped down an expresso, the fuel that jump-starts legions of Parisians, then bumped and "Pardoned" my way out of the *gare* and along the commuter-crowded streets several blocks to the park, which, to my relief and delight, was precisely where the *Plan* said it was supposed to be.

Separated by a green hedge from the hustle and bustle around it, the park was a world apart, a very Parisian one. The high-low cry of an ambulance alarm, so different from the keening wails of our emergency vehicles, wonderfully confirmed it. So did the trimmed hedges and raked gravel paths. From my bench, the sun-warmed sweet smell of the neatly trimmed Spring grass told me it was the perfect place to stretch out after my long overnight trip. I had placed one booted foot over the lawn's low metal fence when an authoritative *"Interdit, monsieur!"* stopped me cold. A gray-haired man in a blue-gray uniform and cap walked briskly toward me and pointed to the small sign near my sacrilegious foot. *Pelouse interdite*, it read, the French equivalent of "Stay off the Grass!" I returned to my bench and reluctantly took out my *Trib*. Having fulfilled his duty to protect the sacrosanct lawn, *le gardien* strolled the neatly trimmed paths like a cop walking his beat, hands folded behind his back. Several laps around the park, with occasional glances in my direction, convinced him I was no longer a threat to his sacrocanct grass and that the rest of the park, like a perfectly arranged place setting, was just as it should be. Then, he took a break. Standing across the park from me, rocking slightly heel to toe, he perfumed the spring air with the smoke from his Gauloise cigarette, its distinct aroma as much as part of Paris as the aroma of an expresso and the very man himself. Now, I, too, at least for that morning, was part of that scene, backpack and all. What's more, in spite of my age, in spite of my fears and "Be careful!" anxieties, I made it! I was tired and disoriented, but it was April and I was in Paris! *Formidable!*

An hour or so later, as noon approached, my hunger told me it was time to take on the world-famous intimidating garçon of a Parisian Café. A café near the park seemed perfect, offering an open terrace and the kind of handsome wooden façade that now is increasingly rare in the city. I had chosen a table at the edge of the terrace so my pack was out of the way and started saying quietly to myself one of the three French phrases Frank had taught me when I heard *"Monsieur?"* Directly in front of me stood a waiter in the traditional black shoes and trousers, white shirt with black vest and black bow tie, and a long white *tablier* (apron) tied around his waist. In his forties, with dark hair and matching mustache, he waited, not with haughty boredom but with consummate professional patience, until I heard myself say: *"Un sandwich jambon et un demi, s'il vous plaît"* — a ham sandwich and a draft beer, please. *"Très bien,"* he said, and off he went. Well, how do you like that? I actually asked for what I wanted in French. The second phrase I had rehearsed, a variation on the first, was *"Un sandwich Camembert et un verre de vin rouge, s'il vous plait,"* a camembert sandwich and a glass of red wine. The third, *"Un express,"* an expresso, I had already used with studied nonchalance in the *gare*. I would need all of them often in the coming weeks.

In a moment or two, my waiter materialized again and with a dancer's graceful dip slipped a small tray bearing a sandwich and beer onto my table. He placed each item carefully on the table and tucked *l'addition* (bill) under a yellow plastic ashtray. What graced my plate was not at all like an American sandwich. No lettuce fringe was visible nor a tomato slice or onion ring. It was simplicity itself, the edges of thinly sliced ham showing between two pieces of a golden brown baguette spread thickly with butter. Ah, but there was magic in that simplicity. As I bit into the crusty bread that tasted as though it had come out of the oven minutes before, a flurry of flakes fell to the table. Then I tasted the rich and slightly salty ham — *jambon* de Bayonne the menu had said––and with it the sweet and unsalted butter. The bread, ham, and butter combination, together with the beer, was perfection. I knew then, without question, that I was in France and relaxed into my chair with deep contentment to savor my sandwich. Over the next few months my linguistic limitations forced me to become a connoisseur of the *sandwich jambon*, but that first one, as is true of so many firsts, was a revelation of sensuous delight no other sandwich could hope to match.

Part of the pleasure of going to Paris is being seduced, and I was eager to let the seduction begin. A sunny spring day, which in itself is part of the seduction, can easily entice you into enjoying that traditional French pastime: whiling away several hours with a single expresso or glass of wine on a café terrace observing the world go by––especially the women of that world, if you are a man. So, on my initial café visit, as the lunch hour waned, I lingered with my post-sandwich expresso and began to hone my skills at people watching. I also noticed that some café customers, as they entered for lunch, took newspapers from a rack just inside the door, a few tables away from me. I needed to test my shaky French, so I walked over and lifted the daily *Le Monde* on its split wooden stick out of the rack. The *New York Times* of France, *Le Monde* I knew would be tough going. With my pocket English-French dictionary at the ready, I turned page after page before finding an article about a new

French film that at least had a headline I could understand. An hour or two, and a couple of paragraphs, later the café began filling up for the mid-afternoon coffee break with *les du café*, the pillars, or regulars, of the establishment. Soon the waiter came directly to my table. *Le journal*, he said, had to be returned to the rack. More puzzled than annoyed, I returned it. Customers going into the café often grabbed a paper from that rack but, I found out later, they did not actually read it. Standing at the *comptoir* (bar), they just leafed through it, checking the lotto winners or soccer scores or trading on the *bourse*, or stock exchange, while downing an expresso and exchanging a few words with other *piliers*. Then, *bises* and handshakes were exchanged all round, including with the barman, who in such cafés is often the owner, and as people went out the door papers were returned to the rack. I had a lot to learn about the complicated café ritual.

Chagrined by my plodding efforts to understand *Le Monde*, I ordered another expresso and buried my head in my grammar book until several hundred children exploded through the doors of the grammar school across the street, wild with the shouted glee of the liberated. The demanding discipline of the normal French grammar school in those days rivaled, I found out, that of my Catholic grammar school. Late afternoon was approaching. Fueled by the expresso, I was ready to set off on the final leg of my trip to Arnaud's.

Backpack in place, I made my way toward the nearest Metro station and descended into the whooshing, jostling world where many Parisians spend hours of their lives. *Mon dieu!* It was rush hour. As my train arrived, the people on the *quai* surged forward and more or less carried me into a car whose doors had slid open in front of me. Everyone in the packed car waited impassively as a voice over the public address system warned people that the doors were closing, a horn blared, the doors clacked shut and, after a slight hiccup, the Metro hurtled into the darkness. Packed around me were tired-looking Parisians, a few of whom actually spoke to me, though even I could tell that those words were not compliments about my nifty orange backpack. *Quoi faire?* (What to do?) If I put the pack on the floor I'd take up space for three people, but keeping it on my back, no matter where I stood, turned it into a barrier people had to squeeze past to get on or off the car. If looks could kill, my trip would have ended right there.

By the time we reached the *Gare* (station) Montparnasse where I was supposed to change lines, a railway station as well as a major Metro interchange, I was as irritable as the glaring people around me. I bulldozed my way out of the car and backed up against a wall until the crosscurrents of coming and going had diminished to a trickle and the Metro horn signaled the train's departure. Then, up an escalator to join the streams of people heading for the station exits. I went right along with them and in minutes was gratefully out of the station. I would walk the rest of the way.

Relieved to be free of the crowds, I put my pack down in a small patch of dirt in a construction area near the door, where I could get oriented without being in anyone's way. Maybe I could even get some help from the young black-haired woman in a knee-length bright red coat and shiny white stiletto-heeled boots standing a few yards away. I fished the *Plan* out of my shoulder bag, found the right page, and enacted the ancient tourist ritual––the turning of the map––to figure out which way I had to walk to get to Arnaud's. Several times I returned the unfriendly glances of my attractive neighbor, giving her my best American smile. She did not smile back. *Au contraire,* she became increasingly annoyed the longer I was there, pawing the ground with her white boots and peevishly flipping her ponytail. The men who briefly stopped to chat with her didn't seem too friendly either.

Finally, I determined my route, hitched up my pack, and set out for Arnaud's, launched by a muttered parting shot from my hair-flicking neighbor. By the time I turned for a final look, another man had taken my place and was chatting with Mademoiselle ponytail, who, after a few nods and a big smile, slid her arm smoothly into his and walked off with him as if they were old friends. I had parked myself in the "office" of *une pute* ("a working girl"), at the busiest time of her workday. With a backpack-lugging American a few feet away, no customer was going to stop and chat with her about her services. *Bienvenue à Paris!* (Welcome to Paris!)

Near the end of my hike to the middle-class neighborhood where Arnaud lived, I encountered another typical Parisian. This one was wearing a T-shirt and shorts and casting about with his ten-year old imagination to see what life had brought into his neighborhood that afternoon: I was it. Falling into step alongside me he got right to the point.

"How much does that weigh?" he asked, ignoring my telltale down jacket and speaking to me in French as if I were another Parisian.

"*Vingt kilos,*" (twenty kilos), I answered, and said I did not speak French very well.

"I can speak well English," he said with a boastful grin. "I can carry that," he quickly added, but in French, pointing to my pack and flexing his arm to show me his golf-ball sized bicep. "I can carry that easily."

"OK," I said, knowing better than to argue. But, just like that, he was off to join a group of kids hailing him from down the street.

To this Parisian *gamin* (neighborhood kid), I was not "another American." In his exuberance, he simply assumed that naturally I could understand him, like everyone else in his world. He might not have been able to lift my backpack, but he certainly lifted my spirits. No doubt sent by Truffaut's cinematic double, Antoine Doinel, to assure me that all would be well with the people here. He was, I discovered, typical of French children, especially if they lived in Paris. Boy or girl, they were usually full of energetic curiosity and confidently direct, even when dealing with adults. They gave respect and they expected to receive it.

Arnaud was home, as he said he would be, and I was able to check out the sofa in his combination living room and dining room, and stow my pack out of the way in his small but comfortable apartment. In his mid-thirties, he had worked for a multinational marine insurance company for more than ten years and as a result could with effort understand a good deal of English. Reserved in nature, however, he spoke almost none. He had short blond hair, was slender, and almost of my height, which then was tall for a Frenchman. In a French I could understand, he said he was exhausted from daylong conferences conducted in English, the lingua franca of such meetings in his multinational company. As we shared a cheese omelet and salad at the table for two in his small but well-equipped kitchen, I suggested that we exchange language lessons. He said that was possible. He would think about it. Then he went to bed, leaving me to consider the rest of my trip.

I still wanted to go to Lapland, but whenever I mentioned that as a destination, people said I was headed in the wrong direction. In London, Mélanie had said it was a long haul and the Scandinavian countries were very expensive. Even worse, they were cold. Go south to Turkey, Frank had said, or the sunny Spanish coast where all the Swedish women go. Even Arnaud, over our shared omelet, said the sunny soaked Greek Islands were the perfect place, or the beaches and mountains of Morocco. Lapland? *On se caille les miches, là-bas!* You'll freeze your ass up there!

I might never own a house--or get married--but my plan was to go to Lapland and that's where I was going to go.   It was the "manly" thing to do, I said to myself. In fact, my decisiveness was more typical of me as a kid, when I refused to eat any kind of fish that did not come out of a can, not even lobster, for god's sake, an ornery twist on my long struggle with my fish-loving father. Happily, my airplane companion, the chatty avuncular priest, was right about the French.   As I might have known from my first bite of that *sandwich jambon,* the French do know a lot about how to live. Lapland quickly became a fanciful memory.

My first task was to transform my French from the language-lab variety to the language spoken by living French people.   From the editing I did in San Francisco and Berkeley, I had made some contacts in Paris who offered to help me find work as a translator if I came to Paris.   First, though, I needed to be fluent in French. Traveling around the country for a few months would help me improve my French and would enrich my knowledge of a country I might want to stay in for a while.   Thanks to Arnaud's hospitality, I could begin by exploring Paris.

❄

Often on these explorations, as soon as I said *"Bonjour"* to anyone, my lack of an American accent led the person to assume that I spoke French, and off they went about one thing or another, ignoring the affably foolish smile of incomprehension that was my only response.   I became so frustrated at times that I wanted to throw a chair through a café window, scream at a waiter, or even go home. "*Tu deviens un peu dingue,*" (You become a bit crazy), Arnaud said laughing. He and his friends, he said, had the same feelings on long business trips overseas or teaching in the Algerian countryside, which several of them did as an alternative to military service. Sometimes, they said, they had to walk away from people to avoid exploding in frustration.

"C'est normal," they assured me, and laughed some more.

It was my slow-growing fluency in French that actually drove me to total distraction at times. It often literally drove my friends out of the room. I knew just enough for others to realize rather quickly that I knew very little. After a few minutes of grade-school conversation and being relentlessly peppered with: *"Qu'est-ce que cela veut dire...?"* What does this or that mean, they went looking for someone who could actually talk to them. I often felt abandoned.

Arnaud and his friends warmly welcomed me to their dinners and walks and agreed to my request that they speak to me only in French. One of them, Jean, spoke English fluently, I later found out, but he never said a word to me, and not just because of our agreement. Though I had lived for more than a decade in California, where people generally speak with a measured cadence, I had not lost the fast-paced, herky-jerky rhythm of speech typical of people from the urban Northeast. Jean could not understand anything I said, he later told me.

I could certainly understand that; I had a similar problem in French with Richard, Arnaud's closest friend, who resembled Charles Aznavour, the star of *Shoot the Piano Player*. Slight and wiry, with a mildly dour look, a quick smile and a Gauloise cigarette often in the corner of his mouth, he exclaimed, when I first met him: *"Mais tu n'as pas d'accent!"* But you have no accent. Encouraged by my few properly pronounced words, for a while Richard would keep talking to me as if I could understand him. Quick with nervous energy, he spoke like many Parisians––and many people from the American Northeast, me, for example––in rapid bursts. Slow down? *"Pas possible. Tu comprends?"* he asked, smiling. Not possible. Do you understand? I did, for once. He had the patience, though, to help me by repeating what he said several times. If that did not work, he drew a sketch on a restaurant place mat to explain himself, or, if we were on a stroll, dropped to a knee and with a finger drew an explanatory picture in the dirt at the base of one of the city's many chestnut trees, white with blossoms in Spring.

I studied my grammar book in cafés, I went to the movies, I listened to the radio, and, unconsciously, I tried to read advertisements on buses or posters, or decipher route signs on the Metro. I even listened in to conversations of my fellow Metro passengers. *Le Monde* was beyond me, way beyond, but I could struggle through some articles in *L'Humanité dimanche*, the Communist Party's Sunday magazine, written in a straightforward style.

Every few weeks I felt I was getting sick, but after sleeping for a day I felt fine. It took a couple of these episodes to realize that I was simply exhausted from the constant effort, conscious and unconscious, of learning French. The process also taught me something about talking with, not to, someone in any language. Whenever anyone spoke to me in French, I had to listen with my full attention and not, while listening, be thinking of a response, the usual tendency when you speak a language fluently. I learned to listen more completely. More surprising, was the discovery I made as my French improved: I became aware of how it brought to life another "me," as my sexual me was brought to life by Charlie in London and Adrienne on the overnight trip to Paris. I used to think each of these different "me's" disappeared when another "me" took over, the way a single strong emotion can sometimes take center stage for a while, or when I slipped into a social role designed to hide my many-sided self. Most of the time, though, the other "me's" are always there, like an unruly bunch of actors waiting for the chance to star. There's the cute, curly, blond-haired five-year-old me; the "husky" (a clothier's euphemism) adolescent me; and a group of 37-year-old "me's. One is in a coat and tie; another in bell-bottoms, beard, and Birkenstocks; another with no love handles; and, of course, there is one who wants to be French. When they don't have a starring role, they do not simply recede quietly into the shadows. *Au contraire!* They burst out laughing at a joke ("What a great sense of humor!"); scoff at a failed effort ("Is that the best you can do?"); groan when I do something foolish for the umpteenth time ("Not again!"); and sometimes offer a bit of help or encouragement as I try to make sense of my life's script. In spite of my frustration trying to figure out that script, which at the moment was in French, learning to play my new role was liberating and exciting.

I kept ordering *un sandwich jambon* or *sandwich camembert* for lunch, yogurt and fruit for breakfast, expressos for a mid-afternoon boost, and tickets for the Metro and bus. With my brain soaking up what my eyes were seeing and my ears were hearing, my vocabulary grew rapidly. Newspaper headlines and magazine covers began to make sense, and, much to my palate's delight, so did menus. I could now enjoy a *salade Lyonnaise,* curly lettuce with a poached egg and bits of bacon; *crudités,* a composed salad of shredded beets, carrots, and celery root in an oil and vinegar dressing; and *poulet frites,* roast chicken with French fries.

I also no longer felt like a deer in the headlights every time someone asked me a question, although people still remarked: *"Vous parlez bien français,"* because of my "Belgian" accent. When you truly speak French well, no one says you do, they just talk to you as though you are one of them––like that *gamin* I met near Arnaud's. One way to tell that you have mastered French is when you can understand a nearby conversation in a café or on the subway about whether François is really going to leave Héloïse.

The final measure, not only of your understanding of French but of French culture, is when you begin to understand French humor. Invited by a girlfriend, I went to hear a wildly popular French comedian,

Raymond Devos, only to sit in sober silence while the people around me, including my companion, could not stop laughing. The comic was a gifted mime, but I did not understand a single joke. Even worse, when having dinner with Arnaud and his friends, I felt completely in the dark as they broke into laughter at a one-word comment. Once in a while, someone tried to explain to me what was so funny, but a five-minute explanation will kill the humor in anything.

The incomprehension went both ways. Arnaud wanted to see Mel Brooks' *Blazing Saddles*, then very popular in Paris, so we went one cloudy Sunday afternoon. During the first few minutes of the film, when I––and no doubt the other Americans in the audience – roared with laughter, Arnaud kept jabbing me with his elbow to ask what was funny. *Pas possible*. It was like trying to explain why "Hi yo Silver" said at just the right moment could cause an eruption of laughter in a group of Americans. When I could understand a bitingly funny Bretécher cartoon in the *Nouvel Observateur* (now simply, *L'Obs*), I knew I was beginning to understand French, and maybe even beginning to understand the people who speak it, although that is a lifelong undertaking.

Twice, desperate to have a real conversation with someone, I went to places where I was sure to find Americans. My first stop was the American Center, where, leafing through magazines in the library, I met the wife of a jazz musician from New York. Alas, just as in my French conversations, I hardly said anything at all. As soon as I asked her how she liked living in Paris, she unleashed an uninterrupted flow of bitter and angry complaints about everything French, especially French men. Her husband, a jazz musician, found a community of other musicians soon after they arrived, some months ago, leaving her mostly alone. She could hardly wait to return to the States.

I tried again in the Louvre where there had to be lots of American tourists. Sure enough, getting lunch in the museum café, I heard a young woman speaking English with an American accent and took an empty place at her table. Attractive and smart, she told me she was a painting student, which meant she had to finish her lunch quickly. Students, she explained, can copy the masters, but only until one p.m. She had to store her easel and other painting materials by then in one of the closets built for that purpose and almost impossible to detect, as I later saw, so naturally do they fit into the wood-paneled gallery walls. Off she went, abandoning me to the company of another English speaker who sat down as she left.. He was a friendly gray-haired rancher from Australia who was traveling in Europe for the first time—I think. I was never sure because, in spite of riveting my attention on his barely moving lips, the only word I could understand was "mate." I smiled and nodded, as I still often did when people spoke to me in rapid-fire French, and he kept right on talking, as lonely, no doubt, as I was for someone who spoke his language. After that, I stuck to my grammar books and newspapers. Whoever was writing the Parisian part of my life script certainly had an ironic sense of humor.

❉

When I arrived in Paris in 1974, most people out for a stroll who needed to use the "*toilettes*," or "*vay say*," the French way of saying WC-- or water closet--went to cafés or restaurants. Women had little choice, but in Paris and other major cities, men could still use the once common *pissoires*, free-standing outdoor urinals--usually a trough screened from public view by an open partition--some dating back to the 19th century. They were rapidly disappearing by the 1970s. The VC's in cafés, usually in the basement, were nominally free, but then, as now, it was understood that if you used them you bought something--*un express* or a mineral water was enough.

To use a VC, however, I first had to figure out they worked. First, I had to get comfortable using a Turkish toilet--two raised foot-shape pedestals at the front edge of a shallow flushing bowl. No problem there. The problem was the second step: turning on the toilet's light. On my first visit I searched without success for a switch on the wall outside the VC, then looked around for a switch inside or a dangling string from an overhead bulb. Nothing. Flummoxed, and in need, I nervously assumed the position while gripping the handle of the door, which I held slightly ajar so I could yell *"Occupé"* if anyone approached. I repeated this perilous ritual several times, feeling so stupid that I would not ask anyone I knew how the damn light worked. Then I noticed one day that the customer before me did something after he entered the WC and again before he emerged that turned the light on and off. It was the door latch! Slide it closed, the light went on; slide it open the light went off. *Formidable!*

❉

One sunny afternoon, I took Mélanie's suggestion about visiting a café called Polly McGoo's, a favorite hangout, she said, for Americans. In case I got desperate, she said, knowingly. I was not yet desperate, but I certainly was acutely lonely for my native tongue. I put aside my farcical experiences with the embittered wife and incomprehensible Aussie, and set out for a stroll to Polly's place on Rue St. Jacques, one of the longest streets in Paris, where street names often change every block. It was mid-afternoon when I got there and though Polly's was crowded and its air was redolent with the distinctive aroma of Gauloises, it was strangely quiet. The reason: the chess games being played intensely by patrons sitting on the banquette that ran along the left side of the café against the wall. The wooden *comptoir*, with customers lined up at its entire length, faced the banquette tables.

I found a spot at a table, took my seat on the banquette and ordered *un express*, the waiter, as usual, shouting *"un express, un!"* to the barman. As is normal in many Parisian cafés and restaurants, the tables were so close together I was sitting almost shoulder-to-shoulder with the man to my right. Clean-shaven but with long, wild reddish-brown curly hair, he sat simmering with impatience, arms crossed, seemingly ready to pounce on his opponent.

I had just taken a sip of my expresso when he erupted with hand-waving outrage and turned to me to enlist my indignation at some sort of forbidden move by his opponent. Pointing to the man across the table, he said something in French that started with *"Cet Américain…"* Though I only partly understood what the American had done to upset him, he certainly was not paying my compatriot a compliment. His opponent, apparently, had touched a piece but had not moved it, a grave violation of the rules. To avoid getting embroiled in what might be a knotty international business I gave my neighbor the noncommittal facial expression used around the world by the uncomprehending and that by now I had mastered. His opponent, leaning over the table so that his long black hair almost hid his face, wore a flannel shirt, which, like my down jacket, usually meant the wearer was American. He alternately stared at the board and glanced up through his hair at his scowling adversary, then, noticing me, gave me a look that was almost a plea for support. I disappointed him. Yielding to my indignant French neighbor who would not be appeased, the *Américain* moved the piece he had touched and pushed the plunger on the timer that sat on the table between the two men. My neighbor quickly made his move, hit the plunger, then, arms crossed again, sat back to keep an eye on *"Cet Américain."*

Polly McGoo's was, I later found out, well known to Parisian chess players. My French neighbor polished off his American opponent, shook his hand in a friendly fashion, which surprised me, then both of them left me to finish my coffee. I never did seek out a conversation with another American. That the French chess-player assumed, like the *gamin* near Arnaud's, that I could understand his French gave me a boost.   Did I look French--or at least Belgian?   Was a transformation taking place? Either way, I was feeling a bit more at home.

During those first few months in France, when I felt frustrated with the language and the surprising foreignness of a place that looked in many ways like the States, I would often play an American song that was on most café juke boxes: "I Can Dance." Its slangy language and jaunty rhythm made me feel both comforted and homesick. Often it brought back to me a memory of sunny days body surfing with friends at Stinson Beach north of San Francisco and dinner afterward in a Mexican restaurant in San Francisco's Mission District. The song and the memories left me feeling in suspension between things I loved about the San Francisco Bay area and things I was slowly beginning to love about France.

I had a lot more to learn about cafés than how to use a WC, and it was not posted like a menu in their windows.   For example, if a woman was sitting alone in a café reading a book or simply people watching, she most likely did not want the company of a stranger. If a *"dragueur"* (a male on the prowl) made a move in her direction, and, as a café regular, she had told her waiter she did not want company, he would quickly send the lothario packing.   Also, Arnaud and his friends said that any woman I casually met in a café would probably be *dingue.*

✳

It was time to look up Mademoiselle Adrienne. The address she scribbled on her boat-train ticket almost a month ago was in the 19th Arrondissement, as far from Arnaud's as possible and still be in Paris. All part of the adventure, I said to myself as I donned my sport coat and turtleneck, full of randy eagerness. The trip took over an hour and did not get me to Adrienne's Metro stop until after nine o'clock. It was probably too late to go out for someone who works, I thought, but maybe we can at least get a glass of wine. Where Adrienne lived, like those eyebrows and her skittish manner, should have set off more alarm bells, but at that point I would have ignored Big Ben. Her apartment was in an old stone building that, like the buildings around it, had no gate or downstairs buzzer and badly needed a facelift. The street was empty and dark except for the lights from a small bistrot down the block. Since I had not seen Adrienne in several weeks and had no way to let her know I was coming, my usual wrestling match between excitement and anxiety was intense.

I climbed the stone stairs, edges worn smooth by decades of use and dimly lit by overhead bulbs, passed a WC on the second- floor landing, and paused at her third-floor door. I listened: not a sound; I pushed the buzzer. *"Qui est là?"* Who's there? she asked. *"C'est Sid, l'Américain du boat-train de Londres."* She cautiously opened the door, recognized me, and, though wearing only a simple rose terry cloth robe, invited me, with hesitation, into her one-room apartment. Sparely furnished with a small stove and refrigerator, a table and several chairs, a bed, a bureau and an easy chair, its only light came from a floor lamp. A well-worn rug covered the center of the room. The decor was less than modest. To my relief, she had abandoned the bizarre eye makeup and her real eyebrows had grown back, dark like her hair, making her even more beautiful.

"I did not think you would come," she said, with a petulant tone softened by her lovely French-accented English.

"I said I would," I answered, "but I am sorry to be so late. I came from the 13th where I am staying with a friend and it took longer than I expected. It is probably too late to go dancing but we could get a glass of wine nearby."

"There are no places nearby," she said, then surprised me by saying: "And it is not too late to go dancing! The discos do not get busy until after 11 o'clock. I will change and we can go to a place I know. But I can't stay late. I have to work tomorrow."

"D'accord," OK, I said. She asked me to turn around while she got dressed. I did, wondering, again, what the hell I was doing there and also knowing exactly what I was doing there. No doubt reading my mind, not difficult at that moment, she asked me to pass her some red shoes that were under the bed. When I did, I caught a glimpse of the black lingerie she was wearing, of her wonderful body, and of her slight smile as she gave me a backhanded wave to turn around again.

"I am ready," she said. Was she ever! Under her bright red jacket, which flared bolero style at her hips, she wore a cream-colored, low-cut blouse. A mid-thigh skirt, bright red like the jacket, revealed exactly what it was supposed to reveal––her strong, shapely legs. Those red high-heel shoes and a black scarf loosely wrapped around her shoulders added the final touches to an outfit both devilishly alluring and chic! *Très, très, chic!* Descending the dark, dank stairway to the deserted street, I could not put this beautiful woman into the place and neighborhood where she lived. *Il y a quelque chose qui cloche* (Something is off.), but when she took my arm and sat close to me on the Metro, I forgot all about it. We went halfway across the city to a discotheque in the Latin Quarter that she had been to before. The doorman and bartender both greeted her by name, which made me both more comfortable and more nervous.

It was already past eleven o'clock, but we were the only people there. After I ordered two outrageously priced beers, Adrienne went to talk to the DJ, whom she also knew, and made some requests. Walking back across the floor in the dramatically dim disco light, she looked like a woman in a film noir, voluptuous and dangerous, with legs that were made for a night of dancing, among other things. She bent low to slide onto the red banquette, offering me a chance to *me rincer l'oeil,* to get an eyeful of her breasts as they pushed against the top of her blouse.

I took a quick swallow of my beer to moisten my dry mouth and asked her to dance. As soon as our bodies met, Adrienne's hands were caressing my neck, pulling my head down to the exposed part of her breasts, which I kissed with heated pleasure, and pulling me toward her swaying hips. Jesus fucking Christ! She lit my fire with such sensual skill I had to sit down after a couple of dances to try to get control of myself-- which I really had no interest in doing. I tried to cross my legs, and asked the cool looking Adrienne about her family.

Unlike on the train, she was happy to talk. She grew up near Bordeaux, she said, in a big house in the country. Her mother divorced her father when Adrienne was nine. Her father, who was in the army, did not remarry, raising her and her older brother alone. Her brother was now also in the army.

"My father is wonderful," she said, "but he made it difficult for me to have boyfriends."

"What did he do?" I asked.

"We lived outside of town, so any boy from school who wanted to see me had to come a long way, usually on a bicycle. When he arrived, my father met him at the door with his German shepherd. He held him tightly on a leash but the dog often growled at the boys and my father never disciplined him for it. The dog was so scary and my father so unwelcoming that the boys usually left without even seeing me."

"Why did your father do that?" I asked.

"He did not think any boy was good enough for me."

"*C'était difficile, mais j"aime beaucoup mon père.*" It was difficult, but I love my father a lot. Without him my brother and I would have been alone. But I wanted more freedom, so I decided to become a nanny in England and then in Paris."

"Was your father angry at you about that?" I asked.

"*Pas du tout. Il m'aime toujours beaucoup.*" Not at all. He still loves me a lot.

It was time to get back on the dance floor. I uncrossed my legs and we jumped into some arm-waving, hip-shaking fast numbers before the pace eased into *slows,* as the French call ballades, though the way Adrienne danced, "hots" was the more accurate description. They were mostly by Johnny Hallyday or Barbara, though I can't say I remember much more about the music. Adrienne demonstrated some new moves, like kissing my ear, and I followed her without missing a beat.

The disco was almost as hot as Adrienne, so we took another break. Since Adrienne showed no interest in my life, I asked her about hers. How long had she worked in London, for example? She had worked for several families, she said, and still had many friends there. She was working now as a receptionist for a real estate company in Paris but wanted to do something else, to make better use of her English, which was certainly better than my French. Also, she said her father was going to visit her in a few weeks to help her find a better apartment and use his influence to get her a phone, neither an easy task in Paris. Then she noticed the time and said we would have to leave soon to get the last Metro to her place, which left a half hour after midnight. We had time for another dance or two to songs that were very, very slow, inviting a body-to-body movement that was more like rocking in place than dancing. In the first dance, she demonstrated that though she had not completely mastered English she clearly had mastered all the subtleties of body language. She drew my hand to her partly exposed breast, and held it there. Then, in the final dance, she pulled my head down again to kiss those lovely breasts and slid one of her own exploring hands from the back of my neck, down my side and to the inside of my thigh, coming close to completing the process of arousing me that her own thighs had started with the evening's first *slow.* I could hear that German shepherd growling.

I paid our bill, which allowed the bulge in my pants to assume a less noticeable shape, then walked a few blocks to the Metro station, with

Adrienne tightly holding my arm. Only a few people waited with us on the quai. This was, after all, the middle of the week. Once on the train, we said little, until Adrienne, who had not pulled her scarf across her low-cut top, whispered to me that a black man at the other end of the car was staring at her. I suggested that perhaps she should rearrange her scarf, a suggestion she ignored. Instead, she returned his look then pressed closer to me. We had one change of trains and our dark, slightly built fellow passenger came right along with us, making us the only three passengers on the next train. From his seat almost at the other end of the car, he repeatedly and insistently looked our way while we pretended to be talking. Mostly, Adrienne kept whispering in my ear about how he looked and how fearful she felt. After a while, her whisperings, her refusal to cover up her impressive décolletage, her snuggling close to me while she eyed our car companion seemed provocative, as if she were taking pleasure in this little bit of theater.

When we reached her station, which was deserted, we got off first and rushed--but did not run--up the stairs to a deserted street, the sharp clack of Adrienne's high heels ricocheting off the station walls. For several blocks the man trailed us by a few hundred feet. Adrienne kept asking me to see if he was still there but I resisted turning around until we were almost at her place. When I looked back, he was gone. We bounded up the dark stairs and in seconds were in her apartment. Still nervous, she asked me to see if our Metro companion had tracked us by taking another route. I opened the door. No one. And not a sound.

There were no more Metro's and only one bed, which I eagerly anticipated sharing with my dancing partner. First, though, I had to descend to the landing half a flight down to use the WC, darker and danker than the stairs. When I returned to gently knock on Adrienne's door, I found not my flame-throwing disco dancer but an Adrienne hidden away under a floor-length cotton nightdress and the flannel bathrobe in which she had greeted me hours earlier. Ignoring that flashing red signal, I moved toward her to kiss her.

"*Pas plus*," she said. No more.

"What was all that seductive stuff at the disco?" I asked with angry surprise.

"*Je ne comprends pas ce que vous dites*," I do not understand what are saying, she said in French, not English, and using *vous* not the familiar *tu* she had used earlier. Then she slipped out of her robe and under the covers, leaving me standing in the small and rather depressing room.

"You cannot sleep with me and I have to go to work tomorrow."

"There are no more Metros," I said, "and I do not have enough money for a taxi. Where can I sleep?"

"In the chair," Adrienne said unsympathetically.

"*Il y a une couverture dans le placard.*" There's a blanket in the closet. After I had gotten the blanket, she snapped off the lamp without so much as a *Bonne nuit!* I took off my pants and shoes, wrapped myself up, and tried to find a comfortable position, so frustrated and angry with the gorgeous Adrienne--an arm's length away--that sleep was out of the question. After I spent a few minutes twisting and turning and cursing, Adrienne, out of the darkness, said:

"You can sleep on the bed, *mais vous ne pouvez pas faire l'amour avec moi,*" but you cannot make love with me, using that damn *vous* again.

"*Merci bien. Comme tu es trop gentille.*" Thanks a lot. You are too kind, I said, emphatically using *tu*.

Wrapped in the blanket, I squeezed between the wall and Adrienne, and discovered, to my surprise, that because it was still somewhat warm she was only loosely covered with the comforter and her nightdress. She lay on her stomach, as rigid as a woman like her can be, arms close at her sides, her lustrous black hair spread out on her pillow. In no time my hand was under those covers caressing her back, then her sacrum, which I knew from studying massage was the source of her sexual energy, then--Glory Be!--her wondrous bottom. And skin so smooth and soft it seemed to invite my caresses.

"*Qu'est-ce que vous faites?*" What are you doing, she asked me, with a tone more curious than annoyed. "I am giving you a massage," I explained, though that seemed obvious.

"*Rien ne va se passer,*" nothing is going to happen, she said.

"*D'accord,*" OK, I said, though we both knew it already was.

Besides, she did not say stop so I continued slowly moving my hand between her now opening thighs, though she stayed on her stomach. Abruptly, she sat up, pulled off her nightgown and slipped back down under the covers, still on her stomach. My God, she was gorgeous!

I kissed the back of her knees, then her thighs.

"*Tu ne peux pas faire l'amour avec moi,*" you cannot make love with me, she said, back to using the familiar *tu*. Jesus fucking Christ!

As she was now lying on her back with her arms crossed over her breasts, her words were a double message squared umpteen times. I kissed her stomach and caressed the inside of her thighs, which were opening and closing with conflicted feelings of arousal.

"*Pas de bruit,*" no noise, she said.

"*Quoi?*" I ask.

"The neighbors are old," she says. "They will pound on the door if we wake them."

"*D'accord. Pas de bruit,*" I say.

Still going back and forth between a "*oui*" and a "*no,*" she pushes herself up toward the top of the bed so the comforter slides off her full and glorious breasts. Then I am on top of her. She is still protesting but now shifting between moving her hips into me as she did at the disco and being physically unresponsive. But she is wet. I am so wound up with a thick mixture of frustrated lust, anger, and sadness that whatever happens between this woman and me will have nothing to do with *l'amour.*

"*Ne me forcez pas,*" she says. Do not rape me; do not hurt me. Angry as I am, I do not want to hurt her. What I want is for her to want me as her disco moves told me she did.

"*Ne me forcez pas!*" she says again. And I do not hurt her. I cry out in pleasure and muffled anger as I take her with spasmodic physical relief but without a hint of any shared pleasure I had hoped for.

Delusional? Of course. What did I expect? She knew almost nothing about me, except that I was an American with some gray hairs on the back of my large hands. All I knew about her, aside from her strikingly voluptuous beauty, was that she had wealthy friends in England and, if her story were true, that she was raised by a forbiddingly possessive father with a testy German shepherd. Adrienne the person, however, was not what I had most in mind that night. I certainly wanted her to be alive to me, to be there with all the lust her provocative actions aroused in me from the time I handed her those red shoes, actions that told me over and over that she knew she had something I wanted. Of course, I did not in fact get what I wanted. Instead, Adrienne stirred up in me a mixture of helpless anger and desire, and a bit of sadness.

At seven the next morning, Adrienne's alarm went off. Part of me, however, was already fully awake, which she was aware of since we were sleeping like spoons. I sat up on the edge of the bed. Adrienne, her flannel nightgown back in place, sat up next to a naked me and noticing my aroused state, reached over and gave my cock a friendly squeeze. "We could have done something about that," she said, smiling playfully, "but now I have to go to work." Back to English, but with a voice that for the first time did not sound tense and wary. She quickly got up, washed at the sink, took a birth control pill, and started to get dressed, doing some of those things that can drive some men crazy.

I got dressed myself, and not turning my back this time, watched her do some of those erotic things I find particularly exciting erotic, like brushing her lustrous black hair or bending forward slightly to settle her wonderful breasts into her bra. I felt again what I felt much more intensely the night before: a mixture of lust and angry frustration. It was a concoction I seemed to find irresistible.

Walking to the Metro, I asked her if I could see her on Saturday night. No, she said, she was going to London for a few days, then her father was coming to Paris to help her find a new apartment, as she had said. On the way to the Metro, the driver of a new Citroën yelled *"Salut, Adrienne!"* She skipped to the curb to chat with him for a minute and came back to me to descend the stairs to the station. The Metro was packed with commuters, the males among them giving Adrienne, in spite of her stylishly conservative work dress, their full attention.

We reached the station where we had to change trains, but before our train door opens, we exchange *bises* and a quick hug. As we part on the quai, she says:

"Write me!"

"Bien sûr," certainly, I say, and give her Arnaud's phone number. "Call me after you move and I will come to see you."

"No you won't," she says, just as she did on the boat train. "Write me!" she says over her shoulder.

"Absolument," I say. Then she was gone.

A few months later, on a sunny fall Saturday afternoon, having traveled for several months and found a job as a translator in Paris, I did go back to see her, though I never wrote to her. Since she had told me that her father was going to help her move I did not expect her still to be in that dark, depressing building. In fact, part of me hoped she would not be, for conflicting reasons, but as on that first night, that part had little say in the matter. Erotic memories of that disco night were dancing through my mind as I looked for her mailbox. *Voilà.* She was still there. Her father was supposed to get her out of there by now. Was anything true that she told me about her father? About anything? Up I went, the stairway clammy and grim even on that sunny afternoon. I paused in front of her door, listening for sounds that would tell me if Adrienne were there — perhaps with company. Silence. I pressed the buzzer several times. She was not home. With a sense of relief as much as disappointment (a version of that old excitement and anxiety cocktail) I walked to the Metro, wondering what I would have done--and what she would have done--if she had been home. Maybe I slipped a note under her door with my office phone number. I cannot remember. If I did, she never called, and I never went back.

That I still remember Adrienne over forty years later makes me think more about what had happened between us. No one could forget her seductive dancing at the Parisian nightclub, or her ambivalent behavior the night we spent together, nor, of course, her remarkable physical beauty. But, and this may be complete illusion on my part, something else happened between us, something I have almost always ignored in my relations with women, though it often is subtle. (In fact, I think something always happens, subtle or obvious, in any of these brief encounters.) In the way women do, she clearly pursued me on that boat train. Besides, how many women ever noticed the hairs on my fingers? None I can remember. Everything Adrienne did or said hinted at serious problems, but who doesn't have problems? In her fashion, she offered me what she had and knew I wanted — what she knew all men wanted from her, including her father, I am guessing. In her ambivalence, with probably some apprehension, she might have hinted at something else she wanted, something emotional. Also, she did, in her fashion, invite me into her bed. To emerge from such an emotional muddle with a bit of wisdom was one reason I came to France. Such a thought is no doubt more romantic malarkey, but I don't think so.

❄

Adrienne's bedeviling behavior would have confirmed Arnaud's view that any woman I casually met would be *dingue,* loony. But a Frenchman's *dingue* could be a Californian's far out chick. This was, after all, the mid-70s, the era of free love, or at least free sex. Paris, however, was not Berkeley. How, then was I supposed to meet suitable women-- through work, as in the States? Not likely, Arnaud said. Co-workers rarely became friends. Then, how? Through family and friends you have had often since childhood: they introduce you to women they think would be good matches for you. For the most part, that left me out in the cold. As generous as Arnaud and his friends were, they did not give parties and rarely went to them. I was on my own.

At that point, my colleagues at work knew me only for a few weeks, though most of them knew that I went to Yale and worked with Clark Kerr, former president of the University of California and my boss at the Carnegie Commission in Berkeley, two facts that, in my case, were misleading. The people at work were as ignorant of the complexities of my American world as I was of their French one. Maybe it would help if I first learned some of the French world's rules of social engagement.

When, for example, should I use *vous* and the familiar *tu* with a woman I had just met, whether in the acceptable social way or on my own? One of the many unreliable books about French culture I had read in Berkeley said that to find out if a woman was interested in moving from a formal relationship to one that might become more than that, you could just use *tu* in a way she couldn't miss. If she used *vous* in response, you had your answer. Arnaud and his friends had used *tu* with me right from the start, and my colleagues at work also switched from *vous* to *tu* after less than a day. Adrienne, of course, used *tu* to express her feelings, not her social standing. Though not the model of "proper" behavior, she knew precisely how to express how she felt by shifting from *vous* to *tu* and back.

A warm Spring day gave me the chance to try out the *vous-tu* dance. I went for an ice cream at one of my favorite small pastry and ice cream shops, which had half a dozen tables but just a single one for four people. In spite of the lovely weather, only one other customer was enjoying an ice cream, so I took the larger table where I could more easily read a newspaper with my dictionary at the ready. The customer lull did not last long, and soon the owner was politely asking me if I would mind making room for a group of four by moving to the table for two next to mine, which was now occupied by a very attractive blonde. *Pas de problème.* I quickly struck up a conversation with my friendly new table partner, who was curious about my experience in France and asked what I thought of its politics and racial problems. She was so candid and amiable, and I was so delighted that I could carry on a conversation in French that was actually about something, that I figured it was time to put my best *tu* forward. When I asked her about the possibility of more *manifestations*, street demonstrations, like the ones that had occurred recently, I put *tu* at the head of the sentence. She could not miss it. And I did not miss her response, which started with *vous*. I was disappointed. But, rules are rules, as Sister Severine taught me in the third grade, and I went back to using *vous*. We left the shop together but went in opposite directions on the narrow sunlit street. I turned for a last look at my blonde table neighbor and found that she, too, had turned to look at me. Later, my friends said that this time I was the one who was *dingue*. The use of *tu* and *vous* in those situations, they said, means *absolument rien*, absolutely nothing. (And I was no longer in the third grade, for god's sake.) People can work together or be neighbors for years and still use *vous* with each other. Sometimes husbands and wives—especially of the *haute bourgeoisie*—use *vous* speaking to each other, a mark of their upper class standing. That was over forty years ago, however, and though the distinction between the two pronouns may still hold true in the upper class, in most cases, when respect for age is not an issue, people largely ignore the distinction.

❄

Back to square one for me, which meant a visit to Le Crazy Horse, to find out if it really offered *"le plus beau spectacle nu au monde"* the most beautiful nude spectacle in the world. At first glance it did not seem to be a good choice. First of all, the club took its very name from a great Lakota leader, who, since my adolescence, had a place of honor in my pantheon of heroes, all of whom--including the Boston Red Sox--were committed to lost causes. Also, my varied adventures in the therapeutic world should have ended my fantasies about voluptuous and inaccessible women that dance through the erotic fantasies of most adolescent boys--and of many men. They were surely nourished during my years in an all-male prep school. A few times a week, the school's day students like myself crowded into the windows of friends who were boarding students to get a glimpse of the girls in gym shorts from our counterpart girls' school across town as they dashed from bus to gym. None of this, of course, answers the question of why I did not go to see Adrienne again.

So there I was at the bar in the back of the room sipping my $20 glass of watery champagne while trying to magically bring closer the beautiful and almost nude women on stage—as far away as I imagined desirable girls to be when I was a "husky," self-conscious teenager. Farther, actually, since whether they posed in dramatically creative or unintentionally farcical tableaux, those splendid looking women always wore the mask of impassivity females start to put on in adolescence, as I learned during my difficult teen years. This combination of physical attractiveness and inaccessibility is, of course, irresistible to many males besides yours truly. I came all the way to France, however, to get rid of those juvenile delusions, to stop seeing such women as I saw those girls of my adolescence—superior creatures with power to invite me into, or bar me from, paradise.

The show over, I left my place at the bar and climbed the red-carpeted stairs to find in the street in front of the club a fleet of cars whose drivers invited unaccompanied male customers to go with them to places that offered, so far as I could tell, opportunities for female companionship of an intimate kind. Delusions intact, I got into a car whose driver immediately stuck on the roof a bogus taxi sign and took off for what he promised was a bar with many available women, *très jolie, comme les danseuses.* Where we went I have no idea. I think it was still in Paris but certainly not in an area I knew. After a ten-minute ride, we pulled up in front of a dark stone building, distinguished from the neighboring residential buildings only by a beefy black man dressed as a doorman, a clue that something uncharacteristic of the neighborhood was going on behind the door he guarded.

The doorman came to the "taxi" as I started to get out and escorted me to the door, which he opened by pushing a buzzer. Inside, a heavy velvet curtain was pulled aside to let me enter and a man in a tux found me a seat at the bar and invited me to enjoy what the establishment had to offer. I certainly could not have found it without his guidance for the place was so dark and smokey I could barely see a few feet in front of me. As I waited for my eyes to adjust, the bartender poured me a glass of champagne, without my asking for it, and said it would be the usual $20 in Francs. The woman closest to me, who appeared to be in her twenties, had African blue-black skin that made her black dress look lighter. Her straightened shoulder-length hair moved stiffly like glistening plastic when she turned toward me and started some sort of conversation that I think included mention of payment for her company. It was hard to tell exactly because her speech, the opposite of rapid-fire Parisian French, was strongly accented, drug-slowed and as heavy with sadness as her eyes. The women in the shadows beyond her at the bar, who also seemed to be black Africans, were all wearing black as well. Blackness and the engulfing sadness of the young woman at the bar and the women in the dark behind her, are all I can remember of that joyless place.

I left without finishing my second watery "champagne" of the night, shouldered through the thick curtain at the door and stepped past the doorman to breathe the fresh night air. No sooner had I reached the sidewalk than the beckoning cries of those "taxi" drivers called to me once again, and once again I answered the call, swirled along on a stream of naïveté, with no idea of where I was going--in Paris, in France, in my life. As we drove through the deserted streets we still seemed to be in the city itself, though our destination this time was in a neighborhood that reminded me more of where Adrienne lived than the upscale neighborhood of my first stop.

There was, of course, a doorman, a buzzer, a bar, and an atmosphere as full of tension as smoke, a different version of the first bar. This time a young woman invited me to come with her to the next dimly lit room where tables ringed a small open dance floor. She shared the drugged look of the woman in the first bar but seemed, as most of the women did, to be from the Arab countries of North Africa, primarily Algeria. I could see no black African women. In a wooden café chair in the pool of light at the room's center sat a small, wiry man dressed in a tank top shirt, loose trousers, and shiny shoes. Even though his back was to me, his slouch suggested a thuggish insolence. Around this bordello Hérodias, danced an attractive Salomé in a pastel peach-colored diaphanous dress. Though its thin material revealed her lithe and attractive body, her narcotized movements were no more erotic than those of the untouchable Le Crazy dancers. My companion asked if I wanted company. With the dancer, I said.

"*Pas possible,*" she said. "*C'est la petite amie de patron. Elle danse seulement pour lui.*" She's the girlfriend of the boss. She dances only for him.

At this point, annoyed that I would not pay for her services, she abruptly moved off through the cigarette smoke to chat up a newly arrived customer. I finished the obligatory "champagne" and having doubled my dose of depression, went back into the night. This time I asked the "taxi" to take me home. Eager to get back to Le Crazy or some other joint, the "cabbie" dropped me off a half mile from my door. No matter, I needed a walk.

Still puzzled about where those bogus taxis had taken me, I wandered back to Arnaud's place through the empty streets, thinking of the titillating and inaccessible women of Le Crazy, the prostitutes of the dismal brothels, and, naturally, of Adrienne. If there were life lessons in any of these experiences, I was not learning them. But I was not doing research for a Ph.D.--I was exploring life, even if I was 38. Such explorations have no age limit. So what if they didn't help me figure out what I was doing in France or where I was going with my life? Who wanted to know, anyway, aside from myself? Was it John Wayne, the man of few words and swaggering walk who was one of my childhood heroes? Not a chance. When people began to take the adult me for Bruce Dern, the only man to kill Wayne in the movies, I finally realized that wanting to have anything to do with the Duke had always been a bad idea.

Chapter 2

Un Flâneur Parisien –
A Walker in Paris

Negotiating the world of French those first months made me feel crazy and lonely, but it also taught me, among other things, about the healing power of profanity. Even when I knew several French swear words, only one--*Merde!* (shit)--did the job of emotional release swearing does. *Fils de putain! Nom de dieu! Zut!* (Son of a bitch! For God's sake! Nuts!) did nothing, *rien du tout.* But "Goddam-son-of-a-bitch" never failed.

Happily, swearing had nothing to do with buying the croissants—chocolate or almond—I usually bought at a local *pâtisserie* (pastry shop) for breakfast and, to complement them, the yogurt and grapefruit juice from an older woman at a local *épicerie,* or deli. I stayed with Arnaud in the Spring, then for a week or so in the Fall, when I again went to that *épicerie* for my grapefruit juice. Apparently, few customers bought it because the short, gray-haired woman who waited on me, her snood neatly in place as always, welcomed me back with a shy smile and, *Ah, l'Américain qui aime le jus de pamplemousse.* Though I felt she wanted to do it, she did not ask me where I had been, so I helped her out, telling her of my travels in France that Summer and early Fall. She gave me a nod this time, with a slightly broader smile. Like most shopkeepers in Paris, she kept track of her customers' comings and goings. If a regular--like me--does not show up for a while, they take note of it and even ask other regulars about the absent person.

I had my grapefruit juice and yogurt at Arnaud's before getting my croissants and enjoying them with a *café au lait* (coffee with milk) at a neighborhood café. Most cafés only sold plain croissants and baguettes, but did not mind, Arnaud told me, if you brought in pastries they don't serve so long, of course, as you ask them first and buy the café to go with them. After that *petit déjeuner,* I became a *flâneur,* a wanderer of the streets, roaming here and there as whim and curiosity took me. When I felt the pangs of hunger, my aimlessness vanished, though I was not immediately conscious of the shift.

After I had been in Paris for a few months, Arnaud invited me to go with him to a party one Friday night. Before he left for work that day, however, he said he would have to work late but I should go on my own. Richard and his wife, Valérie, said they were going. The party was crowded when I arrived and the people--of all ages--were friendly. But Richard and Valérie were not there. No matter, after someone offered me some puffs on a pipe of hashish, I was convinced my French had improved so much that I was not only fluent, but witty. No one noticed. What they did notice was my surprising knowledge of Paris. I mentioned a pastry shop others there knew as one of the city's best, then several *fromageries*, or cheese shops, then a *boulangerie*, or bakery, then a few good inexpensive restaurants. *"Mais, c'est incroyable!"* they chorused, that's unbelievable. Apparently, in my wanderings I had discovered some of the city's gastronomical and inexpensive treasures. How did I find them, they asked? I had no answer then, but during my half-hour Metro trip back to Arnaud's, which, in my hashish haze, seemed to last several days, something floated to the surface of my murky consciousness.

Wandering here and there, I usually followed the lead of my senses. A tap, tap, tap drew me down an alley to a Turkish maker of special shoes. The stillness of a small park enticed me to spend an hour there and find out from the gardener that when new rose bushes are planted in the city's parks, 25 percent are stolen the first night, mostly by Parisians who scale the locked gates and dig them up to take to their country homes. The sound of woodwinds on a street of nondescript shops stopped me to watch artisans in white coats working at a long bench that extended from the window deep into their place of special craftsmanship. As they delicately did repairs and adjustments on oboes, clarinets, English horns and other instruments, they tested them from time to time, which is what I heard. I often found these Parisian treasures by a *flaneur's* luck, but chance alone did not lead me to my discoveries. Hunger triggered my senses of smell and sight, both essential to the task, though it took the remarks at that party to discover exactly how.

As lunchtime approached, or when evening came around, like our ancestral hunters I instinctively began to notice things that told me good food might be nearby: a savory aroma; the sound of laughter and conversation midway down an alley; people by ones and twos walking away from the same place carrying string-tied packages; steamy windows of a café on a small square. I carried no guidebooks, but if I let my senses do their hunter's job--more helpful it turned out than any guidebook-- I'd be sure of finding a delectable blueberry tart, a pungent cheese I'd never tasted, or a good meal with congenial company.

Sometimes I had help. One fall evening, drawn in the darkness to the laughter coming from a restaurant on a narrow street in the Marais, I stopped in its pool of light to read the menu posted on the window next to the door and, looking past the menu, take a peek inside. Suddenly, a stocky woman with short black hair and a black dress pulled open the door and, face to face with *moi*, grabbed the lapel of my down jacket and hauled me into the crowded, animated interior. Wearing a large white apron and a proprietor's challenging but friendly look on her ruddy face, she demanded: "*Qu'est-ce que vous attendez, monsieur?*" What are you waiting for *monsieur?* She pointed to a seat at a long table of lively customers in the middle of the packed and noisy room. "*Asseyez-vous et bon appetit!*" take a seat and enjoy your meal. In Paris, as elsewhere in France, your senses will almost never lead you astray; sometimes you will even get some surprising assistance.

After I had returned to Paris from my travels to Grenoble, Avignon, and the vineyards of southern Burgundy, I resumed for a few days my life as a *flâneur*. On a gloomy Saturday afternoon I followed those senses to a street full of small markets near Place des Vosges in one of the oldest sections of Paris, *Le Marais*, which literally means swamp. On the recommendation of Arnaud's friend, Richard, I had already visited the Place on several occasions during the Spring, but did not discover the nearby market street of Rue St. Antoine until that cool, gray late Autumn afternoon. Among the many shops that lined the street was what appeared to be a popular *fromagerie*, which I visited by falling in with the stream of shoppers as they crowded into its cramped interior. Filling the shop, along with its customers, was a uniquely pungent and slightly acidic aroma. It came from some of France's 350 to 450 cheeses arrayed with artistic flair in the store's case.

I bought some gruyère and some munster, a recent discovery of mine and sharply different from the bland variety that bears the nearly identical name, muenster, in the United States. Made primarily in the Vosges Mountains of Alsace and Lorraine, munster gives off a nose-wrinkling aroma that can repel the casual cheese eater but is irresistible to cheese lovers *comme moi*. That aroma announces what is underneath the cheese's brine-washed orange-yellow coating: a delicious creamy smooth interior with nutty and buttery flavors. Eat it at its peak in Summer and Fall and pair it with a crisp Alsatian Gewürtzminer, and you will be a convert to a gastronomic pleasure that was first enjoyed in the abbeys and monasteries of 14th century France. A sprinkling of crunchy, slightly bitter toasted caraway or cumin seeds gives a balancing accent to the cheese's buttery flavor. You can even spread munster on a boiled potato and enjoy it with a good beer. *Formidable!*

Buying cheese––or anything––in a small shop or a market gives me the welcome opportunity to get to know the person behind the display counter, sometimes as a casual commercial acquaintance, sometimes as more than that. So far as I can tell, my fondness for shopping in such stores goes back to my early childhood in the south end of Hartford, Connecticut, a heavily ethnic lower middle-class neighborhood. Small shops were everywhere. Moreover, even after I was going to prep school as a commuting student, milk was still delivered to my family home early in the day by a milkman who often came into our kitchen in the winter for a warming cup of coffee. The bakery man came to the back door later in the morning several days a week. I've always found that the small commercial contacts essential to making any town or city a welcoming place to live and were an integral part of French life. The markets and small shops in Paris gave me the chance to buy cheese, sausage, bread and other daily necessities––like *jus de pamplemousse*––at the same small shops over and over.

Back out on Rue St. Antoine, my cheese tucked away in my United Airlines shoulder bag, I strolled along the bustling street from one small shop to another, checking out everything from wine to honey to socks. When the damp cold of evening set in and the streetlights came on, I descended into the St. Paul Metro station for the trip across Paris to see Arnaud, who had invited me to dinner. It was Saturday, a big shopping day, so I could only find a seat with three teenage girls.

On Metro cars––and on many Parisian buses––most of the two-person benches face each other rather than the front, so that friends can talk during a trip. Of course, passengers in these knee-to-knee seats are often strangers. A veteran rider of the Metro by this time, I was cooly unruffled by the impassive stares of people who faced me, even if they were teenaged girls. Usually, I had something ready to read, as I did that day. So, ignoring my seat mates, who stopped talking the instant I sat down, I unzipped my shoulder bag and pulled out *Le Monde*, leaving the bag open on the floor between my feet. Almost immediately, my three companions started to quietly laugh. Had I violated another Parisian rule of Metro behavior? Had I– *Zut!*– left my fly open? At first, I did not look up. When I did, the young woman facing me, knee to knee, leaned forward slightly and, smiling, said: "*C'est le fromage, monsieur.*" It is the cheese. Ah that munster! A zesty genie, it was spreading its nose-wrinkling aroma throughout the warm car. By now, other passengers standing and sitting nearby were also smiling. *Merci,* I said to my charming seatmate and zipped that genie up where it belonged. A couple of stations later the three young ladies got off. As the last one pushed by my knees into the aisle, she smiled and said, "*Bon appétit!*"

I have had some interesting encounters on San Francisco Bay Area buses, but none like this. In spite of the fact that everywhere people tend to be on their guard when using public transportation, being physically close to people can sometimes break down public defenses. The incident became *une petite pièce*, a small play, in which my fellow Metro riders happily, if unwillingly, played their parts, displaying an openness to engage the world around them that I often encountered in France.

✻

In a city like Paris--though of course there certainly is not another city like Paris--these quotidian *pièces* happen all the time. Sometimes they involved me as a spectator, and sometimes as an actor without a script, as happened in the Metro or at Polly Magoo's when my French chess-playing neighbor enlisted my support. Or in my office when I became a translator. I used the phrase *je m'en fous,* (I don't give a fuck; *je m'en fiche,* I don't give a damn is used in polite society) having heard a middle-aged woman use it on the bus. My female office mates were indignant. "*C'est tout à fait impoli!*" said one. "*C'est grossier!*" very rude, said another. When I explained where I had heard it, they said: *Impossible!* I had pushed wanting to be French too far.

Gaffes or not, I had opportunities to watch or join in these spontaneous little dramas, which happened almost everywhere. They seemed fundamental to French life, like the open-air markets with unwrapped produce piled up and sold by the weight, the vendor keeping track of your purchases by jotting them down with a stub of a pencil on a small pad. The fabric of life in France, and even in Paris, was more loosely woven than in the States, with the exception, maybe, of Berkeley, and other university towns. This was, of course, the 1970s, not 2020. Times have changed, but some of those small Parisian shops still thrive--in spite of supermarket competition--run by extended families whose members know the names of most of their customers by name.

✳

　While living in France, I sometimes fell into conversation with other French-speaking immigrants, usually male and usually from Africa. In part, it was because I could understand their slower-paced French, and in part because, like them, I was an outsider in a society that did not easily welcome strangers and had complex and deep-rooted rules about class and how you were supposed to behave. Being white and American, however, I was not a target for the hateful discrimination endured by many immigrants, of color, especially those of Arab origin. Still, there was no doubt that I was *un étranger*, an outsider. Figuring out exactly what that meant took time, and it usually got me thinking about what home meant to me. That I might even wonder about something so fundamental would bring a questioning smile to the face of many French people––at least in the 1970s. Forty years ago, a French person from Alsace would no doubt have felt as much like an *étranger* as I did if he visited the Lot Valley of southwestern France, singled out by the natives for his way of speaking if nothing else, but also by his slightly different style of clothing. Had I been a jazz musician or a painter I might have had an easier time fitting in; I would have had a ready-made community open to accepting me, a community with its own language. Basically, however, no matter their regional home and dialect, most French shared the belief one's first responsibility was to be comfortable in one's own skin–– *sentir bien dans sa peau* – which I hoped the French would help me be.

　Before the Marais was gentrified into the upscale neighborhood it is today, a process that started when I lived there in the mid-70s, it was the center of the Parisian Jewish community and, because of its low rents, home to many university students, artists — and Arab laborers. As a result, it was also home to many bistros and unpretentious restaurants with large communal tables where the owners treated their customers like family, literally pulling them in the door if they hesitated about entering.

　On a visit to one of these restaurants, I took an empty spot at a long table opposite a man about my age who told me he had been eating there for years. The restaurant had no menu, not even a simple chalkboard. Instead, either the waitress or *la patronne,* boss, the woman of the couple who owned it (her husband, *le patron,* tended the small and busy bar), just told you what they were serving that day. I had visited it several times before with Arnaud and his friends, who were regulars and did the ordering, bantering with the short, blonde and friendly *patronne*. This time, equipped with my improved French, I was ready to go it alone.

Almost as soon as I sat down, the young waitress appeared, pencil and pad in hand, and rattled off the menu, her words speeding by me like a TGV (a French high-speed train). Since I apparently did not respond quickly enough, she took my tablemate's order for dessert. When she passed my way again, I ordered sausage and lentils, a green salad, and *un quart de vin rouge*, a quarter of a liter of red table wine. In a minute or two she returned with half a baguette and a jar of mustard--both of which she took from her apron pocket-- my wine, and a serving of lentils that almost spilled over the edge of the plate. In their midst nestled two plump sausages. She disappeared, then, in a flash was back with a small green salad that, like the lentils, barely fit on the serving plate, and for my dining companion across the table, a slice of chocolate layer cake. Calling it a slice, however, does not do it justice: it was so large it was on a regular dinner plate like mine, not a saucer-size dessert plate. *"Mon dieu!"* he said, laughing. *La patronne* was quickly by his side to make sure he had been served the piece she herself had chosen. *"Merci, chère madame,"* he said, *"Mais, c'est trop grand pour moi."* It is too big for me. Placing her hand on his shoulder, *la patronne* explained that she had no choice. It was the last piece of the cake and to cut it in half would have made two pieces much too small, especially for a regular customer who liked the cake so much. She had to give him the entire piece. Maybe, she said, *ce monsieur ici*-- meaning *moi*--would have some. Recovering, he smiled and said "*Ça va, ça va. Je ferai de mon mieux.*" That's OK. I will do my best. He did not need my help. Slowly but surely he finished it all, bid me *Bonsoir* and as he left, waved *Au revoir* to *le patron* and *la patronne*.

Not missing a beat, *la patronne* asked if she could join me, then, not bothering to wait for my answer, took his place and started talking a mile-a-minute about how she and her husband--that's him behind the bar-- tried to retire once five years ago, turning the restaurant over to some cousins, but after six months the cousins said it was too much work, and besides, she said, she and her husband missed the restaurant regulars, so they came back. After all, maybe it was a blessing that the neighborhood was changing because this time--they had owned the place for thirty years--they were ready for an easier life *pour de vrai* (really)--though she already felt a bit sad that they would not see the professors and students any more, especially the ones who had become friends, but she hoped some would come to visit them in the country, and of course she would come into the city with her husband sometimes. That's what I think she said, as I tried to keep up with her breathless tale. As usually happened, hearing my good French accent, she just assumed that I could understand her. I could, for the most part, but it did not make much difference whether I could understand her or not: she wanted to talk. She only paused talking about her coming retirement to jump up to visit with other customers, allowing me a moment or two to enjoy my delicious dinner, then came right back and picked up her tale where she left off. As I paid and got up to leave, she got up with me, not to say *au revoir*, until we see each other again, but *adieu*, a more final goodbye, since there was a possibility that we might never again see each other. I said I was sorry about that and would come back for a final dinner. Then, this lively woman, full of surprises, warmly embraced me and gave me *grosses bises*. Several months later, when I finally did go back, a sign on the front door said: *Fermé*.

La patronne's warm *adieu*, with *bises*, was an aspect of French culture I liked right away. The exchange of an embrace and kisses between women and between men and women has long been the custom in France, and during the past thirty years, has become more common as well between close male friends. *Grosses bises* can, of course, be as mechanically meaningless as a "firm" handshake, but kissing someone on both cheeks, feeling the quality and smell of their skin and hair, their physical presence, makes it hard not to be aware of your shared fate as creatures of flesh and blood, no matter how you may feel about each other. The traditional custom of shaking hands when you met friends––but especially exchanging *grosses bises* if the friend were a woman––struck me right away not only as more civilized, but also as a richer emotional experience than our forms of social contact––often defensive and wary––at least as practiced by men.

In fact, I liked the custom so much I brought it back with me to the States. Though shaking hands did not surprise many male friends, trying to deliver *grosses bises* on the cheeks of women friends as they are trying to deliver a friendly "American" kiss on my mouth still leads to some bobbing and weaving in which noses almost always become involved. Nonetheless, I persist in both these habits. Just saying "Hi" without any contact at all, feels incomplete, like eating a fine cheese without good bread.

Near the end of my almost two years in France (with a ten-month hiatus in the States in between two visits) I worked briefly as a potter before realizing that I could not *gagner ma croûte*, my crust of bread, practicing that ancient craft. To earn my plane fare back to the states, I did a stint as a dishwasher at a restaurant near Lyon. Every weekend, I drove there and back with my hosts (the family of Marius, the father in the couple, owned the restaurant) and their young daughter, Emma, from our home base in Grenoble where the pottery studio was located. I will have more to say on my restaurant adventures in due time, but that weekend commute gave me a chance to witness the *grosses bises* ritual in all its Gallic glory. We did the *aller* part of the trip to the restaurant on Friday evening and the *retour* part Monday morning, each trip taking a bit over an hour. On those early Monday drives back to Grenoble we passed through the city of Vienne during rush hour and almost always had to stop for several minutes at a traffic light near the town high school. A low wall, separated from the school by a few feet of lawn, stretched along the front of the school building. It was a favorite spot for students to hang out before they had to start their school day. Twenty or more boys and girls would often be sitting there. Whenever a girl joined the lineup, she walked its entire length, giving *grosses bises* to each and every schoolmate. Each arriving boy gave *grosses bises* to each girl and shook hands with each boy. We so enjoyed watching this ritual that it often took a horn blast from the driver behind us to let Marius know the light was green.

✳

When Spring's sun finally brings blue skies and warmth to Paris, Sunday afternoon becomes a time for a stroll in the air, silken soft and perfumed by the white blossoms of the city's *chataigniers* (chestnut trees). On one of those delicious May Sundays, after I had been in Paris for several months on my first visit, Arnaud, and his friends, Gabrielle and Richard, took me on a walk from the 14th Arrondissement near Gare Montparnasse north along Boulevard St. Michel to Ile de la Cité and Notre Dame. Long and languorous, our stroll gave us—or at least them—time to talk, to look at how the city was changing, and to enjoy the clouds of white chestnut blossoms that floated above us. It also gave me a chance to indulge my sweet tooth with a buckwheat crêpe spread with a swirl of *crème de marron*, a preserve made from sugar, vanilla, and the edible nut of cultivated *chataigniers*, which are called *marrons*. I bought it from a pushcart vendor who spread the *crème* with a painter's flair on a crêpe pulled hot off the griddle then rolled into a cone. The bitterness of the crêpe's buckwheat flour and the sweet, rich crème were one of those perfect culinary marriages that have made French cuisine famous.

As we strolled along, our springtime mood was shattered by the shrill cry of a woman behind us. *Au voleur!* Thief! she screamed. A young man with long black hair, wearing a serape, burst wildly by us on the *Pont St. Michel* that crosses to the *Ile de la Cité*. Before we could move, a stocky man in a suit, his jacket still buttoned, raced by us, running, as the French tended then also to dance--arms pumping like pistons tight to his side, body resolutely rigid--and moving like a bat out of hell. The frantic thief, stolen purse swinging wildly, descended to the quai along the Seine, his pursuer steadily closing the gap. Serape, hair, and arms flying, the thief suddenly realized how exposed he was and bolted up the next set of stairs to the street level, hoping to disappear among pedestrians. Alas, the pedestrians who greeted him were half a dozen Paris policemen taking a break in front of the city's main police station. *Tant pis pour lui,* too bad for him.

After this excitement, we ambled through the Ile de la Cité to the children's playground behind Notre Dame and lounged in the sun for a while. Weaving around us, laughing, shouting children chased each other with bursts of energy, stopping abruptly to confer about matters of great seriousness or wild hilarity, then racing off again. A dozen or so whirled around on a spinning platform they propelled by kneeling on it with one leg and pushing off the ground with their other foot, as if on a round wagon. As my friends talked, I noticed people coming and going from a hedged-in area across the street. I went to explore what was drawing such attention and discovered a world as far as one could imagine from a lovely springtime day in a Parisian park.

I passed through an opening in the hedge and crossed a small green space, at the end of which, on the end of the island, was a low white marble building. People were going in and coming out of the building's very narrow entranceway. Many leaving the building wept. I descended a flight of stairs down toward the Seine. Barely wide enough for my shoulders, the staircase instantly gave me a claustrophobic irrational fear that I might not be able to come back up.

At the bottom of the stairs, there was an open area, off of which ran a long room, its walls covered with 200,000 flickering small quartz crystals, each light representing a French person sent to the Nazi extermination camps. I had entered the *Mémorial des Martyrs de la Déportation*.

Off that main room at the base of the narrow entrance stairway, were several wall sculptures of black angled steel suggesting the violence the *déportées* suffered. Several alcoves only a few strides deep led to barred windows. I entered one, the constricting grip of its walls as disturbing as that of the narrow staircase, and peered through the bars: No sky, no tree, no part of the city was visible: Only the slowly moving slate gray river.

I went back to the main room where I read chiseled on the granite walls words by Camus, Desnos, Sartre and other French writers who spoke of courage and the incomprehensible nature of the human condition. One read: *Pardonne. N'oublie pas.* Forgive. Don't forget. A sign asked for silence. I was among the many quietly shedding tears.

Almost fifteen years later, I returned to the Memorial. Once again it was a beautiful Spring Sunday in Paris. This time, the sun was unseasonably warm, pushing temperatures into the 80s and drawing sunbathers to every park––some of the *pelouses* by then were not *interdites*––and to the quais along the Seine. Half a dozen had spread their towels, oils, and bikinied bodies on top of the Memorial, until, urged by several site visitors, a policeman asked the sun worshipers to move. They did, less embarrassed by their behavior than annoyed, apparently completely unaware of where they were and how their presence could have been seen as insulting. History has things to tell us if we care to listen.

During my mid-70s years in Paris, I saw more than once "*A bas les Juifs*" and "*A bas les Arabs*" ("Down with the Jews" and "Down with the Arabs") scrawled on Metro corridor walls. The extreme right's dislike of all Semitic people was no secret, but toward Jews it was somewhat masked. Toward other "immigrants," by which was usually meant Arabs, the hostility was open. Their preferred target was Algerians, who had been encouraged to come to France in the early fifties to do the hard labor needed for the suddenly booming postwar economy, even though theAlgerian war for independence was at its worst. On the other hand, the Socialist and Communist Parties sometimes supported efforts to integrate Algerians and other immigrants into the French working world and the larger society. (Algeria, conquered by France in 1830, had a long, special, and violent relationship with its colonial ruler, a relationship that became a brutal war for independence from 1954 to 1962. In 2020, the wounds from that war are still not healed.)

Most of my French friends were Socialists, so it did not surprise me that one evening during the Spring, 1974, presidential election, politics became the topic of a heated conversation. Arnaud had invited me to join him and his friends for dinner at a small wood-paneled neighborhood restaurant that had once been owned by Elena, the mother of Hélène, who was Arnaud's girlfriend. A small and cozy place, it had the characteristic warmth of many Parisian neighborhood bistrots, with dark wooden tables and chairs and a banquette of dark red leather that ran along the principal wall, which was covered by a mirror.

Richard spoke of going out at night to paste up posters for the leftist candidate, François Mitterand, over those for his centrist rival, Valéry Giscard d'Estaing, who was supported by the right. "You have to be careful," he said. "You always post a lookout and if you see those rightwing bastards coming, you drop everything and take off. They'll beat the hell out of you, if they catch you. And if they break a few bones or even kill you, too bad for you." Of course, a few people on the left used the same tactics, he had to admit, but people generally agreed that most of the worst violence came from the extreme right group in Giscard's coalition. "What do the police do about the violence?" I asked. "Oh," Richard said, "the police are all fascists themselves," which was, as it turned out, partly true.

The bistro's new owner, a friend of Elena's, overhearing us from his position behind the wooden, zinc-topped bar, said he thought both sides were to blame for the violence, though he, too, was a Mitterand supporter. Then, from across the room, two young men spoke up. Both had short hair and wore wool crewneck sweaters and khaki pants—the "uniform" of the upper class in France that I had worn during my Connecticut prep school and Yale days. The Mitterand supporters were worse, they said, because they were more desperate, knowing Giscard was going to win, which, in fact, he did. Back and forth the opinions flew, a simmering hostility carefully monitored by the vigilant *patron* behind the bar.

After dinner, we adjourned to Elena's apartment across the street. There, settled with our coffee and liqueurs, Richard vowed he would go to war to keep people like those two downstairs from ever getting power. "My young friend, what do you know about war?" Elena asked. Richard, sitting cross-legged on the floor, took a tight drag on his cigarette, said a few more words about those fascist *salauds* (bastards), then fell silent.

A slender man with thick white crew-cut hair and a white turtleneck sweater who was in Elena's apartment when we entered but had not said a word, then spoke from the semi-darkness of the adjoining room. In a gentle, sad voice, he described the days he and Elena spent fighting the Germans in the Alpine plateaus of southern France, about the terror and savagery, and about the many friends they had lost there.

"Nothing," Elena said, "is worse than war. Nothing, nothing! You must do everything you can to avoid it." "It is a horror," the man said, "a horror you can't imagine." On that sober note, Richard, Arnaud, Hélène and I left Elena's to walk home. In spite of the misty rain and the words we had just heard, Richard quickly recovered his combative verve. Lighting another cigarette, he swore that he would never stop fighting fascists like those *salauds* in the restaurant. He'd fight them in the street or anywhere else.

I was a silent observer through all of this. There was no way I could understand what it was like to live in an occupied country for five years, a country where for complex and conflicted reasons a good number of people supported the occupiers and their vicious anti-semitic policies. Richard's passionate feelings told me that the war that ended 30 years earlier was still going on, part of the endless human struggle between those who favor power, order and control above all and those who feel freedom is the highest human value, in spite of the political turmoil that frequently comes with it. Supporters of left and right were still fighting it out in the streets of Paris where, as countless plaques in Paris tell us, policemen, firemen and members of the French Resistance fought a similar battle with the withdrawing Nazis and
lost their lives doing so.

※

The memorial for the *déportées* shook me, as it was meant to do, though the events it commemorated had happened 30 years earlier. I felt like someone who discovers something about himself that makes him feel ashamed.

It also triggered memories of my life in Connecticut. The protestant-dominated Yale world of the late 1950s did not warmly welcome Jews or Catholics (like me). It did, however, make the occasional exception, usually for children of the wealthy, like the conservative Catholic, William F. Buckley, Jr., or students from particular preparatory schools, though never the Bronx High School of Science as many of its students were Jewish. Anti-Semitic and anti-Catholic jokes were not uncommon, and some of my roommates, influenced by that common mix of youthful ignorance and a few beers, occasionally played a record of German marches that included the "Horst Wessel Song," the anthem of the Nazi Party. Happily, sophomoric behavior is usually outgrown. That I did not object to the music, however, humming in ignorance right along with the marches as though they had been written by John Philip Sousa, gives me a twinge of shame even today. Such sidestepping hid my increasing antipathy to everything WASP. During my adolescent and college years, however, my college classmates' behavior was nurtured by a societal structure that, through covenants and quotas, determined who could live where, who could go to which schools, and where one could swim in the ocean or play a round of golf. Yale and other elite East Coast schools--prep schools included--were, of course, pillars of that social structure and the views it fostered. Such views certainly were paradoxical, as those institutions claimed to offer an education that critically examined the irrational basis and often horrific consequences of such views.

Part of my exposure to that paradox occurred on a beautiful spring day during my freshman year in my own all-male prep school. I am sitting in a shade-pulled lecture hall in a World History class at my all-male prep school, where I am a commuting day student. In the sunny countryside of the Connecticut Valley, the school is an Arcadian island of green. With a roomful of other 14-year-old freshman boys I am watching a grainy black-and-white newsreel film of the liberation--actually the discovery--of Nazi concentration camps by American troops, many of them African American, who were stunned to silence by what they found. No one in the class moves. The only sound for the film's twenty minutes is the whirring of the 16-mm projector. When it ends, the teacher says a few words though I don't think any of us heard them. What I still remember, though, are those images of monstrous horror and, when the shades were pulled up at the film's end, the sunlight streaming into the room from the springtime world outside. Even six decades later, I cannot reconcile the two.

❄

In France I often heard and read strong expressions of opposition to intolerance and class prejudice: in newspapers and magazines, in bistro discussions, and in street demonstrations, whether in support of the socialists in Chile or in solidarity with Algerian workers. I certainly did not understand how it all worked, nor how the politics were interwoven with religion and the deep roots of the French class system. As our bistro discussion demonstrated, the French fervently embrace the art of conversation on just about any subject. When it comes to politics, however, as Richard made clear, such discussions can suddenly turn violent; having a bartender as a referee is a good idea.

My initial three months in Paris ended in early June of 1974. One night, I had my pick of any café table on Boulevard St. Michel in the middle of the Latin Quarter; the next night every café was packed with young blonde women--blond men, too, of course, but I did not notice them-- bubbling away in one Nordic language or another. Most were heading south to the beaches of Provence, Mallorca, or the Aegean Islands of Greece. I was headed south as well, but my destination was Grenoble, a major city in the Alps of southeastern France, where the Berkeley friends lived who said I spoke wonderful French. From there, I took a weeklong trip to the international arts festival in Avignon, drove across France to spend a month at a pottery workshop in the Lot River Valley of southwestern France, and finally, before returning to Paris, picked grapes for a couple of weeks in the Macon region of Burgundy. I will write about all of them, but now, Paris is where this story puts me.

When I went back to the City of Light in October, after my stint picking grapes, I felt I spoke French well enough to look for work as a translator. My days as a *flâneur* came to an end for the most part. Paris, of course, was still fascinating and beautiful, but in searching for a job my life fell into the pattern that shaped the lives of millions of Parisians: "*Métro, boulot, dodo,*" subway, work, sleep.

I also still had to dodge such questions as: "What are you doing in France?" Or, "Why do you want to work in France at your age?" Or, the favorite of ten-year olds, "Why aren't you married?" The question I asked myself covered them all: "What the hell am I doing with my life?" It will come to me, I thought. I still believed I would find a "French me" who would be a major improvement over the "me" I had been for nearly 40 years. At that time, any self-respecting Frenchman would have choked on his *sandwich jambon* at such a notion, but maybe not so much now, given how the world has changed. Alas, I had yet to learn that speaking fluent French and sporting a Gabin cap would no more bring about my change than bedding a lithesome dancer from Le Crazy would make me the kind of man I thought I should be. Such efforts at transformation had as little chance of succeeding as my saying "idea" instead of "ideer" could convert me to WASPdom, though my first girlfriend thought otherwise. *Mais, je suis têtu,* I am headstrong. And I had yet to work in Paris. That surely would bring about my transformation, *n'est-ce pas*?

Chapter 3

Tu Sais — You Know

It was almost noon on a hot midsummer Sunday.   In another hour, the market near Grenoble's railroad station would close and city residents who had not fled to mountain retreats would disappear into the cool interiors of their shuttered stone houses, leaving the center of Grenoble, especially its main park, to Algerian men who, without their families, had come to work in France. Ringed by snow-capped Alpine peaks, Grenoble sits on the flood plain of the Isère and Drac Rivers, and in the Summer often bakes in a stifling, humid heat that reminded me of my childhood Summers in the Connecticut Valley.

This was my first visit to Grenoble after I had spent several months in Paris.   The friends I was staying with had invited me to join them on their farm in the Alpine foothills, but I wanted to wander about the city and then visit Julien, a musician I had met at Café Tribunal in Place St. André a few days earlier.   A friend of his had taken a photo of him and his partner, Sandrine, while they were performing in the Place a few weeks earlier and I was sitting in the background. At the café, he had recognized me from the photo and invited me to join the two of them to see *Jazz on a Summer's Day*, an American film about the 1958 Newport, Rhode Island, Jazz Festival. When we parted after the film Julien said to visit him at the railroad station market on Sunday. I was happily surprised, as the French generally make friends more slowly — and more surely — than Americans, especially Californians, who often are effusively affable but weak on follow-through.   Julien 's parents came from Italy and Sandrine's from Belgium so perhaps that made friendship with an American more possible. In different ways, we were all *étrangers*.

I had my late morning coffee at the Tribunal, which, when I returned to Grenoble as a potter, would become "my" café, then started exploring the city before going to the market, which closed at one. To shelter people from the heat in the summer and the harsh weather of winter, the streets in the center of Grenoble are narrow; many are for pedestrians only. As I wended my way along these walkways, barking erupted ahead of me, the sharp sounds clattering off the area's stone buildings. It became more furious the closer I came to its source, which when I reached the end of the block, turned out to be a German Shepherd (again!). It was on a small balcony on an upper floor of a very elegant 18th century building that formed one side of a small square of similar white buildings. At midday, their shimmering whiteness in the intense heat of the midday sun made the entire square seem to float. A heavyset, balding man in a dark suit was standing under the ironwork balcony, apparently inebriated, yelling at the infuriated dog and doing something to provoke it to wilder and wilder barking. When the man caught sight of me as I passed behind him, he turned and pointed to exactly what he was doing: he had unzipped his fly and was shaking his cock at the dog. Unbothered by my entering his surreal performance, he laughed as I left the square and turned back to his dog-taunting game.

Remembering it now, it seems more a dream than real life, the blasting noonday sun transforming that little square into an overexposure in a black and white Fellini film, a perfect fit for feeling slightly out of balance in my new French world. Surprisingly, though, it did not shock me. I just shook my head with amused dismay at a culture that seemed so much like mine but was very different--often in ways I could never have imagined. Even in wild and woolly Berkeley, the man would surely have been arrested. A Grenoble policeman most likely would have told him to zip it up and move along.

That man's bizarre way of provoking a dog struck me as being very unlike what I might encounter in a major city in the States, but a toddler's urgent need to pee during a downtown shopping trip with mom was quite familiar. How French parents dealt with such emergencies, however, was as different as a Speedo is from baggy knee-length swim shorts. During noontime in Grenoble, when as elsewhere in the France of the 1970s, most shops and stores closed for two hours, the only available restrooms were in cafés and restaurants crowded with lunchtime customers. They usually did not welcome a small child in bladder duress. More than once, I saw a mother step to the edge of a crowded sidewalk, pull down her child's pants or skirt, and gripping the toddler under the knees, hold it over the gutter so it could pee. No one--except myself--paid them any attention.

Like traveling to any unfamiliar place, these experiences of daily life challenged my sense of "how things should be." But they did not upset me. I liked what seemed to be, as Janet Flanner said, a view of life that, with reservations, says, "Yes", not the Puritanical and fearful "No" that is so integral to American culture. They touched on what I hoped I would find when I decided to go to France. The French in the 1970s wore western dress, aside from women's monokinis and men's pants without pockets so a svelte silhouette would not be marred; lived more or less like us, though they smoked more; and prepared food so that it usually looked familiar, even if I could cannot pronounce the name of the dishes. The culture, however, can be as different now as it was then, as different as the French language differs from English.

More important to me than these points of cultural friction was what happened during a walk in the country with Julien and Sandrine, though maybe that also revealed a cultural difference. On another Sunday that I spent in town, they took me for a picnic to a favorite place of theirs in the nearby mountains. Generalities of course are always suspect and I barely knew this couple, but from the start of the afternoon, Sandrine, a beautiful woman with a lively intelligence, strong features, long auburn hair and a limber dancer's body, clearly enjoyed flirting with me. I was flattered, but uncomfortable with a nervous tension about male jealousy that usually in such situations caused me to shut down my own liveliness. To my surprise, however, Julien was amused by the game and joined in. My tension evaporated, replaced by a free enjoyment of Sandrine's coquettish game with both of her male admirers. It was a rare experience for me.

A boy's usual love affair with his mom was prolonged into my early adolescence through naps with my mother until I was 13. The experience gave shape to both my emotional and sexual development and messed up my mother as well. It also led to a simmering conflict with my father, even though he finally got my mother to stop those naps. Often, I unconsciously sought out triangles similar to that familial one, and then, faithful to the primal model, hid my sexual interest in the woman by being "boyish," a tactic fundamental to the role of a *tombeur*, or playboy. Not that day, thanks to Julien and Sandrine. Their playful warmth gave me a freedom for at least that afternoon to be fully my self--what I came to France to do. It was a liberating revelation, repeated, with a variation, a few months later in Burgundy.

On that Sunday stroll, my last stop before the market was the city's main square, shaded by large trees. Dressed in dark suit coats and trousers and white or light blue shirts open at the neck, groups of mostly Algerian men filled the air with the graceful filigree of Arabic, from time to time breaking into excited exchanges or bursts of laughter. I entered one of the small cafés on the square for a mineral water and to watch whatever match of the 1974 World Cup was on television. (*football*, soccer, quickly became my favorite sport.) The café, too, was filled with Algerian men, there to watch the game, and often smoking, as were many in the park. Some nodded a greeting as I joined them at the bar to drink my bubbling water. When I heard the church on the square ring out noon, I bid *au revoir* to the barman and my neighbors at the bar and headed for the market.

❊

Since his father's death some years ago, Julien had helped his mother at the family business, selling women's clothing from a mobile van. Several days each week they set up shop at markets in the foothill towns around Grenoble. On Sundays they parked their caravan at the city's main market under elevated railroad tracks close to the main station. It was open every day, but on Sunday it doubled its weekday size and offered everything from cheese to shoes to clothing. Bordering the market on one side was a working-class neighborhood, its air redolent with an aromatic mix of Gauloise cigarette smoke and expresso that came from the cafés near the market.

I had visited the market several times on my own during the week and from my first visit felt as I did in the small Parisian shops I liked-- completely at ease--even though I had known nothing like this market in my life. When I left for France, the San Francisco Bay area began to sprout t such "farmer's markets," but there were only a few. Ironically, in the France of the 1970s, supermarkets were being touted as the newest thing, threatening the existence of such markets. Larger apartments with larger refrigerators, plus convenience and lower prices, made them increasingly attractive. Sadly, these large self-service stores had not yet begun driving *fromageries* and *boucheries* and *boulangeries* out of business. In the 70s, small shops and outdoor city and neighborhood markets still remained the center of everyday shopping life, the food in market displays unwrapped and arranged with eye-catching artistry. Many merchants still used a stubby pencil to jot down your purchases on their palm-sized paper pads and totaling up everything in their heads.

The market extended half a dozen blocks under the elevated railroad tracks, which, in the summer, protected goods as well as buyers and sellers from the punishing sun, and in winter, diminished buffeting by rain or snow. Shoppers entered this sunlight-striped world either pulling behind them wobbly wire-wheeled *chariots de courses*, canvas or oilcloth shopping carts, or carrying several expandable string bags. Some merchants—the white-coated purveyors of meats, fish, and cheese — looked down on their customers from behind their refrigerated, glass-covered cases, which revealed their treasures when the side of the van was swung open and propped up like an awning. And what treasures: rabbits hung with their livers exposed, their darkness telling shoppers how recently the rabbit had been killed; several kinds of chickens; countless artisanal sausages, cooked (*saucisson*) and uncooked (*saucisse*); and regional cheeses — hard walnut-sized goat cheeses, fresh *fromage blanc* (soft and white) to be mixed with green onions or fruit, creamy rounds of local St. Marcellin, and the champagne of French cheeses, Beaufort. Made only from the milk of two species of cows that grazed in strictly defined high Alpine pastures and was a perfect match for the slightly sparkling white wines from the lower Alpine slopes. Much of this array of food could be found only in markets in the Rhone-Alps region, where Grenoble is located, and has been grown or made there for centuries, which is also true for regional foods in France's other regional markets. It was the place to learn more about local fruit and vegetables, try an unfamiliar *saucisson*, and, depending on the patter of the seller and my wobbly French, ask about a cheese I did not know, or a *saucisse*, or pear I had never tasted before. (A *saucisse* needs to be cooked; a *saucisson* is dried or cooked.)

Behind mounds of potatoes, garlic, onions, pears, apples and other seasonal vegetables and fruit stood women vendors in light cotton smocks and aprons or men in sturdy French blues, a blue cotton coat and pants combination, sometimes topped off with a cap, that is worn by workmen all over France. Many of the vegetables had been dug that morning from the fertile, black earth––*la terre noire*––of the Isère River Valley not far from Grenoble, where the river slows its flow to the Rhône. Most of the pears and apples had also been picked that morning in the orchards of the Alpine foothills. Bakers touted their breads — long and thin, squat and thick, dark or light, all with the wonderful just-baked aroma. As newspaper-wrapped parcels passed from seller to buyer, the market air was filled with the singsong *"Merci, au revoir, Monsieur* or Merci, *au revoir, Madame,"* or the combo version, *"Merci, au revoir Monsieurdame."*

By the time I reached the end of the market, where Julien told me his mother's van would be parked, I had stuffed my shoulder bag with bread, several kinds of cheese, and a garlic sausage. Sure enough, the van was there, surrounded by wheeled pipe racks of summery dresses and colorful skirts, in the midst of which was an aluminum-framed beach chair. On the ground next to the chair were two books on painting and music, but no Julien. No one at all, in fact. As I stood looking down at the books, Julien 's mother, dressed in black, emerged from between the racks of colorful summer skirts and blouses. Her black graying hair was pulled back in a tight bun, accentuating her sharp features. Julien now did what had been his father's heavy work of unloading the van and setting up the racks of clothes and then packing everything up when the market closed. "I'm looking for Julien, Madame," I said.

"Dans le café en face, Monsieur," in the café across the street, she said, unsmiling, but not unfriendly. *"Merci, Madame,"* I said and moved past the dresses out into the blinding light of the open street.

I was trying to figure out in which of the three cafés that faced the market I would find Julien when he stepped out of the "modern" one, the last one I would have chosen, and waved me over. I entered its quiet, dark interior and joined him and another young man at a table by the window. Marcel, Julien 's friend since childhood, stood up to shake hands and I ordered a beer.

Unlit to reduce the heat, the café, like many in French cities, had been given a new look: slickly varnished tables of heavy wood had replaced formica ones, amber globe lights were suspended from the ceiling on golden chains, and bar stools were arranged along a counter where people stood in more traditional cafés. To me, it was a supermarket version of a café.

Julien, dressed in black like his mother, was drinking a mineral water. An expresso cup was on the table in front of Marcel, whose appearance was then in fashion among young French men: dark hair cut monkishly short above his high forehead and light blue eyes, a thin bristling beard, a form-fitting peach-colored shirt partly open to the waist., and slightly flared trousers. What, I thought, could Julien, a painter and musician, have in common with Marcel?

When Americans casually refer to this "friend" or that "friend," the French are often puzzled. Until recently, the French, as in other Latin cultures, tended to stay close to home and family when they reached adulthood. Globalization, and the changing job market that goes with it, has modified that pattern but childhood friends still often remain close for life. If you have two or three of these *amis* you are fortunate. You can also have a number of *copains* or *camarades* who share your interests, like a passion for American films or for swimming in San Francisco Bay. *Collègues*, as you might guess, are generally your co-workers; *connaissances* are acquaintances. In the mid-1970s, the traditional lines among these distinctions were already blurring, as people had to move away from home to get work. But, like other distinctions the French make, using them in the right place at the right time was still important in ways that often puzzled me. Trying to sort out when to use the formal *vous* and the familiar *tu*, for example, was continually discombobulating. Only after I was there for a year did I begin to understand the subtleties of such usage, which have by now (2020) largely disappeared among younger people. Like the subjunctive, however, most of these distinctions still have meaning.

"We were talking about the movies," Julien said, "about American movies."

"What films do you like?" I asked.

"The musicals" Marcel said, "like Julien, but westerns, too. You know, the ones that show the enormous spaces of the West in wonderful color, with John Wayne and Gary Cooper. And then the films about the great cities—New York, Chicago, Los Angeles. I would love, *tu sais*, you know, to visit those places. Everything in America is so big. Enormous! There is so much energy there, too, *tu vois*." (*Tu sais*, you know, and *tu vois*, you see, were used then the way "like" is now used in the States, as rhythmic punctuation.)

"It's a big place," I said. "But the movies can fool you, French or American."

"They can't fool you about the space and the energy," Marcel said. "You know, a place like Los Angeles—there's no place like it, the biggest city in America."

As a San Franciscan, I silently gave thanks that there was only one Los Angeles, though the owners of this "modern" café, seemed to have done their best to make an Angeleno feel at home.

"Well, there's no doubt about that," I said, "but New York has more people than Los Angeles."

"*Ah, non,*" Marcel said, with the challenging tone that signaled he knew well a principal rule of French conversation: challenge whenever possible. "Los Angeles is the biggest."

"No," I said, joining this Gallic game, "New York has the most people."

"*Pas vrai!*" that's not true, Marcel countered, taking a drag on his Marlboro.

"Yes, it's true," I said. "Los Angeles covers more space, but New York has more people by a few million."

Marcel shrugged and finished his expresso, making me wonder why he so easily withdrew from the verbal skirmishing that animates so much French conversation.

"Well," Julien added, "whether they lived in Los Angeles or New York, Fred Astaire and Ginger Rogers were the greatest dancers in the movies, and the musicals, like those with Judy Garland, are terrific, too. Great music! The market's closing. I've got to help my mother pack up. I'll be right back."

Wait a minute, I thought, what am I going to say to this stranger? Too late. Julien was already out the door. Marcel took another Marlboro from the pack and after several tries thumbed a weak flame from his lighter. He held the pack toward me.

"*Non, merci,*" I said, but could think of nothing to say.

Marcel looked out the window. I studied a couple talking with the barman in the back of the café, then I also turned toward the street, filled with the shouts of merchants trying to make a final sale. "It's your last chance to buy the market's best eggplant," one vendor cried. "Don't go home without some juicy peaches," another urged. Others were already rolling up their awnings or, like Julien and his mother, packing merchandise away in their vans. A crew of city workers dressed in French blues stood nearby, waiting to dismantle the pipe frames of the market stalls and hose down the street.

"Where do you come from in the United States?" Marcel asked.

"I was born on the East Coast, northeast of New York, '*Nouvelle Angleterre,*" I said, "but I've been living in San Francisco for ten years."

"I know all about San Francisco," Marcel said, tapping his lighter nervously on the table. "Kerouac, Ginsberg, Corso, the Beats. I read them all, *tu sais.* I was crazy about them. About jazz, too. The blues, like Julien. Muddy Waters, B.B. King. I dreamed of traveling to America, *tu sais,* riding a motorcycle across the whole country." He paused to take another deep drag on his Marlboro. "That was a long time ago," this young man said, and with a flip of his finger sent the lighter into a spin. "That's all over for me now, *tu sais.* "

"You don't want to go to the United States anymore?"

"No," Marcel said, and looked out the window again. "I traveled around for a couple of years. Did nothing. Now I've got to get on track, you know, get serious." "How old are you?" I asked, thinking of the 38th birthday I just passed, a birthday that put me, *tu sais,* more than a decade beyond when most young French people feel they have to become serious about their lives.

"I'm twenty-two," Marcel said.

"Well, you have lots of time to travel," I said. "I didn't come to France until this year and I'm thirty-eight. It's my first time overseas." And then came one of the questions I was to hear often in the coming months.

"Why did you come to France?" Marcel asked.

"Well, French movies had something to do with it," I said, "All the great French films of the thirties, especially Renoir, Pagnol, Carné, and then the "*Nouvelle Vague*," the New Wave, you know, Godard, Truffaut, Rohmer. But the language most of all. I have wanted to learn French since I was a kid, maybe because some neighbors were French Canadian and only spoke French. I heard it all the time. I was never very good at it in school, especially the grammar, but I liked how it sounded, its music."

"You speak it very well," Marcel said.

"Thanks," I said. "I understand the language well enough now, but there is so much more to the French and France that is still a mystery to me. The real France, like the real United States, *tu vois,* is not in the movies."

"What do you mean?" Marcel asked.

"The way people communicate without words, just with a look or a gesture, or the way they carry themselves. Sometimes, even a single word can say a lot, like *Bof,* with a shrug. And I never get the jokes. But people who study languages say that humor, often with deep cultural roots, is usually the last thing you ever get when you learn a language."

Marcel nodded agreement, then took another cigarette from the red and white pack. He did some spinning tricks with his lighter, coaxed from it another small blade of flame, and inhaled deeply.

"Last summer," he said, "Julien and I took a trip to Italy. His parents were born there, *tu vois,* so he has lots of relatives —aunts, uncles, lots of cousins. The French, *tu sais,* can be dramatic and excitable, a bit too much sometimes, but the Italians! Always putting on a show, always yelling at each other. And for what? *Rien du tout.* For absolutely nothing most of the time. But they seem to enjoy it. The French, *tu vois,* when we get excited, at least it's about something important. Julien's more French than Italian but he felt right at home, *tu sais.* He thought it all was funny, like a play, or one of his ideas for a song. I couldn't wait to get back here."

"I know what you mean," I said. "

"You know," Marcel said, "it's even harder to travel in a foreign country when you don't know why you're there. Julien wanted to see his cousins, but I took that trip because I didn't have anything to do here. I just went along with him. I was kind of lost." I could understand how he felt.

"Did it help you figure out what you wanted to do?" I asked.

"No. I still don't know," Marcel said. "I'm working now in my father's shop, fixing cars. It's not bad, *tu sais*, but it's hard working with someone over fifty, especially your father. We never really got along that well, we don't think the same way at all, *tu sais*, so we get on each other's nerves."

I ran my hand through my hair, turning gray at a surprising pace, and thought of the years of battle I had with my own father, a battle still unfinished.

"It's hard to decide what you want to do," I said.

"Not in America," Marcel said, putting out his cigarette. "You can do anything you want. You can be anything. Start doing something completely different even when you're older. Maybe even become a movie star," and he smiled. "Here, it's not so easy, *tu vois*. If you don't do well in school when you're young, that's it. They don't give you another chance. They don't think you can ever change after a certain age."

I picked up the cigarettes, thought about having one, then put the pack back on the shiny wooden table. "It's not always that easy in the United States, either," I said. "You've got to make a choice sometime. Get serious, as you say."

"Julien and I went to Venice just to see it, *tu sais*, at the end of our trip," Marcel said. "We had already visited all his relatives in the south and only had a couple of days left. " I couldn't sleep the night we were there. I got up early, when it was still dark, and wandered around. At dawn, I walked into a big square. It was empty, completely empty."

"St. Mark's?" I asked.

"I think so," Marcel said, "I'm not sure. There was no one else there--just pigeons, a lot of them. I walked to the center and looked at the buildings as the sun came up. The light kept changing every couple of minutes. And the buildings changed color, too. It was so beautiful," Marcel said quietly. "When you see things like that, you can't say anything, *tu sais*. You just cry."

Near tears, Marcel looked out the window into the bright midday light of the cluttered street, as I did some spinning bits with his lighter. He leaned forward to see if he could spot Julien and saw him moving through the dispersing shoppers toward the café. "*Le voilà*," here he is.

"All packed and ready to go," Julien said. "You are invited to our house for lunch, both of you."

"*Non, merci,*" Marcel said. "It's Sunday, *tu sais,* my parents expect me home for dinner," observing the national Sunday custom of having the midday meal with the family, still religiously observed in the 70s..

The three of us, all lean, long-limbed and about the same six-foot height, walked into the street filled with vans and trucks maneuvering out of the marketplace congestion. Marcel shook hands with me and hugged Julien, exchanging *grosses bises,* those customary kisses on both cheeks. Then he put on his dark glasses, turned and walked off briskly down the debris-strewn sidewalk, throwing his lighter into a heap of market sweepings. "*A la prochaine,*" he shouted back at us over his shoulder. Until the next time.

Several Sundays later, well after the market had closed and the day had slightly cooled, I watched Julien and Sandrine perform again in Place St. André. Afterward, having a coffee with them at Café Tribunal where we had first met, Julien said a friend had come by his house a couple of days ago to tell him that Marcel had been killed riding his motorcycle in the mountains. He was alone, *tu sais.* We grew up together, he said, looking at the table.

※

During those few weeks of my first visit to Grenoble, I took a side trip to Avignon for the internationally famous festival of contemporary performing arts. Through my university friends, I was able to purchase a seat on a bus for summer school students going to the festival for the weekend. When the bus returned to Grenoble on Sunday night, I stayed for another week in Avignon, where I discovered a rich southern French culture that was dramatically and emotionally different from the more reserved character of mountain-ringed Grenoble.

Chapter *4*

The Land of Touch

Thanks to help from a Berkeley friend, I went to the International Arts Festival of Avignon with a group of students from Grenoble, though I was not an official part of the group. My friend, who worked at the University of Grenoble, got me a non-student pass for the bus, but I had to find my own place to sleep, not an easy task when people who were there for the festival had months before snapped up every decent hotel room. If you were not fussy, though, and liked to meet people, there were other places to stay in this old city, established as a city in the 4th century.

Checking out announcements of such places posted on the bulletin board of the student hostel where the bus dropped me off, I met an exuberant young festivalgoer who was also looking for lodging. A teacher in Rome and a lifelong Communist, as he proudly told me in heavily accented French, he invited me to go with him to a high school where the French Communist Party, according to a colorful flyer, was putting up university students and teachers. Both the Communists and Socialists advertised such dormitory-style lodging during the festival, using the sleeping quarters that were used by students from the surrounding countryside who, because they lived far from the school, spent the week in the city. I took the passenger's seat behind him on his resplendent black Bugatti as he waved off any thought that we needed the flyer's map. He could remember every detail of it, he said, to a very skeptical me. Off we went, turning left and right and left, then left again through the old city's narrow streets to the "Red" hostel. Because of my new friend's precise knowledge of the hostel's location, we only had to stop a half dozen times to ask directions, a task he left to me.

When we arrived, it was mid-afternoon and almost all of the beds were available in the men's dormitory room for forty. By the time we had settled in, however, a steady stream of travelers was arriving. A trio of men in their early 30s were from Florence, we soon found out, for when they heard my Roman friend singing a popular Italian pop song, they introduced themselves to him, saying that they of course knew where he was from because of his strong accent. That's all it took. Off they went, joking and jiving about food and accents and regional habits until the

Florentines started singing the popular song right along with their Roman compatriot.

Later, after the Roman had gone off on his Bugatti, I sat outside with the other Italians at a table near the school playground, the men having been joined by two Italian women, also teachers, who were staying on the dorm's second floor. They all were French teachers near Florence, they said, and started to talk in Italian about the evening's schedule of events in what was called "Festival Off." The principal festival had become so dominated by famous groups, that younger, relatively unknown performers of all kinds had started a parallel festival––like off Broadway––putting on performances in cafés, bistros and smaller out-of-the-way venues. After talking for a moment or two in Italian, the man closest to me in age suggested that they speak French, since I did not speak Italian. The graciousness and warmth of that gesture was my first clue that I was in a southern Latin world.

Before I had gone to Grenoble, I had the romantic idea of bicycling along the Mediterranean coast, starting at Toulon and ending up at the Italian border, and maybe going beyond it. Avignon was a possible stop on my trip. I bought a fine red Gitane bicycle in Paris and had it shipped first to Grenoble, then on to Toulon. Getting my new bike out of the baggage shed at Toulon should have been a warning that this trip was maybe not the best idea. The stationmaster, curtly official in his spiffy khaki uniform––with shorts––and neat military crewcut, stated with impressive authority that my bike was not there.

"*Mais, non,*" I said. "*Il faut qu'il soit là!*" It has to be there."

"*Il n'est pas là. Je suis certain,*" he said.

"*Pas possible,*" that's not possible, I said.

"*Mais oui, c'est possible, parce que je le dis.*" Yes, it is possible because I say so, he said, raising his voice.

"*Quand même, je voudrais le chercher,*" Nonetheless, I want to look for it, I said, raising my voice to match his.

"*Les Americains sont tous cons!*" he shouted. Americans are all jackasses, clearly failing to notice my Belgian accent. Then, red-faced, he told me where I might go to look for it, and probably where I might go in general. One step into the high-ceilinged baggage shed at the end of the platform, and *voilà*, I could see my resplendent new red Gitane among a group of tagged bicycles. They were all vigilantly guarded by a couple of rail workers in French blues trying to escape the heat by enjoying an afternoon *maïs* cigarette and relaxing in low-slung beach chairs. "*Allez-*

y!" Go have a look," one said. I quickly wheeled my red and white beauty through the other bicycles awaiting their owners, gave the baggage man my ticket confirming my ownership, and wished him and his assistant, neither of whom had moved the slightest bit from their comfortable chairs, a *"Bon après-midi."*

I took a room at the Hôtel de la Gare, across the street from the station, stowed my bike, and went to the café next door to have a beer and watch the 1974 World Cup, my new addiction, so intense that I already found nil-nil matches exciting. The place was packed, so when I saw an empty spot at the bar, I stepped right up and ordered *un demi.* No sooner had I turned to watch the TV in the back of the café than an older man returned from the restroom and took the spot at the bar behind me. Almost immediately, I felt a hand on my arm and turned to see the smiling face of my neighbor, who asked me to move a bit so he could see the TV screen. In Grenoble or Paris, the request might have been just as polite, but probably with no hand on the arm. I was in the South, the land of touch.

The gracious warmth of both the Italian teachers and the man at the bar came, it seemed to me, from the same cultural and geographical place, a place of warmth and sun where people are more emotionally open and inclusive, and more willing to make contact — even if the contact can be heated and obnoxious.

✳

When the weekend ended and the students and their bus went back to Grenoble Monday morning, I stayed to see more of the festival, especially a Saturday night performance by Alvin Ailey's Dance Troupe, whom I had seen in Berkeley. Without my pass, which expired Monday morning, I had no connection to the University of Grenoble and could no longer stay at the dormitory. The hotels in the middle of the festival were naturally full, so the first night I slept on a dock that was floating on the Rhône. The spectacularly illuminated Palais des Papes nearby and other illuminated buildings across the river soared into the night sky, protecting me, I hoped, from any scoundrels. They could not, however, protect me from the river, whose soft lapping sounds first lulled me into dreamland then woke me up as the water started to rise over the edges of my floating bed.   I grabbed my sleeping bag and backpack and skedaddled to the nearby beach, covered with baseball-sized rocks, not sand, but beyond the river's reach. Pawing   away enough rocks to clear a space for my body, I settled down again. and quickly fell asleep.

The next morning, when the heat of the sun began to cook me in my down sleeping bag, I opened my eyes to see two scuffed black shoes a few feet from my nose. Down near the river, someone was shouting, in Arabic it seemed, at the person standing in those shoes, who, as I looked up at him, was a silhouette against the bright sky, his face in dark shadow. Dressed as the Algerian men I saw in the Grenoble park--dark suit coat and pants, white shirt buttoned almost up to the neck--he must have been standing there looking at me for a few moments, as his friend's cries were increasingly insistent. Hearing those cries and knowing instinctively that if he had intended to hurt me, he would not have stood there long enough for me to wake up, I said *"Bonjour."* My morning visitor, who could have hit me on the head with a rock and rifled through my sleeping bag for money and the always valuable passport, said nothing and simply turned and walked over the stones down to the water where his beckoning friend was waiting for him.

These young men were two of the several million like them from the Maghreb—the part of North Africa made up of Morocco, Tunisia, and Algeria—who lived and worked in France.   Most of them are from Algeria, which has a special relationship with its former colonial ruler that allows Algerians to come to France without the usual immigration requirements.   I had pushed my luck on that beach. Both instinct and reason told me to find a safer place to sleep.

I ended up in a small hotel that was affordable and simple. My room was dusty and had only cold water, but the sheets were clean, the bed surprisingly firm, and hot water and a shower were in the bathroom just down the hall. It also was quiet: I neither saw nor heard any other guests, which, like an empty restaurant, should have told me something. The elegantly cordial owner, however, calmed my apprehension by assuring me he would stay up until I returned at night, no matter how late, and he did, always graciously welcoming me, whether I returned at 10 or after midnight. A tall, slightly stooped man, with thick smoothed-back white hair, a long face and an aquiline nose, he told me he was born in Egypt and asked me where I was from. I later found out from a friend who grew up in Avignon that the hotel was in an area that was not safe, especially at night. I made a typical tourist's mistake, but was lucky again, as I was never bothered. Besides, it was very close to Place des Corps Saints, where I spent many a pleasant hour enjoying a leisurely coffee and observing the square's daily theatrical events.

On one end of that long *place* a family-style restaurant called Bistrot Pascal served people young and old from the neighborhood, who all seemed to know each other as well as the woman and her mother who owned the homey place. The main dining room was always full at dinner and lunch, the smaller room beyond it served as a backup dining room, and the room beyond that as the owners' combination living room and dining room, complete with a TV. A grandfatherly man with a white neatly trimmed beard, often sat near the kitchen doorway so he could keep an eye on the cooking as well as greet arriving customers. The son of the younger female owner usually played in the rear room but in shorts and T-shirt often rode his dune buggy among the tables in the evening wishing diners *"Bon appétit"* as he made his way to the street.

Pascal had bright yellow tablecloths, good local house wine and a variety of salads, pastas, and omelets, all savory and reasonable in price. On my second visit I was with a group of my university companions speaking different languages and laughing at each other's wacky pronunciations of French, when a wonderful looking older man with a broad, tanned face and imposing Gallic nose made a grand entrance with his shorter, shyly smiling wife. Announcing their return after a vacation, he said with a big smile *"On arrive! On arrive!* We are here! Many diners waved welcome home. After one more visit, I was treated like a regular: Pascal became "my" restaurant. Choosing "my" café, however, took a bit longer.

Place des Corps Saints was shaped more like a Y than the traditional square. The main road that entered it from the end near Pascal splitting into two narrower streets when it reached a large, raised terrace with a fountain situated in the crotch of the Y. On the narrow two-lane branching streets that bracketed the terrace, which was shaded by several large plane trees, were three cafés: two on one side of the street, just as it split, and one on the other. All three cafés had tables and chairs on the terrace, their different colors––red, yellow, or blue––indicating which café they belonged to. I settled on red.

Waiters for all three cafés served their customers using a similar technique to deal with the steady flow of cars, mobylettes, and bicycles. When a customer chose a table, a waiter from that café Fred Astaired his way across the street to the terrace, took his customer's order, returned to the café to fill it, then moments later, balancing a full tray of coffees, pastries, or sandwiches, sashayed back through the flow of traffic to deliver his order. I never saw one spill a café or drink, though occasionally one had to use some deft footwork and a shouted curse at a cheeky driver as he quickstepped through the traffic. The same waiters also took care of patrons inside their cafés, popping out to the sidewalk from time to time to scan their terrace territory for interlopers. These garcons, which basically means boys, an odd name for such respected professionals, made a game of it, pretending to serve a wrong-colored table, then feigning innocence when warned off by the proprietary shout from across the street.

This *place*, I found out later from a friend who was born in Avignon, the same friend who warned me about the hotel, was special for more than just the pleasure of watching the waiters. It was Avignon's most popular gathering place for artists, writers, musicians, and leftists, strategically located in the borderland between one of the city's poorer quarters, where my hotel happened to be, and the large, upscale main square a few blocks away, where well-to-do foreign festivalgoers generally sought refreshment. From where I took a morning coffee in the *place*, I could see the regional headquarters of the Communist Party, whose local members gave me warm welcome as they gathered most mornings for coffee, sitting, naturally, at the red tables of "my" café. They seemed to know everyone, inviting other café customers to join them and calling out to horn-tooting friends who waved from car or mobylette as they passed by.

Their most boisterous greeting was given to a couple in a classic 1950s BMW motorcycle with sidecar that slowly entered the *place* from the far end. The driver and his female passenger, both with gray hair, were in full leather gear of the same vintage as their gleaming black rig. As soon as they came into view at the far end of the *place,* they drew *ooh*s and *ahs* from the patrons of all three cafés, who rose to their feet to cheer when the purring machine came closer. The BMW's driver, goggles pushed to the top of his leather helmet, slowed to a parade-like pace. His smiling passenger, whose full head of silver gray hair was now helmet free, then rose to her feet and, gripping the windshield with one hand, waved like a queen with the other in gracious queenly acknowledgement of the suitable tribute.

❄

One evening, during the middle of the week, while I sipped my wine and read the local paper at my café on the *place*, its tranquility was disrupted by the laughter and shouts of customers at the side-by-side cafés on one side of the island terrace. What provoked their merriment was an unusual couple strolling along on the other side of the place. The man, short and black-haired, was sporting a white summer suit, a bright blue tie, and a Panama hat. His female companion, holding his arm in the most courtly fashion, was broad-shouldered and towered above him. She matched him, however, in her stylish attire: a red wide-brimmed straw summer hat, a hip-clinging, white dress with splashes of blue and green, and red high-heeled shoes. The calls and shouts built as the odd couple sauntered toward the door of the lone café on their side of the *place*. When they reached it, they dramatically paused and turned to face their admirers gathered on the sidewalk in front of the two cafés across the *place*. The man removed his hat and bowed in a debonair manner. His companion then turned her broad back to the applauding gallery and with a saucy wiggle of her hips bent forward and flipped up her skirt, revealing white underpants and a very broad, very male bottom. Cheers, hoots, and whistles followed them into the café. My waiter told me the couple were well known to the habitués, or *piliers,* of the *place*, which, I later found out, was also favored on their time off by the prostitutes who lived in the area. With every change of season, the odd couple delighted their admirers by showing off a suitably stylish outfit, their appearance always touching off a rambunctious reception.

❄

Though I considered Place des Corps Saints my "home" neighborhood––when I travel I never feel at ease until I establish one––I had to visit at least once the city's main square, with its fancy restaurants and high-end cafés, its public buildings, and its cathedral. I chose the late afternoon of the festival's final Saturday, the hottest day of my week in the city, and settled into a terrace chair at a café next to the cathedral. Sipping my *citron pressé*, a lemonade from freshly squeezed lemons, and relaxing under a terrace umbrella was the perfect way to pass an hour or so before a performance by Alvin Ailey's dancers, my last festival event. Perfect, that is, unless the devilish mistral, which can howl in all seasons, decided to pay a visit.

This cold, dry and often violent wind blows fitfully all year and had already made many appearances during the festival, coming out of the snow-covered Alps to roar down the Rhone Valley to the Mediterranean, often at speeds up to seventy miles an hour. Always unpredictable, the winds blow sometimes once a day, sometimes three or four times a day; sometimes for ten minutes, sometimes for an hour. Wind in general seems to throw all of us out of balance, but the mistral's fitfulness is especially unnerving, putting people on edge, and, some say, causing a rise in suicides. This devilish wind paid a visit to my last festival event that evening, but it was far from disruptive. It became part of an offering by a superb performer who gave us all that night an unforgettable gift.

As at Place des Corps Saints, I played spectator on this more fashionable square, sipping my lemonade, watching the comings and goings of expensive black Citroën sedans, high-fashion ladies with their leash-straining small dogs, and the careful play of well-dressed children. The jubilant clamor of cathedral bells startled me out of my musings and announced the emergence from the cathedral of a newly married couple in tuxedo and flowing white gown followed by their smiling tuxedoed and gowned wedding party. Several flower-bedecked limousines waited at the curb. But first came the photographs. Smiling and talking, the happy group arranged itself at the church's door for the traditional wedding shots. The photographer was still giving them directions when a white van, horn blaring, careened into the square and screeched to a halt in front of the couple's waiting limousine. Out of its flung open doors leaped a film cameraman, a female audio technician, and a pair of male lighting assistants, who all bounded up the stairs, long hair flying, cables trailing behind them––all of them stark naked. Like revelers from a Picasso painting, they swooped and leaped around the bride and groom, who, after a moment of shock, broke into roars of laughter. In a minute or two, it was all over. The nude quartet dashed back to the van, jumped in, and, waving and tooting goodbye, sped away from the cathedral and their startled friends.

That never would have happened at any church in the Irish-American world I knew, and probably not at any American church of any denomination. That it happened in Avignon on a square of upscale cafés reminded me again of the difference between American and European culture, at least the culture of southern France.

The last event for me in Avignon was born of a cross-cultural love affair that had been going on since the pre-World War II days of Josephine Baker and Sidney Bechet––an affair between the French and the jazz, blues and dance of African Americans. Tonight's performance under a clear sky was a celebration of that love affair. As the sunlight began to fade, Alvin

Ailey's dancers, then mostly African American but now multi-racial, took the stage in the main courtyard of the Palais des Papes, a magnificent fourteenth century building that from the festival's beginning has been the venue for its major presentations. The sold-out performance was packed with an international audience that knew Ailey's work and was abuzz with anticipation. When the dancers appeared on stage to take their first steps, wild applause greeted them. Every dance received a foot stomping, whistling expression of the crowd's affection. The final piece tlhen of every Ailey performance was "Revelations," its spiritual music and rhythmic dances expressing the joy and strength of the African-American people as they struggled through the horrors of slavery and subsequent violent discrimination. It was an audience favorite. I had seen Ailey's troupe perform it once in Berkeley, and, as it did then, it brought the cheering, applauding crowd to its feet.

Whistles and foot stomping went on and on until "Cry" was announced as a second encore. A tribute to a black woman who travels through a cruel world and finds the courage and strength to prevail, it was a solo piece created for the troupe's superb Judith Jamison, a tall, powerful and supremely graceful dancer. Until that point in the evening, the mistral had not made an appearance, but Jamison's long white dress, wound around her like a sash, seemed to invite the entry of the capricious wind. Within minutes of her first steps onto the stage, as if it were responding to a cue, the wind swept into the Palais. Jamison embraced it, spinning and running so her white sash unwound and was carried wildly up and out by the wind. When it billowed upward she leaped, arms outstretched, as if to follow it; when it collapsed to lay quivering on the stage like an animal, she joined it in clenching and upthrusting movements; when it whipped out straight, she twirled to wrap it around her, then let it spin out again in soaring billows. No one in the audience moved, and for several moments after Jamison triumphantly bounded off stage, her white sash spinning out behind her, there was complete silence. Then all of us exploded out of our trance with cheers, whistles, and foot-stomping applause. Jamison, first alone, then joined by the rest of the troupe, took bow after bow, smiling all the while, as all of us in the audience were smiling. Bouquets of flowers were placed along the front edge of the stage or handed to some of the dancers, but the applause thundered on under the star-filled sky. Several times the dancers ran off the stage only to be called back by unabated cheering and rhythmic applause. Three, four, five times, they bowed and waved, then returned the applause and blew kisses. Finally, smiling and laughing, the dancers went into the audience to embrace and exchange *grosses bises* with their happy and affectionate admirers, sharing with them the extraordinary joy of this unforgettable experience.

I floated out with the smiling, jubilant crowd into the warm Provençal night and almost danced slowly back to the waiting Egyptian owner of my hotel. The following morning, I boarded a bus for Grenoble and points unknown, hoping to give my life's dance a new joyful expansiveness.

Chapter 5

Valeilles and its *Village Naturiste*

"*J'arrive*," I'm coming, chimed the response when I rapped on the door of a silver "*caravan*," or mobile home, parked at the edge of a pine wood. The chime became a hum as I waited at the foot of the caravan stirs next to a folding table with a thin binder and a bouquet of colored pens in a crockery jar. To the left of the caravan, a silver-haired man wearing dark-rimmed glasses sat in a camp chair reading a newspaper in the shade of the woods. Seeing me at the caravan door, he nodded a greeting. Then the humming stopped and the caravan door opened. Slowly, as if descending a sweeping chateau stairway, came a black-haired woman in her forties, as voluptuous as a Maillol statue, tanned to a warm nut brown and wearing a red, floppy straw hat, spike heels––and nothing else. What did I expect? After all, she was the manager of this *village naturiste* – or nudist center – in southwestern France. Nonetheless, I was so surprised that when she looked directly at me and said "*Bonjour, monsieur,*" in her warm voice, I was speechless––in English and French.

I had frolicked on several nude beaches near San Francisco, and even taken nude massage classes, yet every time I doffed my clothes I still had a brief tussle with my father's sly admonition to my brother and I that our genital equipment was so inferior we would be "lucky" to find a woman. Clothes-free, my energy usually took over in such situations, and I dispelled that wily undermining voice, relishing the freedom of being unencumbered by either clothes or inhibitions.

My cavortings on nude beaches, however, did no more to prepare my Irish-American self for this woman than French tapes had readied me for her "*Eh, alors, monsieur?*" That she delivered this query with a coquettish smile after settling her tan round parts into the embrace of a canvas chair did nothing to help me find the right French words for a response. Eventually, however, as I feigned looking at the surrounding scenery, the caravan, even at the smiling woman's mischievous brown eyes, anywhere but at her Rubenesque body, at which, of course, she knew I wanted to look most of all, I was able to say "*Bonjour, Madame*" and ask the price of admission to the *village*. With a voice full of teasing pleasure at my discomfort, Madame explained the prices for day and week passes, that it was strictly forbidden to wear clothes anywhere on the grounds—only shoes or sandals were allowed—that the changing rooms and swimming pool were up the road a short ways, and, smiling coyly, that a couple of beautiful young women had gone up that road a few minutes ago.

I paid for a day pass, which she recorded in her notebook. Then, she looked up from under the rim of her red hat and handed me my receipt, making her ample breasts gently quiver. *"Merci, Madame*, I said. As I turned to start up the dirt road, she cheerily wished me *"Bon après-midi, Monsieur,"* and bent to her bookkeeping tasks as though in a Paris office. The man reading the newspaper called to her: *"Tout va bien chérie?"* Everything was definitely going fine for *"chérie"* and, I imagined, for him as well.

Chérie was the manager of a *village,* or resort, for *naturistes,* people who believe that living close to nature, eating a good diet, and dispensing with clothes are essential for a healthy life. A small sign on a two-lane country road indicated where this *village* was--a half mile off the same road that passed through the hamlet of Valeilles, fifty miles south of the Lot River in Quercy, a rich agricultural region of southwestern France.

The couple who was my hosts in Grenoble--they had moved from Berkeley several years earlier--knew I made pottery and suggested I get in touch with a friend whose wife, Rose, was taking a ceramics workshop in southwestern France. There were still openings for the first two weeks in August, apparently, and Marius, Rose's husband, and Emma, their two-year-old daughter were driving to join her in just a week or so. I registered by phone and in one leisurely day near the end of July drove with Marius and Emma some 400 miles to Valeilles.

The trip, which started at dawn, gave Marius and I a chance to discover that we both like poking along country roads and exploring small towns. In fact, that was exactly what we did on this trip, taking mostly two-lane roads, which provided me with a tour of the Auvergne's Massif Central and its ancient volcanoes. More importantly, as it turned out months later, our trip gave me a chance to learn about the restaurant run by Marius's parents. Emma dozed most of the time or watched the countryside, which changed every hundred kilometers or so, as it often does in France. We stopped once for a coffee, since we left at five that morning, and again for a picnic lunch near a small mountain town. By late afternoon we reached Valeilles. Rolling along at a leisurely pace, we had driven from the Alps to just a hundred miles or so from the Atlantic, almost two-thirds of the way across France. No wonder the French can't believe how large California is, to say nothing of the United States.

❄

The pottery workshop was one of several organized for the first time that summer by Paul and Isabelle, a married couple who were professional ceramicists, and Jean-Baptiste, or JB, the new owner of the town's only bistrot. All of them had moved to Valeilles several years earlier. In addition to the two-week pottery workshops, they had also organized similar workshops in black-and-white photography and the secrets of cooking the specialities of the region. Among those savory dishes were goose stuffed with the wonderful local prunes, a variety of duck dishes, and cassoulet, a slowly cooked stew of white beans, duck, goose, pork, and sausage. A one-page flyer promoted a grand program of summer events to complement the workshops: rock concerts, performances by an Occitane dance and music group, and barbecues with a *boum,* or dance party, afterward. The presence of the *village naturiste* was discreetly noted in small type at the bottom of the flyer, which, designed like a simple road map, put Valeilles in the center, with directional arrows guiding one and all to the Lot River Valley's new hub of culture, as *The New Yorker* did once, showing New York as the center of the entire United States, greatly reduced in size around it.

In keeping with most publicity, these claims had little to do with reality. Not only was Valeilles far from being a regional cultural center, it was far from everything, so small it did not even have its own bakery. Nonetheless, in the Summer of 1974, this hamlet surrounded by gently undulating pastureland and fields of vegetables, grain and maize (feed corn), was buzzing with activity. Set just below the mesa where the *village naturiste* was perched, its fifty or so houses were strung along both sides of a two-lane road that topped the crest of a low rise. Made of white stucco or light gray stone, the houses were roofed with traditional red tiles. Behind them, sloping down from the road, were vegetable gardens and small plantings of wine grapes.

At one end of town was the village square, which was only more or less square, as it was bisected by the area's principal two-lane road. One half of this skewed square was formed by the town hall, the adjoining bistrot, and the gravel area in front of them; the other half, across the road, was made up of a small gray stone church, which faced the road, a stone rabbit hutch that abutted the large, barn-like corrugated shed housing the pottery studio, and, across from the church, the white stucco post office. A gravel area in front of the pottery shed and post office was used as a town parking lot. In the summer's blistering heat the shed's doors were kept open most of the day, revealing in its high-roofed interior twenty or so potter's wheels, several kilns, mounds of clay, and every morning myself and a dozen or so members of my workshop.

Several of these aspiring potters lived nearby, including Martin, who was an internationally known water skier and owned a VW, rare in the land of the Deux Chevaux, the small "roll-top desk" Citroën so popular in France at that time. Other workshop members were put up by families in town. The rest of us, including myself, stayed at an abandoned stone farmhouse a mile or so outside Valeilles. I camped outside in a tent, as did Marius, Rose, and Emma. Three women stayed in the farmhouse, which offered only cold water. A rickety wood-plank outhouse was available for life's daily needs. Though that summer's drought brought relentless heat, and a heavy storm would have given us a cooling break, we were lucky the rain never came, for it would have made living in and around that farmhouse a muddy misery.

Few tourists—even French tourists—ever visited Quercy. Like California's Central Valley, it did not offer a lot for visitors, being largely agricultural. Moreover, the nearby Lot River was polluted and the swimmable Dordogne was 80 miles to the north. As a result, the workshop impresarios knew that they had to have something to spice up their workshop ragout. The *Village Naturiste* with its small pool was it. Its allure was sure to attract the city folks, in particular workshop participants from Paris. Oddly enough, though, the workshop organizers did little to promote it. Perhaps because it was a bit risqué for the socially conservative people of that rural area—*la France profonde*—the less said about it the better.

In JB's bistrot one day, where members of the photography and pottery workshop often ate lunch, an aspiring photographer said she went to the *Village* pool almost every day with her visiting husband and kids. They all had a fine time, she said, and the *Village* was just an easy half-hour walk from town. I asked her if she were nervous about the nudity. *"Mais, non, pas du tout. Pourquoi?"* Not at all, she said, why? France was the land of the monokini, after all. I spent the first workshop afternoon or two shaping clay in the oppressive heat of the ceramics shed, but memories of those California nude beaches kept dancing through my head. On the third afternoon, they led me out of the baking town to the hand-printed wooden *Village* sign, then slowly up the gravel road to the round, sun-browned madame in the floppy red hat and teasing smile.

Those two *jolies femmes* who had arrived just before me could well be frolicking in the pool, I thought, as I bid *chérie "Au revoir"* and started up the road to find out, hiding my eagerness––and nervousness––by slowing my walk to a saunter. At the end of a short stroll I emerged from the sweet-smelling pine woods, mounted a slight rise, and found myself standing next to a small but inviting pool of shimmering chlorine green–– completely empty. From where I stood, I could see across gently rolling fields and pastures all the way to the Pyrenees, a hundred miles or more to the south. There was, however, no trace of the *jolies femmes*. Not even the sound of a voice broke the heat-swollen silence. Where had they gone?

I entered the small brick changing house and started to undress, stuffing my clothes into my airline flight bag, when from the pine woods came Plock... Plock... Plock. Someone was playing ping-pong, most likely those *jolies femmes*. I had felt at ease tossing a Frisbee around on California nude beaches, but was I ready for nude Ping Pong in the woods of southwestern France? Wearing only sandals, I followed the "plocks" along a sandy path through the woods and quickly came to a clearing. "*Voilà*," there they were––all three of them. The two women, both in their twenties, were casually rallying at the ping-pong table. Off to the side, a muscular, dark-haired young man energetically did push-ups on the edge of the sandy clearing. The women paused to introduce themselves: Andrée, from a distance, with a cool nod; Sabine with an open smile and a warm handshake. The pusher-upper jumped to his feet, said his name was François and shook my hand with appropriate vigor, then abruptly started windmilling his arms and stretching this way and that––a routine, I assumed, designed to bring him a conquest at more than just the ping pong table. His body glistened with sweat. Sabine handed him her paddle and François, bouncing around as though on center court at the French Open, started rallying vigorously with Andrée, who was as dark as a Gauguin Tahitian beauty.

I stood to the side with Sabine, who had long, wavy, reddish-blond hair, a full-breasted figure, fair skin, and a coy, flirtatious manner. She watched the game with amused attention. I did, too, more or less. My French was still clumsy, but I was more interested in playing a flirtatious game with Sabine, taking her occasional smile as encouragement, than challenging the formidable skills of Andrée. In fact, I had no more luck in my games with Sabine than François had with Andrée. Cooler than Sabine, but equally beautiful, the olive-skinned Andrée's strong features, framed by chestnut-brown hair cut shoulder length, betrayed self-assured pleasure at whipping François and testy unhappiness when he won an occasional point. In the end, the Frenchman's pre-match calistlhenics were useless against his opponent's paddle skills.

He badly missed a sharply angled forehand that ended a second game and handed me his paddle, saying "*La belle France contre Les Etats-Unis,*" seeing the match as yet another opportunity for the French to stick it to the Americans. Who was I to pass up such a challenge? I'll tell you exactly who I was: a lustful 38-year-old eager to put my frosty opponent in her place and Sabine in my sleeping bag.

Andrée, seemingly irked by the attention I was paying Sabine, approached our contest with a determination that darkened her already dark features. We had barely rallied, when she asked me if I was ready, impatient to put me in my place. *"Oui, je suis prêt"* I am ready, I said, knowing I was far from it and still a bit self-conscious about my nakedness. I had to forget about it, though, if I was to have any chance of beating Sabine. We rallied for serve. Surprisingly, I won. I should have quit when I was ahead, for I quickly found it impossible to forget about Andrée's nakedness. Even on my serve she quickly taught me the stiff ping-pong price I would pay for my prurient eye, putting me down five to zero.

She came at me with everything she had, which was plenty, as Humphrey Bogart might have said. Slamming and slicing and top spinning, she was always in the background, stretching her lovely limbs this way and that, her pubic hair peeking over the edge of the table, her thighs taut, her breasts quivering slightly with every shot. No wonder François had succumbed so quickly. But I had my pride, and a lingering if ill-founded hope that a victory would win favor with Sabine. I dropped the first two games quickly, winning only a few points in each, before shifting my focus in the third game from Andrée's distracting curves to dealing with her hard-to-handle assortment of shots. I backed off; I moved in. When she smashed, I blooped; when she sliced, I sliced back. I felt a surge of confidence. Andrée won the third match, too, but I had begun to give her a battle. She was feeling the heat. Her tight jaw got tighter; her sang-froid began to melt. Rivulets of sweat trickled down between her breasts as she pushed strands of hair off her damp forehead. François cheered on La France. Sabine, enjoying it all, sent me oh so lovely smiles from time to time, but, alas, saved all her cheers for my opponent. In the end, I pulled out the fourth game. Or did she, out of boredom, let me win one? *Pas possible*! There was no way this woman would let any man beat her. Her smug pleasure at trouncing François and her readiness to depart after I finally won a game made that clear.

Finally figuring out how to best such a haughty opponent was certainly satisfying, but I could have happily spent all afternoon losing to Sabine. Surprisingly, as I was inviting her to play, Andrée quickly gathered up her things, and clearly speaking for Sabine as well, curtly said–– in English––that they had to leave. She then brusquely walked away without so much as an *au revoir*. Andrée taught English in high school, Sabine said, as she turned to follow her *copine*. I was left with a playful over-the-shoulder smile and the image of a voluptuous woman, all white and pink and curly reddish hair, disappearing into the dancing shadows of a sweet-smelling pine wood.

"*Comme c'est curieux*," that's really odd, I said to François. Andrée did not say a word in English until the end. Perhaps she was shy, he said, smiling. We both knew better. "*Enfin, elles sont copines. C'est la vie, quoi,*" he said, as we walked up the path to the pool. *Copine* (*copain* for men) has several meanings in French: partner is one.

❉

Some children were splashing around in the pool and half a dozen sunbathers lolled about at poolside, including the photographer and her visiting husband and children. The somber Andrée and lovely Sabine, however, were nowhere to be seen. At one end of the pool, a man in his seventies, wearing a well-worn straw hat, quietly stood up to his waist in the cooling water, smiling at the children's aquatic antics and playfully splashing them when they got within range. Two of the children Pierre, 14, and his sister, , twelve years old going on twenty, greeted me from the side of the pool with waves and cries of "*Seed, seed, viens ici!*" Sid, come here. Pierre and Corrine's mother had died of cancer several years ago, I had been told, and their father was constantly busy trying to make ends meet, so, along with Marie, who was Corrine's age, the two children adopted me as their exotic "uncle."

I had met Marie first, when, curious about the new group of potters, she had wandered across the street at the end of our half-day workshop and joined me at the faucet where I was cleaning my tools outside the shed's front door. With my improving but still shaky French and my American ways, she found me, she later confided, even more unusual than the odd Parisians. She had short, tight curly blond hair and boney arms and legs like most kids her age. But unlike Corinne, she was quietly curious in almost an adult way, thinking about my answers to one of her many questions before she asked another one. Since I was slower at cleanup than my workshop colleagues, we had time to talk. When I was finished, we sat under the plane tree that shaded the gravel courtyard in front of the shed and shared information about our families and the differences between France and America. Marie, whose family had only moved to Valeilles from the Jura Mountains a few years ago, said it was hard not having her cousins and aunts and uncles close by. I talked of my difficulties living in a country with a different language as she laughed and shook her head of curls at my mistakes.

Often Pierre and Corrine joined us in their energetic fashion, and they all made jokes about how funny the Parisians were who came to the workshops. Some of them were shocked if, during our break, the postmistress happened to carry a rabbit by its hind legs out of the hutch next door and dispatched it with a sharp blow to the back of the neck. Compared with the Parisians, however, an American--especially a man my age--was like a visitor from Mars, though this trio never made me feel that way. Besides, having no kids of my own, which I have regretted from time to time, I enjoyed their company.

Most of all, when not laughing riotously at my French, they asked me questions about my life and America. We traded lessons on language, on different ways of doing things--Americans don't exchange *"grosses bises"* when they meet or leave each other--and talked about the size of the American houses and cars they had seen on television. Pierre shouted *"Pas vrai,"* as did Marcel in Grenoble, when I told them how big California was or how many people lived in New York. *"Incroyable! Pas possible!"* Did I know any cowboys? Had I ever seen any *"peaux rouges,"* or "redskins?" How could I be in France alone, without any family? Of course, they also wanted to know what I was doing in France. And how did I find out about Valeilles? As I searched for the right French words, I marveled at how unself-conscious they were, how at ease in talking with an adult, a trait they shared with other French children I met, like the boy I met on my first day in Paris. They saw themselves deserving of the same respect they gave to me. That I was an American old enough to be their father, which they also found *"incroyable,"* made no difference.

When the church bell rang noon, Pierre and Corrine went home for lunch and Marie's father called to her for help. *"J'arrive!"* she shouted, I'm coming, and galloped loose-limbed like a colt across the road to help set the tables, have lunch, and help Gina, the waitress, clean up. I was left, very unBuddha-like, under the plane tree, wondering, as they did, what I was doing in that place and why I had such strong feelings for a country I barely knew.

When I approached the pool, the self-consciousness that I had lost playing Ping-Pong, returned--but not for long. As on the beaches of California, I quickly got past the first few introductory moments of glancing discreetly at everyone's private parts—like dogs sniffing each other—then joyfully yielded to the children's exuberance, which of course was completely free of imprisoning inhibition. The three of us jumped in, our wild entry spraying the old man and his sporty hat. He smiled and splashed us back but otherwise did not move an inch, not even to adjust his slightly askew *chapeau*.

Pierre wanted to wrestle, but Corrine shooed him off and climbed on my back, holding me tightly around the neck to leave no doubt who was in charge. With imperial flirtatiousness, she demanded that I tow her around. *"Oui, mademoiselle,"* I said, going wherever she directed me. From one end of the pool to the other we went, circling the old man. All the while, I was aware that the wriggling young girl clinging to my back and pressing her mouth to my ear to be sure I heard her commands, already had, consciously or otherwise, blossoming feelings about my maleness. I wanted to respect the woman she was becoming, moving in the wink of an eye from being twelve to being eighteen and back again, but I did not want to curb her exuberant affection. I had little time to think about it, however, because Corrine's intense, sinewy energy gave me little time to think about anything except how to get this girl-woman to loosen her grip so I could breathe.

After Corrine softened me up with half-a-dozen turns around the pool, urging me to go, *"Plus vite. Plus vite. Encore plus vite,"* faster, faster, even faster, Pierre took me on for a tag-and-dunking match, which, of course, he--and France--won. Whenever we got within range, the older man in the straw hat did his laughing best to splash us. I finally conceded to Pierre that I could not beat him, *jamais,* never, and the two of us hauled out to rest in the sun, a bit apart from the others: It was time for a man-to-man talk.

With Corrine busy elsewhere, Pierre was able to talk to me without fear of being interrupted and started a serious conversation, a bit to my surprise. Of course he asked the question the French I met, sooner or later, always asked, no matter their age. Why was I in France, to which, as usual, I had no clear answer. Then came, why wasn't I married? My answer to that was also full of uncertainty, but I think was more honest than any I would give an adult. With these children, I did not feel I had to lie to protect some image of myself or to defend what I was doing. I said to Pierre that I was in France partly to forget a love affair that came to a messy and unhappy end, and, beyond that, that I just had not found the right woman, which might even have been true. "*Les femmes!*" Pierre said, looking as serious as a 14-year-old can look when commenting on this subject, "*Elles sont vâchement difficile à comprendre.*" Women, they are are really difficult to understand. To which I could only say: *C'est absolument vrai, sans aucun doute!* Absolutely true, without any doubt.

❄

The half-mile walk back to Valeilles was all downhill, but without the cooling water and mesa breeze, I quickly felt the strength-sapping weight of the heat. As I neared town, the older man from the pool spun by on his black moped (a generic name for a cross between a bicycle and a motor scooter), his hat pulled down tightly, his eyes focused on the twisting two-lane road. A few minutes later, he and I were sharing a table at JB's café, a cold draft beer in front of me, a *citron pressé* in front of him. He'd love to have a beer, he said, but he still had a few kilometers to go before reaching home in the neighboring village of Dausse and with French drivers on small roads, you have to keep your wits about you, especially, he added, when riding a two-wheel putt-putt like mine.

"It's so hot! Why don't more people from town use the pool?" I asked him. "Too risqué for country folk," he said. "They imagine all kinds of wild things go on there. I just give 'em a wink and let 'em think I'm having a hot time." With that, he quaffed the last of his lemonade and set his hat securely on his head. "*A demain,*" see you tomorrow, he said as he shook my hand and walked out to mount his moped. He pedaled vigorously for a few seconds until the engine caught, then kicked up the parking stand and, after checking for traffic, pulled out onto the road, spraying pebbles behind him, and buzzed off for home.

Soon after he left, the town's unofficial "grandpa," or *Pépé*, abandoned the bench in front of the café to enter it for his afternoon ritual. Except for the midday hours, he kept an eye on the comings and goings at JB's bistrot and the town post office and pottery shed across the street. In the morning, he was on his bench to enjoy the sun's warmth, and there again during the late afternoon when the bench was in the shade. He greeted and smiled at everyone who passed him, even the peculiar workshop people from Paris and other foreign places who came from that pottery shed across the street to eat at JB's. As soon as he entered the bistrot bar Pépé started a ritual that I had the pleasure of observing several times. Wearing, as always, a soft leather golf cap and plaid *pantoufles,* or soft-soled slippers, he paused just inside the door, acknowledged me with a *"Bonsoir, Monsieur,"* and kidded with Gina, the waitress, feigning to give her an affectionate embrace but settling for *grosses bises.* Then he took his station at the bar and yelled for JB, who played his role, as always, by not responding. Only after Pépé's third shout did *le patron* mosey in from the adjoining restaurant and ask, in mock annoyance, why the mustachioed *Pépé* was shouting. All he had to do, JB said, was call for him in a normal voice, like other customers did.

"*Mon dieu, je voudrais un pastis, comme toujours,*" for God's sake, a Pernod as always, Pépé said, reaching across the wooden bar to tug the beard of the uppity Marcel. The café owner promptly put on the bar in front of his now smiling customer a clear eight-ounce glass, poured into it two fingers of amber-colored liquid, then put next to the glass a bowl of ice cubes and a carafe of water. *"Content?"* Happy, he asked, then reached over the bar to give a tug to grandpa's formidable mustache and went back to the café's kitchen. *Pépé* removed his cap to run his hand through still heavy long brown hair and shook his head, as usual, in mock consternation at *le patron's* rude behavior. He tumbled a few ice cubes into the glass of *pastis,* added water, which turns the amber liquid milky yellow, and, after a short pause to savor the moment, took a generous swallow of the licorice-flavored drink that, to my surprise, is wonderfully refreshing in hot weather. His sigh of satisfaction rose softly to fill the café's stillness.

But the ritual was not over. Wham! Like the crack of a rifle, a folded newspaper slammed on the bar at Pépé's elbow, causing him to almost jump out of his *pantoufles.* He turned to confront the rude disturber of his peace, another older man, whose fox-like features and bright eyes were shaded by a snappy Panama hat. *"Oh, c'est toi!"* Pépé said, as usual, and the two friends, after shaking hands, fell into lively conversation. I missed its subtleties, but I overheard enough to know that it covered everything from the drought and its heat to the nudist *village* to the workshops and the people, *un peu bizarre,* who were everywhere in town this summer.

Was Valeilles ready for all this? Pépé asked. Why not? answered his friend, and—Wham!--slammed the newspaper again on the bar. Pépé's mustache didn't even twitch.

Rituals of daily life like the ones I saw repeated at JB's café had for years been part of small-town life all over France—right along with the postmistress gossiping with neighbors while snapping *haricots verts*, green beans, farmers leading their night-wandering bulls home at dawn, and just about everyone making daily trips to the baker for fresh bread. Similar rituals are characteristic of many small towns all over the world, binding people and their shared lives together in casual but important ways. When, like the once obligatory family Sunday lunch in France, they happen with regularity in both city and countryside and are entrenched for many decades, they become, as Marcel Proust observed, threads of a pattern that, woven together over time, give people a sense of belonging to the same culture. The French now live in a modern industrialized country, of course, and new ways of living have loosened this fabric of daily life. With every change--like the introduction of home butane gas canisters--something is gained, of course, but something is also lost, though we often pay little attention to how those losses affect us and our particular world--until they no longer are there.

Since most of my fellow farmhouse potters were French and had, like Rose, attended the preceding two-week pottery workshop, they had already created a number of daily rituals, which happily became part of my Valeilles life as well. Right after dawn, while the air was still slightly cool, Marius and I, sometimes joined by Martin, drove in Marius's car a mile or so to a nearby farm where the dairyman filled our two-gallon can with milk from the day's first milking. One morning, as he skimmed from the centrifuge the still warm milk, rich with cream, he told us of the latest wanderings of his bull, who had managed to stroll more than two miles from home last night. "How did you get him back?" Marius asked. "*Tout d'abord, il me connait,* first of all, he knows me, the farmer said, so I can get close enough to carefully put a rope in his nose ring. Then I can lead him home like a calf. Have a look at him, he said, and took us to view the roaming sire of his herd.

Entering the darkness of the cowshed from the brightness of the centrifuge room, we had to wait a minute or two to realize that what seemed to be a black boulder the size of Martin's VW Beetle was, in fact, the dairyman's prize bull. He stood about twenty feet away, motionless but for the occasional fly-shooing swish of his tail. Hearing us enter, he slightly turned his head to fix on us a large eye, which in my imagination expressed nothing but mythic malevolence. Then, with our fresh milk, still warm, we headed for Dausse, another short trip, where we bought from the region's flour-dusted baker a golden-crusted yard-long, foot-wide work of his centuries-old craft. As warm as the milk, it was the most beautiful, most delicious tasting French bread I've ever eaten, so irresistible that Marius and I, and anyone else who had come along with us, always tore off a chunk or two on the five-minute drive back to the farm.

Waiting for us to deliver the milk and bread, our hungry fellow potters had already started to make coffee and had set the table with jam, local honey, butter, and a tin of powdered hot chocolate. The milk was quickly heated and the bread was sliced and piled on the table, along with pots of hot coffee. Every day, admiring the golden loaf on the rough-hewn wooden table in our all-purpose kitchen and living room, its plank floor smooth from ages of use, I marveled at how eight of us could polish it off in one sitting. Yet, every day we did just that, leaving only scattered chips of crust and an empty milk can, washed clean and ready to be filled again the next morning.

Some of us added a second ritual at day's end: a sunset walk to Dausse for an after-dinner drink. Dausse had the same kind of stucco and stone houses as Valeilles, but twice as many. It was a town, not a hamlet. Because of its size, the bakery, and the fact that it boasted two bistrots, its citizens, people from Valeilles told me, looked down their noses at the *ploucs*, or hicks, from its smaller neighbor. We reached Dausse as the day's heat relaxed its grip on the countryside and the last summer light was slipping from the sky, though it was nearing 10. Rarely was anyone out and about, not even during those warm evenings: houses and shops were dark and closed up tight. One café, though, was open, at least for us. When we knocked on the door of a small grocery store that adjoined the café, Monsieur Ricou, *le patron*, emerged from the back room and without a smile but with a welcoming *"Bonsoir, mes amis,* let us in. Not wanting to let the rest of the town know he was open, though, he did not turn on any lights. Instead, with the military briskness his crew-cut suggested, he guided us through the semi-darkness of the café to the wood bar, calling out *"Fais gaffe!"* heads up, as we slowly wended our way among tables crowded with upended chairs.

Then, stationed behind his *comptoir*, Ricou asked: *"Et alors? Eaux de vie?"* some fruit brandies? To our enthusiastic *"Bien sûr!"* he responded by calling out the name of each as he took the announced bottle off the shelf behind him and placed it with dramatic authority on the bar. Bam!--*Pruneaux* (prune). Bam!-- *Pêche* (peach). Bam!--*Noix* (walnut). Bam!--*Mirabelle* (yellow plum). Bam!--Armagnac. My favorite was prune, rich and clear with a marvelous balance between the strength of the alcohol and the chewy sweet flavors of prunes. It is made from *prune d'ente*, an important a variety of plum grown widely in the southwest of France. The name changes from *prune* (plum) to *pruneau* (prune) when the plum is dried into the wrinkled fruit that is known as *pruneau d'Agen*, Agen being an important town in the region. The prune is also called the Black Gold of Aquitaine because it is considered by chefs and connoisseurs of such matters to be the finest prune in the world. When a few prunes are put into bottles of Armagnac, also regional, it is sold as Pruneaux d'Armagnac, a perfect topping for ice cream.

Monsieur Ricou said that for us his café was never closed. The warmth of his *eaux de vie* and the warmth of his welcome, which bubbled along beneath the surface reserve often found in some French, lasted the entire easy stroll back to the farm. I pulled my sleeping pad and bag out of my tent into the soft warmth of the windless star-filled night, deciding to take my chances with any roaming bulls, and drifted to sleep as with easeful thoughts of the pleasurable new rituals I had discovered. My weeks in Valeilles were so enlivened by a sensuous mixture of aromas and tastes and human encounters of all kinds, that I felt life itself was giving me *grosses bises* every day.

Strangely, it all felt familiar, as if I became aware slowly that what Valeilles offered me was something I had needed for a long time, maybe even since my childhood in the culturally diverse neighborhood of the south end of Hartford. For certain, it let me put completely out of mind the badgering questions of where I was going with my life.

❄

On the Sunday halfway through my two-week workshop, the withering heat of the summer-long drought convinced some of us to head west to the Atlantic Ocean. Marius, Rose, Emma, myself, and one of our farmhouse mates set off in Marius's little station wagon accompanied by Martin and two more workshop colleagues in his Beetle. Our destination: the broad beaches of Les Landes, just a few hours away. As the group's only habitual swimmer, I could hardly wait. Could this be a French Stinson Beach? No stops on the way, we agreed, though Marius and I made that a real test with our shared love of poking around as we traveled. We failed the test. Though Martin kept right on going to our next arranged destination on the coast, Marius could not resist pulling over at a roadside stand that was selling flats of those delicious local *pruneaux*. Its hand-lettered sign said they had been oven dried for only a third of the 24 hours it takes to convert them to prunes, just long enough so their bluish-purple skins were swollen to the point of bursting. After the vendor gave us all a sample, Marius insisted on buying a flat, in spite of warnings from his passengers. They were irresistible, their sweetness exploding in our mouths and all over our hands. The entire flat was gone within minutes. Prunes doing what they usually do, we then had to make more than a few emergency stops before reaching the Atlantic.

We met up with Martin, as planned, in a small beach town just minutes from the ocean, and bought what we needed for lunch. Marius went to an *épicérie*, or deli, for cheese, *charcuterie* (ham and sausages), and wine; Martin went to a *boulangerie*, to buy some baguettes; and I, with some hesitation, entered a small, unlit produce store near the *boulangerie* that had bananas and apples displayed outside. Peaches were still in season, and once my eyes adjusted to the small store's unlit interior, I saw an inviting display of them, some too large for a group to share but others just the right size. Behind the display stood a short wiry woman, with gray curly hair and a defiant look. A slight nod was her only response to my *"Bonjour, madame."*

"Je voudrais des pêches, s'il vous plait, madame," and chose several smaller peaches. Quick as a store cat pouncing on a mouse, she rounded the counter, took the smaller peaches from my hand, put them back and assumed a defensive position in front of her display of peaches.

"Non!" she said. *"Prenez celles-ci,"* take these, indicating the large ones. Surprised by her reaction––after all, a sale is a sale––I explained that I wanted the smaller ones.

"Les grandes seulement," only the large ones, she said.

I gave her my best American smile, and tried again.

"J'ai besoin des plus petites, madame," I need some smaller ones, madam. *"Absolument pas!"* madam snapped, arms folded like the proprietor she was. *"Seulement les grandes!"*

Almost speechless, but willing to be peachless, I gave up.

"Enfin," I said, *"pas de pêches du tout!"* Well, no peaches at all. *"Au*

revoir, Madame," I said. She did not say a word, and I walked out, letting in a few flies as I did.

My companions were disappointed when I returned empty handed, but laughed when I told my story. They were not surprised. Sometimes small-town French people can be like that. *"Rigid et déraisonnable?"* I asked, rigid and unreasonable. *"Non, non, ça, c'est trop,"* not that bad, Marius said. "We can be stubborn, but only once in a while," he said. Rose rolled her eyes.

At the beach, I was the only one eager to jump in, or go anywhere near the water. Too cold, the others said; the waves are too big, they said; and there were no showers or places to change. *Tant pis pour moi,* too bad for me. I got my feet wet, but the rest of me had to wait for another visit to that pool at the *village naturiste.*

On the way back to Valeilles, the ever-curious Marius waved Martin to stop and convinced him to turn off the regional road we were traveling and investigate a woolen mill and the hand-woven clothing announced by the typical small hand-printed roadside sign you found then all over France. We wended our way along a rutted dirt road until we reached a sprawling two-story wooden mill that must have been built in the 19th century. Deep in the mill, a man with long white hair and a white beard that came to a neat point, sat working at a loom powered by the stream that ran underneath the mill. The soft golden rays of light coming through the windows in the building's unfinished plank walls transformed him into a weaver from another age. I bought a sweater, taupe in color, a blend of the fleece of the brown and white sheep raised in that region. It cost $50, a lot on my skimpy budget, but over forty years later, I still wear it and get compliments about it, though, like me, it is a bit frayed. Made from untreated fleece, which is rich with the lanolin natural to sheep, it still repels a mist or light rain and takes a week to dry after I hand wash it.

❊

Every two weeks, a series of special events in Valeilles marked the end of another round of workshops. Photographers hung their black and white images in the café, potters displayed their pots, plates, pitchers and bowls in the pottery shed, and, under the culinary guidance of Madame Bunniel, members of the cooking workshop spent a morning preparing a lunchtime feast of regional specialties for all workshop participants. Her husband, Sébastien, was the town's most prosperous farmer and

Sébastien's mother the town's bean-snapping postmistress and tobacconist. After World War I, the government reserved all tobacconist positions for *les mutilés de la guerre,* wounded veterans and their immediate descendants. Sébastien's grandfather had been killed, like millions of other young Frenchmen in that obscene and insane bloodbath.

To accommodate the thirty or so guests, planks were set out on sawhorses under the large oak trees in front of the Bunniel's modest one-story stucco home, which sat on a slight rise and was surrounded by pastureland. The improvised tables, some on wobbly supports, were draped with red-and-white checked tablecloths that were held down by bottles of wine, though in the noontime heat, they hung still and straight. Picnic benches and chairs from the house and from JB's bistrot provided seating.

While we chatted in the comforting shade of the oak trees, a fizzy, dry white wine called *Perlé*, from about thirty miles away, near Albi, prepared us for the first course, garlic soup. Carried in tureens from the kitchen, it gave off steaming clouds redolent of that potent relative of the onion, but to our surprise
––or at least mine––the garlic's piquant flavors had been tamed by long hours of simmering in beef stock, enriched with butter, a bit of Armagnac and ingredients known only to Madame Bunniel and her half-dozen workshop sous-chefs. The result was rich and savory, balanced with a touch of sweetness.

It was followed by a cassoulet, filled with morsels of duck, goose, and sausage, and thick with white beans. With it we drank a dark red wine from the Lot Valley. It was so dark, in fact, that in the 70s it was still called the "black wine of Cahors" the chief city of the Lot area and the center of the wine's production. Its high tannin gave the wine, with aging, a fullness of body that made it chewable, as the French say, a perfect match for the cassoulet.

After a green salad to clean the palate, we all helped clear the tables to make room for preparing the dessert. Under Madame Bunniel's watchful eye, pairs of her sous-chefs carried outside one at a time round, tissue-thin sheets of pastry dough, four or five feet in diameter, and spread them like tablecloths on the tables. What would they become? Certainly nothing appetizing if I did not stand watch to keep away the flies, which came from every direction, first by ones and twos, then by the dozen, then by the hundreds. I swung my arms about, waved my newspaper, and finally took off my shirt and swirled it over the drying pastry. *"Ne vous en faites pas,"* Madame Bunniel said. Don't worry about it. The heat of the oven will take care of everything. It was a moment for the Gallic shrug, which I executed to perfection before refilling my glass with more of the "black wine" of Cahors.

Ten minutes later, Madame Bunniel tested the sheets of dough for dryness, declared them ready, then demonstrated precisely how we would help her turn them into a specialty of Quercy. First, she said, cut off a piece of the malleable pastry about as big as a saucer for a coffee cup. Hold it in your open hand so that when you slightly curl your fingers, the piece forms a shallow cup. Then carefully make half a dozen overlapping folds in the dough as you slowly close your fingers. The final result should resemble a blossoming flower, the "petals" supported by your curved fingers, the stem end in the center of your palm. Finally, place the blossom, open side up, narrow tip down, in a pie dish, starting at the rim and leaning blossom against blossom in circles from the outside rim toward the center until the dish is full. Madame Bunniel sprinkled each finished dish of "blossoms" with Armagnac and brown sugar and popped it into her very hot oven. Four or five minutes later, the first few "tarts" were done and, after a quick dusting with powdered sugar, were delivered to the table outside. The "blossoms," dark at their open ends and gradually becoming lighter toward the bottom, were like brown and golden flowers, and as crisp as ice-cream sugar cones. Cries of *"Magnifique!"* greeted their arrival. As soon as the first batch was devoured, we started chanting *"Bis,"* encore, and more came out, and then more. It was a fitting finger-licking end to that sumptuous meal. We raised our glasses to toast Madame Bunniel and her assistants, who, Madame declared, were now true chefs of *la cuisine de Quercy.*

Full, hot, and a bit tipsy, we took down the tables, carrying some to the Bunniel's barn and stacking others for JB to collect later. Before walking the mile or so back into town, though, I had to visit the WC, or toilet. Where would I find it, I asked the ten-year-old Bunniel son. *"Dehors,"* he said, outside. *"Où ça?"* where? I asked. "There's an outhouse near the barn, he said, but for the rest, anywhere you like." These people were not poor, but like many farmers they made use of everything—night soil included—and lived simple lives that to city folks were sometimes rough around the edges. A natural gas delivery system had only recently been set up for the region, Madame Bunniel explained. Until then, we heated all our water with wood. "Now," she said, "the gas does the job," pointing to the blue canister hanging on the wall near the kitchen sink.

"But," she added, "we still drag the tub into the kitchen for our Saturday night baths." A real bathroom was next, she said.

As I lay under the stars that hot windless night, I couldn't help wondering if the Bunniels weren't living the good life, in spite of their less than modern plumbing. After the student-led eruptions of the late 1960s in Berkeley and in Paris in May, 1968, many young city-dwellers romanticized about the slower-paced, earth-centered life of the small farmer and the close community of a country town. I did, too. Without a mate, however, and close to 40, my only "farming" experience was with my family's World War II Victory Garden and, years later, tending a small plot behind my Berkeley apartment. I had second thoughts--and third ones as well. I asked Sébastien Bunniel how he liked living in Valeilles, in this land of wheat, corn, dairy farms and foie gras. "It's quiet," he said. "Very, very quiet. In winter, a flock of doves flying over can be the most exciting thing that happens for days."

❄

The next night--my last in Valeilles—would feature the Soirée Folklorique that was given every two weeks as both a farewell party for those whose workshops just ended and a welcoming party for those about to start new sessions. It was not going to be a big bash like the one announced for mid-September that would put a finishing touch on the workshop season. An unnamed "*super groupe*" was promised for that, as well as singing folk songs around a camp fire at the village naturiste--in the nude?--competitions at *belote*, a popular card game in France, and *pétanque* or *boules*, like lawn bowling but on gravel or dirt wherever there is enough space. My less elaborate soirée was going to offer Occitan folk singing and dancing, a barbecue in the small grassy area behind the town hall, and a *boum*, or party, in the town hall basement, which for the occasion would be transformed into a discotheque. It sounded good to me. My colleagues on the farm decided not to go, having been to the preceding one, which I had missed, so I put on my Birkenstocks and went alone, walking the mile or so to town as the evening began to turn down the day's heat.

Small announcements of the program had been posted in JB's bistrot: a performance by the local Occitan folk group would kick off the evening, literally it turned out. Occitan derives from *langue d'oc, oc* meaning yes in the regional language spoken for centuries in southwestern France.

Langue d'oil (*oil* also meaning yes), the dominant language in northern France, became the national language after the French Revolution. Nonetheless, like Provençal, an Occitan dialect spoken in Provence, and Breton in Brittany, Occitan was spoken in daily life until well into the 1930s.

In the 1970s, no autoroute cut through the region to bring tourists, French or otherwise; phone service was as skimpy as blue canisters of butane; and television sets were generally found only in cafés, where they were hidden behind cabinet doors and turned on only for telecasts of the Tour de France, matches in the national sport of football (soccer); and rugby, then only a big sport in the French southwest but now popular all over the country. Much like Germany and Italy, modern France is fairly new as a unified nation state and for several centuries had to contend with strong regional identities and their distinct languages, which the "back to the land" movement often revived. On my last night in this quiet corner of France, I would have a chance to enjoy the benefits of this movement, a cultural cassoulet that was a mixture of the old France of Occitan and the new France of Johnny Hallyday, who would no doubt dominate the music of the *boum*, with the Rolling Stones adding spice to the mix.

The music and dances of the *soirée folklorique* were performed in the gravel courtyard in front of the pottery shed. Pierre and Corrine both participated and were in full costume: loose white blouses with billowing sleeves, broad red sashes around the waist, long black skirts for the women and black pants bagged out like knickers for the men. Bright red stockings up to the knee and shiny black shoes completed these simple but dramatic costumes.

To get things started, the group sang some Occitan songs, which seemed Slavic or Arabic in their harmonies and rhythms. Then in pairs or as a group, the two dozen dancers stepped into a series of dances, inspired by the beating drum and wailing, looping sounds of bagpipes and flute. Both gracefully slow and skipping fast, the dances featured high kicks and leaps, rhythmic hops and tricky spins to display the dancers' skills.

A feat of terpsichorean daring topped the dance part of the program. The two dozen performers took their places in three circles of eight dancers each, with the alternating men and women in each circle roughly of the same height, important for this dance. At first, the dancers started to shuffle slowly in circles, like a carousel just beginning to move, arms on neighboring shoulders. As the rhythmic rat-a-tat-tat of the drums increased, the circling dancers, arms more tightly locked on shoulders, shuffled faster, then trotted, then, skirts twirling, pants flapping, ran at a dizzying pace, sending dust and gravel flying. When the centrifugal force of the turning dancers was at its peak, the women raised their feet behind them, each woman locked in place by the tight grip of the men on either side of her. Red-faced and sweating, the men ran faster still, until the women, extended their legs out fully behind them so their bodies were almost parallel to the ground. We gasped, then exploded into whistles and wild applause until the dancers slowed their pace and the women lowered their legs until their feet touched the ground, skipping to a stop and a final rousing cheer.

After they had caught their breath and wiped the sweat off their faces, the singing and dancing troupe sang several more Occitan songs, as dramatic in shifts of tempo and key as their spectacular dance. The director then announced a special number: the women would choose partners from members of their appreciative audience. I hoped, of course, that one of the attractive young women dancers would pick me and I got my wish. In a flash, a smiling young lass came to stand in front of me and took me by the hand. At twelve, however, Corrine was a bit younger than I'd hoped for. No matter, having sat out the circle dance she was full of high-stepping energy and, as she had in the pool of the *village,* quickly took charge, pulling me into the dance area of the gravel courtyard and telling me what I was to do––follow her lead exactly, *bien entendu,* of course. The trio struck up some polka-like music, but in spite of Corrine's instructional skills, I made a complete fool of myself, causing my charming partner to shake her head in dismay and her brother, Pierre, to hoot and whistle at us both. When the dance ended, Corrine and I bowed to each other and I tried to thank her for choosing me, but she was too quick, running off to join her laughing brother. The troupe ended their Occitan evening with a set of drinking songs: It was time for beer, barbecue, and *boum.*

I crossed the street and with other spectators and some of the dancers went down through the City Hall's not-yet "*booming*" basement to the small yard behind the building. There, I found my ceramics teacher, Paul, who was keeping an eye on some sizzling red and spicy merguez, North African sausage. His long auburn hair and thick mustache gave him the look of a pirate, the perfect persona for the owner of a fire-engine red 1960s Pontiac convertible that he drove with hair-blowing, bare-chested bravado over the narrow roads of Quercy, leaving locals to shake their hair in his wake.

"You!" he said, staring at me, "you, I almost threw out of class."

"Moi?" I said, as he had hardly spoken to me since the first day of the workshop. *"Pourquoi?"* Why?

"You would not follow my directions," he said.

Well, he had me there. I stubbornly balk at following anyone's directions––about anything. That approach to life has its drawbacks, but my contrariness helped me survive parochial school and the spirit-breaking strictures of the Catholic Church––Irish-American version. Right from the start, Paul had seemed to sense my recalcitrance, looking back at me over his shoulder after showing me the approach he wanted us to use when we centered clay on the wheel. In my defense, I did try his approach, but quickly reverted to a technique of centering clay on the wheel that, unorthodox as it was, worked for me in Berkeley. It did not escape Paul's attention. He came back later in the morning to correct my California style and we went through the ritual again: I bent intently over the wheel and did my best to follow his step-by-step directions. Of course, as soon as he moved on, mumbling about me under his breath, I reverted to my wayward behavior, as he knew I would. The next day, Isabelle, his wife, replaced him at my elbow. After a little flirting on my part, and maybe hers, she accepted the fact that my heretical approach worked fine for me. I also told her that I was not fond of the time pressure the wheel demanded and preferred hand-building. Paul never came near me after that first day, having taken my stubbornness as a challenge to his authority. I, however, had forgotten all about it, so his angry tone at the barbecue surprised me.

"*Oui, oui. Vous! Exactement! J'en avait marre de vous.*" I was fed up with you, he said, poking the sizzling sausages. "My wife said she would teach you, though, so I gave you a second chance."

"*Merci,*" I said.

"Thank Isabelle. She is a great teacher," then he quickly put out his hand and smiled.

"She is why you ended up being the best in the class."

Of course Paul could not have known that my resistance to taking directions was nothing personal. This contrary and stubborn streak is, in part, no doubt, why I was drawn to the French, who some feel are cursed with a characteristic that is not always considered charming. In fact, however, challenging another's views seems built into their language. It certainly is built into *moi*.

As the sun went down, the music started up in the disco — the Stones and the Beatles, and, of course, their French imitator, Johnny Hallyday.

The weather was hot, the music hotter, and sweat-slick dancers jammed the floor, shedding as much clothing and decorum as allowed in this small French town. In the 70s the French danced with great energy, but usually without the freestyle abandon of a Californian. With arms held close to the body, they stayed within a smaller dance floor space and rarely leapt about with the wild swings and spins of the style I knew. After a half-hour or so of bumping bodies and pounding beat, almost everyone sought the cool night air — and the cold beer — outside where the merguez were piled high on a platter. But the Stones played on and I kept dancing with anyone who cared to join me. Finally, a grinning Sébastien Bunniel, beer in hand, took the floor opposite me. Both of us stripped to the waist, he, short, black-haired, and barrel-chested, I tall and lean, we whirled and jumped and stomped in a bacchanalian dance, carried along by wailing guitars, and by Mick Jagger's sensual voice and driving energy. At tape's end, both of us exhausted and dripping wet, we headed outdoors to drink a cold beer.

The cooling night air revived me quickly so I returned to the dance floor to join some of the new arrivals, whose workshops started the next day and who had reached Valeilles too late for the Occitan folk dances and barbecue. Among them was a young woman with that striking Mediterranean combination of coal-black hair, light olive skin, and light blue eyes. Her straight shoulder-length hair framed a face that suggested a Hemingway heroine (not Ingrid Bergman): high cheekbones and strong brow, straight almost prominent nose, and those enchanting blue eyes.

I quickly invited her to dance. And dance again. Her name was Ariane and she was from nearby Albi, she said. Tomorrow she would begin the pottery workshop. We had a beer. We danced some more, including a slow, which brought us closer together. Wishfully thinking I was still in Berkeley, I asked her to spend the night with me in my tent. No, she would not.

"*Vous partez demain, non?*" she asked, holding me apart to look directly at me with those remarkable eyes.

"Well, yes," I admitted. "But perhaps I will change my mind if you spend the night with me."

"*Non, je ne le ferai pas,*" no I will not, she said, though she smiled this time, and moved closer.

Then apart once more, to make sure I understood her: "I've been traveling this past year or so, trying lots of things," she said. "It's time I became serious," becoming serious as she spoke. It was time to settle down in Albi, where she was born, and begin to become the potter she wanted to be. At least she had to give it her best, to find out if she had the talent and discipline to succeed. Even with my still simple French, I could understand how strongly she felt.

She was in her early twenties and I was 38, yet she was the one who had decided to become serious. Young people, many French believed then (some still do), need to spend a year or so after high school traveling and finding out about life and themselves. If we don't do it when we're young, they feel, we'll end up wanting to do it later, when it can cause havoc with lives that have usually become more settled and complex. Of course, for Americans — who might change careers two or three times or more — life's phases have for years not been so clearly defined. In fact, today they are now not so clearly defined for some French either.

I was following this wise course the French urge their young people to take: trying to find out who I was by exploring the world and themselves, though I was a bit late setting off on such a venture. That I hoped this process would actually change me at the age of 38, the French did say, was bordering on absolute folly.

When the *boum* was over, the city hall clock read one a.m. It was time to walk back to the farm.   My black-haired love, eager to start her workshop the next morning, had gone to the home where she was staying, leaving me alone to wend my way along the two-lane road back to my sleeping bag. As I neared each farm, its watchdog announced my approach with barks that bounded over the moonlit hills in all directions, fading out just as I reached the next farm and its canine sentinel got the roundelay going all over again. In the warm, still night, with the barking dogs and bong-bonging of the belled cows, I felt the presence of people who had farmed this land through centuries of war and peace, storm and drought, and winters perhaps too quiet even for them.

Tarn et Garonne, France

In the cool kitchen of the fieldstone farmhouse,
we waited, Emma and I,
as dinner talk in French danced around us:
I, new to France,
she, only two, new to everything.

Both of us could only ask the simplest questions,
only understand the simplest answers.
She watched us large above her;
I watched her small frustration grow
to gargantuan proportions, until,
jaw set, she reached
for anything she could turn over,
anything that would crack open
this world neither of us understood
and get her carried out of it
to her family's tent and sleep's embrace.

Outside, too, where I feel the weight
of the night's drought-heavy heat,
I still am lost for words in any language
to tell me why, so far from home,
I feel at home
in this deep countryside of France.
The barks of watchdogs continue to rise and fall,
as across slow centuries of hills,
the cows' carillon of bells
softly sways me to sleep.

The next morning, I rose with the sun, took down and packed my tent, rolled up my sleeping bag, and stuffed my bright orange backpack with clothes and books. Then. with fellow potter, Martin, drove in his prized VW Beetle right to Monsieur Ricou's in Dausse. The *patron*, ever-present twinkle in his eye, seated us, for once, outside in the sun, and, even though it was not yet nine, poured us drinks of pastis large enough to make walking, let alone driving, hazardous. They were on the house, he said.

Martin asked me what I was going to do next. I wasn't sure, I said, but I had some contacts in Paris who told me they would help me find work as a translator. "You could become a potter here with me," he said. "We can set up a studio in Penne or Agen." The offer came out of nowhere. My first thought was that living on the Lot would put me within dancing distance of Ariane in Albi, and it was a chance to live in France, something I thought I wanted to do. But I had not forgotten Sébastien Bunniel's words about the area's "quiet winters," and I hardly knew Martin. He was a vegetarian and––*Mon dieu!*––did not drink wine. But aside from that, I only knew that we shared an abiding anger at the Catholic Church, which had scarred both of us.

On a trip to pick up some clothes at his family's home nearby in Penne, we had stopped at a couple of churches––simple, handsome, stone structures. At each, he insisted that I take his picture as he sat in a chair on the altar like a longhaired, jeans-wearing bishop. To end each visit he left his own mark, as a dog marks its territory, on the church's stone wall, a gesture of contempt far less enduring than the marks the Church had clearly left on him. Our shared feelings were a bond, but was what I knew of this gastronomically unique Frenchman enough for a highly risky venture? Like staying to pursue Ariane, it would mean a dramatic change in my life. Was I ready to completely leave my life in California and my aging parents? I wrote down his address and said I would write to him fromParis.

We shook hands with Ricou, then very, very slowly we headed back to the café in Valeilles. The skies were overcast for the first time since I had arrived, the uncertain light and unsettled quality of the air reflecting my feelings about leaving this part of *"la France, profonde"* the French soul. At the café, we said our goodbyes over the usual breakfast—bread from our baker in Dausse, local butter and homemade fig jam, steaming pots of coffee, and hot milk for the powdered chocolate. JB even helped Gina serve us and sat with us for a few minutes, a rare gesture from a man who was always worriedly busy.

We helped ourselves, as usual, until we could eat no more, and each paid the French equivalent of a dollar for it all. As a farewell meal, it was perfect, lessening a bit my sadness at leaving my young friends, Marie, Corrine, and Pierre, my pottery teacher, Isabelle, and even Paul, her husband, but perhaps most of all at leaving Ariane, that black-haired, blue-eyed woman from Albi who had decided to become serious about her life.

Partir, c'est mourir un peu, to leave is to die a little.

Chapter 6

Monsieur Renaud and Danielle

In wine book illustrations and on wine shop posters, vineyards at harvest time are always awash in sunlight and the pickers, dressed in colorful clothes, are all handsome lads and lovely lasses. You can almost hear the folk songs they must be singing. In France, the wine grape harvest is called the *vendange,* but the same ritual, with variations, takes place wherever wine grapes are grown, and, at least in Europe, is always depicted in the same enticing way. A sunny happiness reigns.

When I arrived in Lyon, a hiring center for working the *vendange* in Burgundy, some friends I had met through Arnaud put me up for a night. I told them of my wine-picking plans and they quickly warned me that those poster images were a total fantasy. Naïvely, I thought my friends were exaggerating and continued to believe what those alluring images promised, lock, stock, and barrel—or in my case women, sunshine and song. I did, however, heed their advice about footwear. After all, they had done several *vendinges.* Rubber soled with thick canvas tops, the boots I bought looked sturdy enough to be a match for whatever the vineyards had in store for me, though I really had no idea what I was getting into.

The agricultural office in Lyon had no work, so I called a vintner whose name had been given to me by Mick, an Englishman I met as we both scanned work offers on a bulletin board at the Lyon train station. The vintner's land was in the Mâcon region of south-central Burgundy, an hour's train ride from Lyon. It was known for its fine Pinot Chardonnay wines, the best of which is Pouilly-Fuissé. I telephoned the vintner (showing a new confidence in my improved French). "*Allo, oui,*" said what turned out to be the vintner's cheery wife, Madame Percot. We are almost done picking, she said, but Monsieur Renaud, across town, will need people as soon as we're finished. You can work a day with us, she said, then, after a day off, work ten more days for him. She told me what the pay and lodging would be, which would be the same for her and for Renaud. That all seemed fine, so I agreed to meet the good Madame at the train station in Macon later that day. I was tall, I told her, and would be carrying a bright orange backpack, hard to miss.

As soon as I walked out of the small Macon train station, I heard

"*Monsieur Américain*" and spotted Madame Percot standing next to her car and waving. A short, spirited lady with curly blonde hair, she was only a few years older than I and drove as though determined that neither one of us would get much older. To calm my suddenly jumpy nerves, I focused on the narrow road that spun out before us, twisting and turning over the vine-covered hills like a riled snake and barely wide enough for two small cars. Knowing this rustic byway like the back of her cigarette-holding hand, my chatty chauffeur drove right down the middle, showing absolute confidence that, like the Grand Prix ace many French drivers take themselves to be, she could easily deal with whatever lay around the next curve or over the next hill. During the entire wild half-hour ride, she deftly shifted her attention between her high-speed negotiation of the road and her breakneck conversation with me, her white-knuckled American passenger. Several times, she slammed on the brakes, almost knocking the ash off her cigarette, and each time just avoiding a collision with a putt-putting tractor. The drivers of these vehicles, armed with *priorité à droite* (yield to the driver on the right), a law that has the force of papal infallibility, showed not the slightest interest in whatever kind of vehicle might be about to bring his life to a dramatic end. Caps firmly on their heads, unlit *maïs* cigarettes (made from corn) set in the corner of their mouths, they were unshakeable in their conviction that the *priorité* would protect them, and told us so by not even deigning to glance in our direction. Not to worry. The good Madame tossed off a few curse words and switched to practicing another French driving pastime — tailgating — until the road straightened out enough for her to squeeze by the tractor, tooting her horn all the way and giving a friendly wave to the tractor's sublimely indifferent driver. Not once did she use the rear-view mirror, feeling no doubt that talking with me and watching the road ahead of us, more or less, were quite enough to manage at one time.

In the small town of Davayé, we came to a halt in front of a gray stone building, on the main street. Knees still shaky, I followed Madame Percot up some well-worn, sagging wooden stairs to where the pickers lived who worked for her and eventually for Monsieur Renaud. They were all in the vineyards, she said, so just find an unoccupied mattress and get settled; the others will return at sundown. She said she would see me tomorrow night when she and her husband would throw the dinner for the *vendangeurs* that is traditional at harvest's end.

It was after four by the time I got settled and went out for a stroll. Like many small French towns Davayé was built along a two-lane road that linked it to similar towns nearby, small clusters of buildings on ridge crest or hilltop that seemed to hold together the patchwork of vineyards surrounding them. The two-story gray stone houses on the town's main street presented a uniform wall to passersby, their few narrow windows shuttered and set above the heads of any walkers. When the gates to a house opened up for a car or a tractor pulling a cart, I caught a glimpse of the large interior courtyards behind the street-side facade. Bright with flower beds and boxes hanging from second story balconies, they offered vistas of the vineyards that rolled out and around the neighboring towns.

With the *vendangeurs* all working, the town was empty and as depressing to me as the leaden, lowering sky. I felt very lonely and somewhat lost, feelings I had a number of times in France that almost always brought up that nettlesome question: What the hell was I doing there? Living my life, damn it, I said to that nagging voice, then returned to the dormitory to take a nap, a practical stratagem in such situations.

✳

Clumping boots and voices woke me up. The pickers had returned, including Mick, the Englishman I had met in Lyon. Two brothers were from Germany, but the rest of the pickers were French, several from the area around Davayé. They told me the Percots made one of the better St. Vérans, though as Pinot Chardonnays go it was a notch below the nearby Pouilly-Fuissé. As an employer, however, Monsieur Percot fell far short of the wine he made, showing up in the vineyards only to complain that the pickers were not working fast enough. Even worse, he served food that varied little from day to day, an unacceptable affront to anyone French. That night, the entire crew was going to a country restaurant for their own *fête de vendange*. I was welcome to come along. Some would go to the Percot *fête* the next night because they liked Madame; the rest would skip it.

The trio that shared my room — Danielle, Luc and Émile—welcomed me with an offer of Cognac. Émile then played his favorite Bob Dylan tape, "Bringing It All Back Home." All three, especially Émile, who owned the small tape deck, thought Dylan was *"formidable, terrible,"* and *"chouette."* In other words, he was the best. When I offered to do a bit of translation, Émile bluntly turned me down as if I had insulted him. None of the three spoke more than a few words of English, but Dylan's words apparently did not really matter. I felt the same way about listening to Léo

Ferré and Jacques Brel: the music and their distinctive voices made the lyrics less important.

Then we were off--four small cars, filled with smoking, singing celebrants, a mechanized caravan wending its way through the now misting night. After a half hour ride over the rolling hills of the Mâconnais region of southern Burgundy we pulled into a gravel courtyard surrounded by three or four houses on top of a small rise. One of these buildings was our restaurant, though with vineyards all around it and no town nearby, it looked like someone's home, which it was, in part. It was also a restaurant, though there no sign, lit or otherwise, told us so.

Establishments like this were common in rural France, often open early mornings and late afternoons, and on weekends, or just when the owner felt like it. Customers are usually locals the owners know or relatives of their own extended families. Because the personal relationships that keep these places going are embedded in the life of an area, strangers usually are not welcome. Once, in Valeilles, a group of us went with Martin to such a place where he was well known to make a reservation for dinner. When he came back to the car full of his fellow potters, he said, with annoyance, that the owners told him they were full. Without explicitly saying no, they made it clear that they did not want a group of strangers in their place, and that's what we were.

Percot *vendangeurs* who came from the area were not strangers to our hostesses, of course, and neither were the German brothers. They had worked several picking seasons in the vineyards around Davayé and had brought other pickers with them on their seasonal visits to the restaurant: all of them were as welcome as locals.

The welcoming in this case was done by two reserved country women in their forties, whose coy but warm smiles told me they clearly liked having these young people--I was the exception--in this homelike place, which they owned. Under their direction, we pushed together enough small tables to form one long one, draped it with red-and-white checkered tablecloths, both cotton and oilcloth, and set out an assortment of chairs that folded, wobbled, rocked, and teetered. As we took our places, loaves of bread, bottles of Beaujolais, and plates of several kinds of sliced local sausage were placed here and there on the table, preparing us for the crudités — shredded raw carrots, celery root, and cooked beets in a dressing of wine vinegar, olive oil, and tart mustard. A few minutes later, when the wine had loosened us up, our hostesses and the *vendangeur* helpers who had earned the status of "locals," carried out of the kitchen pots of lentils and sausage, platters of stewed rabbit, and bowls of potatoes boiled and buttered. The feast ended, *comme d'habitude* (as usual), with several kinds of local cheese — soft and hard, mild and sharp, cow and goat. It was a grand feast served by gracious hostesses who cruised calmly in and out of their kitchen domain, replacing empty platters and bottles of wine with full ones, telling Danielle how pretty she was, and joking with the *vendangeurs* they had come to know. When we toasted them and the dishes they had prepared for us this rainy night, they blushed, smiling with a mix of professional pride and maternal affection. Where that restaurant was, exactly, I never knew.

How would I fare the next day after this evening of food and wine and familial warmth, not being used either to eating so well nor to a long day among the vines? Mick had arrived a couple of days earlier so already was used to the work. At dinner, he filled me in on what I could expect the next day. "It's not that hard. You get used to it pretty quick. When it's drizzling like now, though, the mud keeps you from moving along on your knees. You've got to work bending over.and that's a bit tough on the back." I had another glass of Beaujolais.

Back at our damp, unheated lodgings in Davayé, we bundled up in heavy coats and woolen hats and huddled together in one room, prolonging the festive evening by sharing brandy and by getting to know three young women who were friends of one of the local *vendangeurs*. The German brothers, who had gone right from the dinner to Lyon, soon clumped up the stairs to join us and happily share some hashish from Lyon. In no time we had not only warmed up, we had moved to a higher plane and were totally out of touch with any thoughts of tomorrow's work.

As I took puffs on the pipe that was passed around, I speculated on the relationship of my three young roommates. Danielle seemed to be with Luc, then sometimes not; Émile was a friend of them both, though not either's lover, so far as I could tell. In spite of my "free love" years in Berkeley, I was no more prepared for this wrinkle on intimacy than I was for nude ping-pong at the *Village Naturiste*. The California me was still going toe to toe with the Catholic Connecticut me, and though I had won some rounds on the nude beaches of California and with my last girlfriend, the outcome of the fight had not yet been decided. In any case, whatever intimacy existed among the trio had to be shared, I thought, since they all slept in the dormitory's only double bed, a tight snuggle for three. Were they a real life *Jules et Jim* right here in Davayé?

I stopped musing over that three-person puzzle when one of the local young women smiled at me from the cocoon of her heavy coat, her delicate, sharp features set off by her short black hair, still slick from the rain. Just 20, if that, she was visibly uncomfortable in this room of a dozen people she barely knew, most of them men adrift on gentle swells of brandy and hashish. I rode my particular wave across the small room and sat next to her on a mattress on the floor, where she was doing her uneasy best to look at ease. We had barely introduced ourselves when Danielle came over and stood directly in front of me.

"*Venez*" Come, she said with a commanding voice, and reached down to grab my hand, giving a sharp, quick glance at my companion. "*Où?*" Where? I asked, letting her pull me up.

"*Dehors. Vite!*" Outside. Quickly! she said, pulling me away from the black-haired woman, out of the room and down the stairs. Where was Luc?

"*C'est bien, la pluie.*" she said, tilting her face to the rain and holding my arm tightly as she guided me through the darkened town. Slipping her lithe body under my open down jacket she pressed it against mine, the two of us leaning into the veils of light rain until we passed almost beyond the light of the town's few streetlights. The drizzle soaked our faces and set a fringe of glistening droplets on Danielle's curly brown hair.

"*Par ici,*" she said, walking with short purposeful steps and talking in an over-the-shoulder French too fast for me to understand. What I could understand was that Danielle had a definite idea of where we were going and no doubt what we were going to do when we got there. When the town had become a huddle of buildings behind us, she turned us off the road into the sea of vines, their leaves glinting with light from the town's distant streetlamps and sprinkling us as we passed, a kind of Bacchic benediction.

Out of sight of the road, Danielle stopped on a grassy area between two rows of vines, picked a bunch of the ripe grapes and turning toward me reached up to press their sweetness against my lips. Then, all rain-slick sinuous energy, she pressed her body against me and kissed me deeply with her quick tongue, blending our tastes, the rain, the grapes. Opening her jacket, she put my hand on her warm breast and deftly undid my pants, freeing my erect cock. Pushing me down then until I was kneeling in the wet grass, she slipped her jeans and panties over her slip hips and straddled me, guiding my cock into her with her warm hand and riding me until we both shuddered with release in the mist-filled darkness.

Kissing me with her darting tongue again, she said, *"Sacre baiseur,"* which means someone who likes to fuck, which I surely did, even in those rainy vineyards.   After our burst of quick heat, I was in a state of baffled satisfaction, the bafflement increasing as Danielle abruptly got to her feet, rearranged her clothes in a businesslike manner and headed out through the vines toward the road, not caring, it seemed if I followed her or not. I followed, zipping and buckling, until I caught up with her. Then I noticed coming toward us, backlit by the town lights, the figure of another man, whose appearance Danielle obviously expected.

"*C'est Luc,*" she whispered, letting go of my arm.

"*Salut,*" she said sweetly as he reached us, then quickly moved close to him.

"I needed a walk after that brandy."

Luc said nothing, but looked at me intensely in the dim light. Danielle put her arm around his waist and pulled him close, then, excited and confident, jauntily walked between us as we returned to the town and the party. Luc, I was sure, had gone through this before. The *Jules et Jim* scenario I had imagined for my three roommates had become complicated though I had no idea what, if any, my role might be in the new script.

At the party, the black-haired young woman had left, along with her two companions, which for some reason disappointed me. For the rest of the evening, Danielle purposely avoided looking at me and stayed close to Luc. He did look at me, however, and not with a kindly eye.

Midnight came, and the end of the brandy and hashish. Dylan's last song — "Lay, Lady, Lay," I seem to remember — dissolved into the sound of the now heavily falling rain.   I crossed the landing and slid into my sleeping bag, trying not to think of Danielle, who now was all cozy with Luc and Émile in their shared bed. They were leaving as soon as they were paid at the end of work the next day, Émile had told me at dinner, heading south to the Beaujolais region, where they heard they could make better money. I felt a twinge of lustful regret at the news, but also relief that this *ménage à trois--ou quatre*, if I fancied myself part of it--would not have the Truffaut film's tragic ending.

*

Ten hours of slogging through drenched vines the next day, feet swaddled in pounds of mud; ten hours of searching for grapes hidden under layers of dripping leaves; ten hours of a steady, soaking drizzle turned Mick's "A bit hard on the back," into the epitome of English understatement.

At day's damp end, my only goal was to crawl into my sleeping bag and rest my tortured back. My friends in Lyon had given me due warning. What they had not told me was that in most years, picking does not begin until Autumn's first light rains mark the end of Indian Summer's sunny warmth. The grapes need every bit of sun they can get, but not heavy rain, so scheduling the start of the *vendange* each year is a bit of a gamble, hedged by years of experience and knowledge of the weather that doesn't come from TV weather forecasts.

After an hour's rest, I managed to get my back to straighten out and slowly walked to the Percot's harvest dinner with Mick. Though Madame Percot did her best to liven things up, the *fête,* as predicted, was a sad affair, with bland food and the lowest quality Percot wine. The climax of the event, at least for Monsieur Percot, was the dandling dance he did with his small white dog cradled in his arms.

The next day was filled with glorious sunshine, large white clouds sending undulating shadows racing like flocks of birds over the vine-covered hills. Mick and I wandered around the small and empty town, located the house of Monsieur Renaud, where we would meet early the next morning, drank a few expressos in the town's only bistrot, napped, and read. For dinner, we went back to the bistrot and scanned the hand-printed menu on the chalkboard just inside the door, as though we were comparing it to some other place in town when we well knew there was no other place. This was it, so in we went. Some men, most of them wearing French Blues and soft golf caps, already occupied a couple of tables. The unsmiling woman behind the bar was *la patronne,* who owned the café with her husband--*le patron,* of course. Madame Percot, who knew them both, said their food was *pas mal,* not bad. *La patronne* said all they had left--at least for us--was lentils and ham with a small green salad, which she quickly prepared and brought to us without a word. For the most part the men sat quietly, drinking their wine without taking off their hats, smoking Gauloise cigarettes, regular or *maïs,* and, smiling slightly at Mick and me, two more of those odd-looking strangers who drifted into "their" bistrot for a few weeks every Autumn. So ended our day of freedom before ten straight days of dawn-to-dusk picking at Renaud's. I moved my backpack across the hall to where Mick was bedded down and where I found a slightly better mattress.

❄

Thump, thump, thump. A pounding on the door followed by *"Levez-vous! Le petit-déjeuner dans quinze minutes."* Get up! Breakfast in 15 minutes. I squirmed reluctantly out of my warm sleeping bag into the damp, cold room, where the windows were completely fogged over and my breath visible. Someone had turned on the single overhead bulb and carried up from the downstairs bathroom––the only one in the building––a bucket of water, our "bath," which, until the trio departed, had been heated, one small pan at a time, on Luc's butane camping stove. A splash of that icy water snapped me out of whatever dreamworld I happened to be in. In addition to the Englishman, Mick, my other new roommate was Vincent, who had just turned eighteen. Laya, from Normandy, and Didier, from Paris, two university students, settled in the room across the hall vacated by the trio. All but Mick were up and out the door before me and probably enjoying their first cup of coffee. I washed, shivering, pulled on some clothes and trundled down the wooden stairs to join the waiting Mick for the short walk across town to Renaud's. A tractor chugged by in the opposite direction, pulling a cart full of pickers bundled together against the penetrating pre-dawn mist. The temperature had dropped overnight to near 40 (5C), but as the sky lightened, it looked as though we would at least get some sun today. The humid closeness of the air and a scrim of light clouds, however, said that rain was near. Ah, those deceptive posters.

In the Renauds' sand-floor cellar, redolent with the aroma of fresh bread and coffee, we met our *patron,* Monsieur Renaud, a bear of a man, six-feet tall, bald, with large, soft hands, and a slight but kindly smile. The mugs of strong, hot coffee, tea, and chocolate warmed our hands as we quietly rose to the surface of our senses and finished off a couple of baguettes. Then, led by *le patron,* some of us bundled into a cart pulled by a small tractor driven by Armand, Renaud's foreman. The rest of us set off on foot with Philippe, Renaud's son-in-law. That day's vineyard, like all of Renaud's holdings, was only a ten-minute walk away. Behind us, the town was being roused from sleep by the pale brightening sky and the coo-coo-ri-coos of its resident roosters. Fortunately, the day of sun had dried the ground enough to let us move along on our knees as we picked. Unlike Monsieur Percot, Renaud picked with us every day, something he must have done for years as his round face was red and weathered from a life outdoors. His body was as solid as Solutré, the massive outcropping of rock that stood watch over the entire area and was a symbol of Pouilly-Fuissé. He said little, but his few words, his sharp eye, and his movements revealed an attentiveness that did not miss much. As we gathered around him at the vineyard that first morning, he predicted the weather: *"Soleil aujourd'hui. Pas de soleil, demain. La pluie vient ce soir."* Sun today, no sun tomorrow. Rain is coming this evening. Whether he consulted the experts on the radio or knew from his years of experience, the predictions were a daily ritual and always accurate. Then Renaud assigned us in pairs to particular rows and, when we had finished a row, checked our work to make sure our picking was thorough. *"Américain, mettez-vous là. Anglais, mettez-vous là."* American, you work there. Englishman, you work there. He always put Mick and me back-to-back––thoughtfully, I felt, because that way we could to talk to each other and occasionally sing Beatle songs. We found out later, a bit chagrined, that his real reason for putting us back-to-back was that he quickly realized we were the slowest pickers and did not want to pair us up with the others, who all were much faster. Every hour or so, Armand put aside the harmonica he played as he waited for the cart to be loaded, hopped on the tractor, and towed back to the town's cooperative crusher a lashed-down stack of grape-filled bins.

    With the weather dry, we were able to work on our knees all that first day, to my back's great relief, but a light rain came that night, as Renaud predicted, and stayed with us as mist or drizzle for all but the last of our remaining nine days in the vineyards. That meant working bent over at the waist, lugging a couple of pounds of boot-clinging mud with each step as we inched along. The rows were the same 50 yards long as the rows on our first rainless day but under those conditions seemed twice as long. Sheltered from the elements by the leaves, the grapes were usually out of sight, forcing us to grope for the stem of each bunch to be clipped. After just a few minutes of work, my hands were so numb with cold that I began to snip off the fleshy end of my left thumb or index finger as they gripped a hidden stem. Mick had the same problem, as did most pickers, I soon found out. Some Percot pickers told him how to deal with it: squash a grape or two on the nick; the alcohol stanches the flow of blood and quickly closes up the cut. At least until you do it again farther along the row. Every half-hour or so, the call came to pass our buckets to where an oak bin was waiting to be filled and carried to the tractor cart. Every time, my stem-seeking left hand would be streaked with blood. The other more experienced members of our crew, though faster at picking, did not do much better.

In addition to being a *vintner,* Renaud had for decades been a master *pépinieriste,* vine grafter, which I found hard to imagine given the size of his hands. His skill became essential in wine country after phylloxera, a burrowing root louse, got to Europe from America in the 1870s and 1880s and devastated most of the continent's vineyards. Once the French realized in the 1890s that American vines were resistant to the louse, all French varietals were grafted onto the stock of American grapes. As master of vineyards and vine, Renaud, I thought, surely would be so experienced at the *vendange* and the handling of sharp tools that he would fly through the picking without a nick, even though he used a traditional cutter about the length and shape of a pencil and topped with a small, curved razor-sharp blade. A couple of days into the harvest, *le patron* was picking in the row on the other side of where I was doggedly and bloodily bent to my task. At the cry of *"Enlevez les seaux,"* pass the pails, I hefted my bucket over the vines to Renaud. Our hands met on the pail handle, his as blood-streaked as my own.

Every day, at almost every break, Monsieur Renaud discussed the world of wine with his son-in-law, Philippe, his experienced foreman, Armand, who was struggling to beat the alcoholism that had put him in the hospital a couple of times, and Pépé, Renaud's contemporary who said little and had not taken care of his teeth. Would this year's weather be better than last year's? Would this year's wine be better, demanding a higher price? *Le patron* explained why Pouilly-Fuissé was superior to St. Véran, though both were made from the Pinot Chardonnay grape and grown but a few kilometers apart. It was the difference in their *terroir,* the natural characteristics of the soil where the grape is grown, especially how that soil's features are combined––whether it is rocky or not, and what kind of drainage it provides. The *terroir* contributes a particular taste and character to good wines. The soil of Pouilly-Fuissé and the area around Davayé were not similar so their grapes had different *goûts de terroir,* different taste and character. A *terroir* can be small, very small.

❊

Renaud also shared most of our meals, which were prepared by his wife and daughter. For ten days, at dawn, noon, and dusk, these two stocky, curly-haired ladies, wearing dark cardigan sweaters over flower-patterned, light cotton aprons, clomped downstairs in knee-high rubber boots from the Renaud's second-floor kitchen, and picked their way through the mud- puddled courtyard to our basement "dining room." They brought fresh bread, hot coffee, stewed rabbit, homemade pizza, cheese-filled omelets, roasted chicken, and local red wine. Before every lunch and dinner, our rotund *patron*, with a proud smile, brought out his gleaming silver *tâte-vin*, shaped like a scallop shell, and invited us to taste his own Pouilly-Fuissé––pale gold, unfiltered, and deliciously complex. *"Venez boire un goût,"* come have a taste, Renaud beckoned, standing at the doorway to the cave, the small dark wine cellar next to the room where we ate. Not only did a few of us accept his offer at lunch that first day, we also enjoyed a glass or more of the red *vin de table*. Big mistake. Rising from the table after lunch, I had absolutely no interest in returning to the vineyards for another five hours of picking. A nap is what I wanted, a lovely siesta. The younger pickers felt the same way, so from then on, Renaud, Phillipe, Pépé and the wiry Armand did the midday drinking, the four of them finishing at least a half dozen bottles at every lunch. How they managed to do it and return to work in the vineyards was beyond me.

Lifelong habit no doubt had a lot to do with it, especially when the habit was reinforced in the vineyards whenever we had a break. Each row took over an hour of snipping and slogging to finish, though Mick and I usually needed a bit longer than that. Then it was time for *le casse-croute*, the breaking of the bread, a few minutes to rest our backs and have a bit of bread, cheese, salami, and, most importantly, water mixed about half and half with red wine. I had learned my lesson about wine that first day so my drink at break time was plain mineral water, to the dismay of the crew's older members. *"Mon dieu!"* Armand said. *"Mais non!"* Pépé exclaimed. *"Pas possible!"* added Philippe. Plain water, they all believed, would sap my strength and make me sick. *"Non! Non! Mauvaise idée!"* A bad idea, *sans aucun doute*, without a doubt. In spite of their protests and concerned advice, I stuck to my water.

For an American of any age to be working the *vendange* was unusual, to say the least; to be doing that kind of work at 38 baffled the entire crew, especially Renaud and his son-in-law. They thought that either I was looney or was a liar about my age. The truth was I needed some money and I wanted to see what this part of French life was like. Those enticing posters had deceived me, of course, but when picking ended, my illusions about the *vendange* were almost as crushed as the grapes I had picked. Nonetheless, as did my future stint as a dishwasher in a restaurant near Lyon, it gave me a view of French life that deepened my understanding of this country I found so attractive.

I was lucky, though, to find work with Renaud. Based on what other pickers told me, this easy-going bear of a man and his family was an exception, as was our small crew of *vendangeurs*. Neither of the students, however, made it very far in the ten-day harvest. Laya, slight of build, simply found the work too hard and left after one day. The next day, Didier got a phone call that told him he had to return to Paris to take an exam for the engineering school he was about to enter. A general agreement between pickers and vintners, at least in this Macon region over forty years ago, required that pickers had to complete the entire picking period to get paid, usually about ten days. If they left early, for whatever reason, vintners were obliged only to give them enough, more or less, for train fare home. Laya and Didier only got some of that, as they worked but one full day. Their departure had Renaud worried. As a member of a cooperative, he had ten days to complete the harvest and crushing of his grapes. To complete picking on time, our small crew would have to work extra hard unless he found more pickers.

✳

In the dawn darkness of our third day of picking, a barefooted Danielle glided through my room on her way to the "bathing" room. What was she doing here? Then I heard the voices of Luc and Émile. Renaud *a été sauvé*: Renaud was saved; the trio had returned. With them came Luc's camp stove and hot water. *Super!* Since using the bathing room was a one-at-a-time affair, giving each person a chance to do a bit of washing up in private, I waited with happy excitement for Danielle to exit. And I waited. And I waited. With only a few minutes to get to breakfast, I finally knocked, hoping to give my vineyard love a welcome-back hug and *grosses bises*. Whoa, Nellie!

"*Entrez,*" Danielle said.

Surprised and pleased, I pushed open the door to see "Her Litheness" brushing her hair by using the steamed up window as a mirror. I smiled — at her back — and said "*Bonjour.*" Danielle returned my greeting without missing a brush stroke, and, to my disappointment, not even looking at me. I stepped closer and put my hands around her waist. Then she turned.

"*Ne faites pas ca!*" Don't do that, she said, using the formal *vous* form and quickly stepping away as she continued brushing.

"*Pourquoi pas*?" Why not, I asked.

"Because I don't want you to," Danielle said, her face the mask of smug indifference females learn to put on when they reach adolescence. She stuffed her hairbrush and other toilet items into a small knapsack, explained how to turn off the stove, and walked out without saying another word.

Danielle's return brought frustration, liveliness, and a few surprises to my remaining days in Davayé, which otherwise were as routinely cheerless as the town, the gray skies, and the long rows of vines. To break the monotony, we sometimes went to the town's lone bistrot, where Mick and I had already made several appearances. If we were lucky, we arrived before the owners seized on the absence of customers to bolt the door and pull down the shutters. Not that we could blame them. During the *vendange* most of Davayé's citizens and its visiting *vendangeurs*, bound as we were to the harvest's cycle of long days of hard work, retired early. The couple who owned the café seized the opportunity for an early retirement themselves closing up as soon as there were no customers. When we showed up, they had a conflict: They wanted to keep us out, but they also wanted our business. Several times, we arrived at the bistrot door as *la patronne* was about to lock it. Each time, after glaring at us, she let us in. Without a word, she took our orders, served us, then joined her husband behind the bar, where the two of them stood with arms folded, waiting for us to leave.

Its dour owners notwithstanding, that bistrot was our bar and nightclub rolled into one. We took our places at one of the wooden tables scattered about the black-and-white squares of the linoleum floor and Luc and I continued our competition for Danielle's attention by seeing how far back we could tilt our wooden chairs before an arm-flailing crash to the floor. We quickly learned that we had to select a chair carefully and, once astride it, pay close attention to its squeaks and wobbles. Tilting back a bit too far, suddenly shifting my weight, or looking at Danielle to make sure she was looking my way, brought me crashing to the floor, feathers ruffled but ready to try again. Luc did not fare any better. Danielle's only reaction to our silly flopping was laughter, which happily made light of this adolescent competition. The owners, however, did not laugh, coming to our table to tell us to put an end to our shenanigans. Sometimes, if we arrived at the bistrot early enough, the men Mick and I had seen on our earlier visit chatted with us, or rather with Danielle, Luc, and Émile since both my English friend and I had difficulty understanding their local accent. Most of these regulars had come right from fields or vineyards to eat, staying after dinner to enjoy, like us, a smoke and a glass of *eau de vie,* brandy.

Renaud's cooperative took most of the grapes around Davayé, bottling them as a regional Pinot Chardonnay; a few vineyards, a bit higher in quality, were bottled as Saint-Véran. The daily jumble of pulp, seeds, and skins from the co-op's crusher were dumped next to the waterless fountain in the center of Davayé. A regional producer hauled them away at day's end and pressed them into *marc de Bourgogne,* giving each vintner, in exchange, an agreed upon number of bottles of the powerful spirt. Without color and almost without taste, *marc* has a punch like Italian *grappa* or Serbo-Croatian *slivovitz,* as we all found out at the *fête de vendange* at picking's end.

Though our picking was bedeviled by a cold drizzle, only once was it heavy enough for us to stop working. A steady rain puts too much water in the bins, which then goes into the crusher with the grape and dilutes the wine. My row-long conversations with Mick, occasional evening visits to the town's bistrot, and Renaud's steady temperament helped keep me at my task, but Danielle's flirtatious ways and provocative pranks gave an extra spark to the entire crew. She led the teasing of Mick and me for how slow we worke d, as we always finished a row just as the rest of them were done with their break. To put an end to their insults, we decided one morning to forego singing Beatles songs and zip to the end of the row faster than our mocking tormentors. We did, impressing even *le patron* himself––until he inspected our work. Our speed had come at a price neither he, nor the rest of the crew, wanted to pay, as all of us had to scour the row again for the many grapes we had missed. Renaud discouraged any repetition of the experience and for the next few days the rest of the crew bombarded us with an even stronger barrage of jibes and sarcastic comments. From time to time, as we rode the tractor-pulled cart to town at day's end, Danielle's teasing took the form of stuffing a handful of grapes down the back of my shirt, squashing them to make sure I couldn't get them out. The still-watchful, still-edgy Luc sometimes added a fistful for good measure.

Dinner was the highlight of the day, since we could have a glass of wine or two without fear of slipping into a siesta under the dripping vines.

Midway through the *vendange*, I got to the farmyard a bit before dinner and came across the Renauds as they skinned a rabbit, which they did every couple of days. The sight would have made the vegetarian Danielle cringe, which made me, miffed at her teasing, want to lure her to the courtyard when it was happening. Like most French people who have the space — even a small backyard area in a crowded city — the Renauds raised rabbits for the protein. Waiting for the others to arrive, I went to have a closer look at the handsome animals, since even from a distance these rabbits were unlike any I had ever seen. *"Faites attention! Les mâles mordent,"* Renaud warned. Watch out, the bucks bite. Peter lRabbit relatives they were not. Renaud warned me that the aggressive bucks will bite the end of your finger off if you give them the chance. Both the males were French lop-eareds, their drooping ears long enough to almost touch the ground, and both were strikingly handsome, one a dark mahogany brown, the other light rust and white. They were the biggest rabbits I had ever seen, each carrying about ten pounds of kicking muscle and pent-up randiness. (No wonder the slang phrase for someone who is "hot to trot" is *chaud lapin* for a man, *chaude lapine* for a woman.) Below them in four other cages were the does, smaller and less aggressive, but still inclined, Renaud said, to take a nip at any finger that came their way. Next to the cages, in what was once a horse stall, a dozen young rabbits were hopping around in loose straw. When five or six months old they became one of the delicious stewed dishes Madame Renaud prepared for us several times. In fact, one was a main course at our *fête de vendange*.

Renaud put off until the last day the picking of his single patch of Pouilly-Fuissé grapes for that luscious unfiltered wine he offered us before each meal. Older than the rotund *patron's* 65 years, the vines were grown without trellises and barely reached a height of two gnarled feet, demanding, if the light drizzle persisted, just the kind of stoop labor to make a back scream. Happily, the sun broke through and stayed out the entire afternoon, allowing us to pick from our knees for the first time in over a week. Handling those small almost brown grapes, I knew they were the fruit of decades of carefully tended life in the rich alkaline clay that makes them thrive. Our good spirits, Danielle's good looks, and the warm sun almost qualified our crew to be on one of those damn posters.

Grapes in, crush done, and a *patron* who valued our work made for a *fête de vendange* worthy of the name. Ours started with Renaud's expected *"Venez boire un goût,"* and this time we all did. Even Danielle, who did not often drink, had a taste from his silver scalloped shell, his *tâte-vin*. Beautifully balanced between clean acidity and the fruity sweetness of those old grapes, it was the perfect introduction to the meal that followed. For the occasion, the two unfinished wooden tables had been covered with the ubiquitous red-and-white checkered tablecloths, places had been set, and several bottles of sparkling white wine stood ready. Called *Clairette de Die,* it comes from the Drôme River Valley in the Alps in the country around the town of Die, and is famous for its peach and apricot flavors and flowery aromas. We started to take what had become our customary places when Danielle objected. On this night, she insisted that Monsieur Renaud sit next to her, not near the head of the table with his son-in-law. Smiling as coyly as this large man could, the *patron* yielded to Danielle's insistence. After a volley of pops signaled the opening of the sparkling *Clairette,* a toast was made to a successful *vendange*: Renaud toasted us and we all stood to return the gesture, toasting him and his wife and daughter, who lingered for a few minutes after bringing us platters of *crudités* (that simple and delicious a mixture of shredded vegetables in a simple vinaigrette), local pâté, and sausage. Next came the main course, *lapin au moutarde,* rabbit in mustard sauce, served with rice. Bottles of red *Côtes du Rhône* followed the *Clairette* and were emptied and quickly replaced. Platters and breadbaskets crisscrossed the table, travel plans were swapped, and compliments for the wonderful meal delighted to blushing embarrassment Madame Renaud and her daughter, who, in spite of our cajoling pleas, would not join us at the table. Voices rose with excitement as modest plans became grand adventures, trips to Rome became tours of Italy and Greece and even Turkey, then to anywhere that was more exotic than anyone else's destination; people rose to their feet to toast with good luck the announcement of each extraordinary journey. Finally, wine and exuberance and the uneven floor got the better of me and, arms windmilling, I toppled backward to a laughing thump on the soft sand, my glass still in hand, held high for a refill. Monsieur Renaud, having seen it all before, remained his steady, good-tempered self, though his weathered rosy complexion became even rosier.

Madame Renaud and her daughter brought us several platters of regional goat cheeses as dessert before we wound up our grand dinner with a couple of bottles of the powerful Marc de Bourgogne. Our festivities were not over, however, as Danielle's flirtatious coaxing persuaded a more than willing Renaud to tell us stories of his life in 1930s Paris. In those tension-filled years on the eve of World War II, he worked in the rough and tumble world of Les Halles, the city's now demolished wholesale produce market. He also supported the Popular Front government of socialist Léon Blum, elected in 1936 against the tide of European fascism already in power in Spain and Italy.

When Yves Montand replaced The Beatles and Dylan on Émile's tape player, the smiling Danielle, showing an uncharacteristic shyness, charmed our *patron* to his feet for a dance, which he would do only to a certain song by Montand, a waltzing ballad about *"le temps des cerises"* the spring season of cherries and young love, both sweet and painfully short. The rest of us moved the tables to clear dancing space as Monsieur Renaud, in girth three times Danielle's size and more than a foot taller, deftly guided his infatuated partner with wine-softened attentiveness over the uneven sand floor. We were eager to do the same with Madame Renaud and her daughter, down from the kitchen to clear the last dishes and wish us well, but we lacked Danielle's charm and the two ladies retreated, laughing, to the second-floor safety of their house. After Monsieur Renaud ended dancing with his beaming partner, she turned quickly to Luc and pulled him to her for the next spin around the uneven sandy floor. A couple of dances later I received one of those surprises France happily gave me. Danielle and Luc reached out together and pulled me into their twosome jig until all three of us, tipsy from the wine, the rollicking dance, and the soft floor, tumbled laughing into the sacks of flour and sugar that lined the room. It was not the *Jules et Jim* scenario I had envisioned ten days earlier, but this was Hollister, not Truffaut, and for that I was happily grateful. In fact, little had happened to me as a *vendangeur* had followed any script since my wild ride to Davayé with the spirited Madame Percot.

✳

The wine and *marc* gone, and our legs and minds as well, we straggled back to the dormitory, most of us tumbling exhausted into fully-dressed sleep, oblivious to the damp and cold, appetites satisfied––at least some of them. All but Vincent, the youngest member of the crew, who had no interest in sleep and wanted to talk. He was a bit nervous about his coming trip and who better to talk to about it than a "hippie" from California. Of course, he did not know how unhippie-like my life had really been. But that did not matter to him any more than my desire for sleep. At dinner, he had told me he was going to travel somewhere by motor scooter, but we got distracted by the wine, the food, and the general frivolity and I never found out where exactly he was headed. Now, I was going to get the whole story. When he told me India was his ultimate destination, I was flabbergasted. No wonder he was feeling nervous. I had felt a lot more than nervous when I left California on this trip and I was only going to Europe. "I want to learn more about Yoga and meditation," Vincent said. "And even if I don't make it all the way, the trip itself will be a kind of meditation." That seemed not only "far out," but "right on."

As we walked in a light mist from one of the town's scattered pools of light to another, Vincent talked of what he would pack, what books he would take, how long the trip might last, and what kind of work he might find along the way. "What do your parents think of your trip," I asked, knowing he came from a small town in the Vosges Mountains northeast of Macon. "My mother is worried some, but I come from a large family and on our farm there is only enough room for a few of us. I had to leave sooner or later." Old enough to be his father, who felt the trip was a good idea, I wished him well, gave him encouragement, and offered him a few practical tips I'd picked up from my six months of living out of a backpack––take a sewing kit, an extendable clothesline, and a Swiss Army knife. They are all essential. Vincent's trip would certainly change him in unexpected ways, as mine, I hoped, was changing mine, though I was a bit fuzzy on what those changes were. As our walk ended, he asked me what I was going to do next. With as much savoir-faire as I could muster, I said that I was going to Paris to look for work as a translator. *"Super!"* Vincent said. "I've only been there once, but that's where I'll go when I get back from India."

Then we climbed the dormitory's worn wooden stairs and tried to go to sleep, Vincent still excited about his adventure, and I trying to quiet the sharp-toothed anxiety that his questions had awakened from a two-week nap. Vincent was right: Taking a long trip is, in itself, a kind of meditation, opening the traveler both to an interior emotional world as well to an outside physical one. On such a trip, the possibility is always present that something unexpected in the outside world will bring suddenly to the surface a memory or feeling from the interior world that startles with its eruptive force. Danielle and Luc pulling me into their dance did exactly that, reminding me of the peace I wanted with my father.

At dawn the next day, goodbyes and good wishes were exchanged, including *grosses bises*, those kisses on both cheeks that can be accompanied with a hug. After the evening before, I was not completely surprised that Danielle offered me both *bises* and hugs with affectionate warmth. When Luc did the same, however, I was astonished. The French had a lot to teach me about life. Renaud's son-in-law, Philippe, then drove Mick and me to the autoroute toll plaza near Macon. He said it would be easy to pick up a ride from there to Paris. Mick, heading for England and the hop harvest, pulled his long hair into a neat ponytail and we flipped a coin to decide who would have the favored front position for oncoming cars. I won. The first driver looked me over but kept right on going until he stopped to pick up Mick. Must have been his guitar case. In a couple of minutes, a young couple from Nice stopped for me and stuffed my backpack into an already stuffed trunk. With barely any conversation, they took me out of Burgundy's vine-quilted slopes, past gleaners scouring fields for turnips or potatoes the mechanical harvesters had missed, and finally through the valley of the Seine into the pulsing, cacophonous energy of the City of Light.

Chapter 7

Paris — From *Flâneur* to Translator

I returned to Paris in October of 1974, still in a winey cloud from my time in Monsieur Renaud's vineyards. Arnaud generously said I could stay with him for a couple of weeks while I looked for translation work, then I would have to find a place of my own. Being a translator would not fit my father's definition of the "real job" he hoped I would get, but it certainly was a lot closer to it than picking grapes.

When I decided to go to France and leave my Berkeley life behind, I had to do a head-down charge as if I were blindly attacking a bully, reality be damned. Not only did I have to ignore all those parental "Be carefuls" in my head but anything else that would cause my always vulnerable excitement to do a flip-flop into anxiety. As a result, I blithely ignored any effects the worldwide oil embargo might have on my French job prospects.

Only when I arrived in Paris did I find out that the French government had barred almost all work opportunities to anyone not a citizen of a country in the European Economic Community (EEC). That meant all translation work from French to English was reserved for English-speaking French people or French-speaking citizens of the United Kingdom. But there was a loophole: I spoke "American," as the French call it, not the English English that most French learn in school, so there was still a need for people who could translate French into American. I hoped my Carnegie Commission connections might push open a bit more that slightly open door just enough for me to get work. If that happened, my life would change, as looking for work quickly made clear to me. My carefree springtime life as a Parisian *flâneur* would dramatically change. No longer would I be able to go wherever my whims took me, checking out a *boulangerie* at midafternoon, or a shop that sold regional honeys, or a *fromagerie* where I could spend hours exploring its display of wonderful cheeses.

One *fromagerie*, in particular, became my favorite. As soon as I stepped in the shop's door, I was in cheese-lover's heaven, intoxicated by the pungent, slightly acidic aroma of puck-sized rounds and rust-colored cones, cinder-dusted pyramids and blue-veined wedges, cheeses wrapped in grape leaves, and cheeses rolled in herbs or crushed pepper. Some were hard and crumbly, others soft as warm butter; some were goat, some sheep, some cow. It was time to pull out of my shoulder bag my new cheese book, Androuet's classic *Guide de Fromage*. As I stood in front of the shop's main case, tracking down where and how a particular cheese was made, I noticed that from time to time someone peered down at me from the spaces between the bottles and tins on top of the case. After a few minutes, this *maître fromager,* the shop's master cheese merchant, joined by his equally curious assistant, asked me the name of my book. I held it up so they could read the cover. "*Alors, c'est Androuet!*" said *le maître,* and both men smiled approval. When I told them I was American, they were surprised again; not many buy Androuet's *Guide.*

Exploring a colorful eruption of flowers and greenery down a pedestrian walkway or what was causing an unusual noise in a quiet alley would now have to wait for the weekend. I would probably miss, then, the invitation of a Turkish shoemaker working in his open alleyway shop who invited me to stop and asked me about the States. As he continued to work with a small hammer and other fine tools on a pair of ankle-high black shoes, he told me he made such shoes for people with special foot problems. Years ago, he said, when he and his brother were young men, they stopped in Paris on their way to the States. He met the woman who became his wife, found work as a maker of these special shoes, and stayed to raise a family. His brother made it to Chicago. The shoemaker had visited him several times, and after every visit, back in Paris, dreamed again of finally reaching his long-ago destination. But his home now, he said, was Paris where his wife's family lived and his children and grandchildren. Such encounters revealed a bit more about Parisians, people who were both like me and unexpectedly and profoundly different. They also helped me get in touch with the French-speaking "me." When I was in Grenoble in the summer, a friend who taught English to French first-year university students told me to get rid of what she said is a linguistic crutch, my French-English dictionary, and start using a French one. I already spoke better French than some of her French students, she said. That was hard to believe, but I had a habit of denying whatever view of myself that did not conform to the image of the adolescent I persisted in thinking I was. I came to France, however, to banish that image and my friend's advice told me I was succeeding. After all, I could now carry on a lively conversation in French––more easily of course after a glass of wine. One has to be willing to be a fool to learn another language and I had willingly played that part long enough to develop a different persona. Pleased at this transformation I pushed aside any uneasiness I felt about being almost forty.

The new dictionary changed my linguistic life *tout à coup,* instantly. Looking up one French word in my hefty new paperback *Petit Robert* usually forced me to look up half-a-dozen others used in defining that first one--something I like to do, even in English. These hunting expeditions pushed me into thinking more in French, reinforcing another new habit: listening with full attention to the person speaking to me. When speaking English, I often thought about what I was going to say as the other person was talking to me, something most people do. When speaking French with someone, that was impossible. Still short of fluency, I had to focus fully on what a person speaking to me was saying. Day by day, however, as I learned about cheese and struggled to tell a respectable woman from a *poule de luxe,* or high-class prostitute, I began actually thinking in French. *Incroyable!* Unbelievable! This new linguistic confidence strengthened, of course, my illusion that I could become French. That was truly *incroyable,* though I was certainly not the first or the last American to be seduced by such a fanciful notion.

Looking for work did not mean I had to completely give up a *flâneur's* encounters, but I now had places to go and people to see, so I put myself on a schedule and became familiar with the sixth and seventh Arrondissements in central Paris where I went for most of my interviews. I began to feel like other working Parisians and also began to absorb French at an accelerating rate, soaking it up from advertisements, newspaper headlines, and posters. I even fancied that I had mastered the Gallic shrug, which comes with a *"Bof,"* and perfectly expresses an attitude of existential acceptance. I also often rode the Metro with commuters and saw on their tired faces the effects of the life-draining triplets, "*Métro, dodo*"--the *Métro* to *boulot,* work, then at day's end back to the *Métro* for the trip home and *dodo,* sleep. Cameron Quigly, an old prep-school friend of mine, had worked in Paris for ten years, so I sought him out for job-seeking advice and other tips he might have about how to get along in Paris. He could not help me much on the work front, but told me over lunch one day how he fought against that *ronron quotidien,* the daily grind, that can numb you to the beauties even "Living in a city like this must change how you look at the world and even how you see yourself," I said. "I feel better about myself just being here. How could you possibly fall into a rut?"

"The routine of work does it," Cameron said, "even if you like what you are doing. Once you get a job, it's easy to stop paying attention to the life around you, especially if you commute underground." "I can't imagine ever getting bored here," I said. "I've been here ten years," Cameron said, "and I feel that way, too, but the trick is keeping that feeling alive. For me, walking is the key. "What do you mean?" I asked.

"Once I found a job, I looked for an apartment within a mile or so from my office, then mapped out half-a-dozen walking routes to and from work so every walk would be different. And I kept adding routes," he explained, "taking longer walks on the way home in the longer days of Spring and Summer. I made it a point to pay attention to the different neighborhoods I walked through every morning and evening and to how the seasons changed them."

"That's what I did when I first got here," I said.

"But when you work," Ben said, "you have to make those walks a part of your day. What I noticed didn't have to be dramatic, it just had to be something I hadn't paid attention to before––the changing light on the Seine, or a café I had passed by, or a shop owner standing at the front door of his or her shop with windows full of hand-woven scarves or regional honeys. Sometimes I would stop at the café or visit the shop, and maybe even buy something. It gave me a chance to get to know the owners.

"I almost forgot. I'd walk through parks, not around them so I wouldn't miss seasonal changes, which are important to me. "

"What a great idea!" I said.

"It works," Ben said. "Those little pieces of Paris remind me almost every day of how lucky I am to live here."

When I found work, I would follow Cam's plan, I thought, and not fall into the *métro, boulot, dodo* trap, turning Paris into––*mon dieu!*–– Hartford, Connecticut.

❄

It was time to see if my connections could open for me the almost closed door of employment. I had reference letters from Clark Kerr, who was director of the Carnegie Commission on Higher Education in Berkeley where I had worked as an editor for several years, and from a few

Commission members. First, however, I would get in touch with Alain Touraine, the author of a Commission book I edited who had invited me to call when I got to Paris. As a Marxist socialist (he has since moved to the conservative end of the spectrum, a *bobo*, as the French would say, a bourgeois bohemian), he supported students on the barricades in what the French call *Les événments de Mai '68*. Frustrated by the sclerotic system of higher education, students mounted increasingly larger *manifestations,* demonstrations, that became highly disruptive of Parisian life, especially in the Latin Quarter, where demonstrators cut down trees and pulled up paving stones to build barricades. They finally were repressed with ferocious violence by the *Compagnies Républicaines de Sécurité* (CRS), a riot-control force that is part of the French National Police. The brutality of the CRS brought from all over France more supporters of the students' cause, vague as it was, and to the streets of Paris and other major cities. Protests were staged against the pro-government radio and television network and even against the national theater. Labor joined them and staged a crippling general strike that challenged the presidency of Charles De Gaulle. Six years later, the memories of those chaotic days were still fresh for many, especially those in the academic world.

Touraine's work compared the French and American systems of higher education and was one of a Carnegie Commission series by foreign scholars who had taught in the States. Editing his book was one of the best professional experiences I have ever had and introduced me to a Marxist way of looking at educational institutions and society. Touraine liked my work as much as I liked his, so I felt confident calling him, but still not all that confident about talking with him in French. Sitting in Arnaud's living room, recommendation letters in front of me, I bit the bullet and picked up the phone. In my best Belgian accent, I introduced myself in French to Touraine's secretary. He was out of town, she said, but she would tell him I called and to call back again in a week.

Formidable! I can actually do this in French! Not wanting to lose my momentum, I quickly called one of Kerr's friends, a high-level administrator for the French Senate, and late in the afternoon of the following day went to see him in an imposing 19th century building that housed the staff of the French Parliament and Senate. At the gate, I gave my name to the formidably solemn guards, waited as they checked their guest list, then followed their directions into the world of state power, monumentally intimidating as such buildings are intended to be.

Climbing the well-worn white marble stairs from one floor to the next I became increasingly nervous about my somewhat long hair, my English cord trousers and American sport coat and tie, and, of course, my Belgian accented French. Off the top floor foyer was a reception area for the administrator. His secretary said he was expecting me and quickly told him on the phone that I had arrived. She then ushered me into a deeply shadowed office where a tall gentleman with close-cropped white hair, dressed in tails and a white bow tie, was seated at a wide, dark-wood desk, partially backlit by the semi-circle of a large window behind him. While getting up to shake my hand, he made a friendly comment about "*Mon cher ami, Clark Kerr*," then invited my still nervous self to sit down and tell him how he might help me. The imposing setting and his elegant attire would have turned my French into gibberish if not for his welcoming manner, which quickly calmed me down. I told him of the translation work I was seeking then almost fell into a trance as I listened to his clear and impeccable French. I could understand every word he said and was able to respond easily to his questions. He could do little to help me, he said, but would have his secretary call me if something came up. In fact, though he did not know it, he had helped me enormously. When I went down the stairs I had climbed just a few minutes earlier, crossed the courtyard of marble paving stones, and walked past the guards, I was almost airborne. My French was *terrible,* which in the France of 1974 meant terrific!

The next day, when I called Touraine, his secretary said he had recommended me to a colleague who was looking for translation help on a French-American journal and that she had made an appointment for me with this colleague for the next day. His office was at the *Maison des sciences de l'homme* (MSH), a center for advanced research in the social sciences on Boulevard Raspail. Was that convenient, she asked? Well, I should say it was. All I remember of the appointment is that I was offered a job as a translator of articles from French to American for a sociology journal published in the States and in France. Though the pay was barely enough for me to get by, I could have vaulted over the Eiffel Tower. I was going to work in Paris!

❄

Though he often came to the *Maison* from his nearby offices, Touraine never made an effort to meet me. I was puzzled, since he had so highly valued my editing that he wrote in his book's acknowledgements that I should be considered the co-author of the English edition. He was, I was told, very reserved with everyone, in spite of being out there with his students on the barricades in '68. A neighbor from Berkeley, Antoine, whom I met in the MSH cafeteria in one of life's surprising coincidences (he had heard my French language instruction records coming from my window across the street) said that it was probably a matter of class, which, to my complete surprise, trumps a lot of things in France--and in the States for that matter. Touraine did exactly what I hoped--helped me find work--but without the social interaction that normally goes along with such relationships in the States. It was a cultural difference--one of many--that took getting used to.

A French friend, Antoine, who was doing research in the MSH library, understood Touraine's attitude, but did not understand my disappointment, even though he had spent a year studying in Berkeley. After staring at each other in the cafeteria several times in puzzlement, I approached him one day and said I thought I knew him but couldn't remember where we had met. What he remembered was meeting me a couple of times as a neighbor living across the street. More importantly, he also remembered hearing the *"Répétez après moi"* of my French records sailing out the open door of my balcony. I had only been in France long enough to understand the basics of French social behavior, but not much more than that, so Antoine's two years in Berkeley gave him an advantage over me. Neither one of us, however, grasped the more subtle cultural differences between our countries. Some American behavior--well, maybe just mine--still baffled him at times, as it did one winter evening.

Once in a while we would grab a beer in a café across the street from the MSH before heading home. One night, as we sipped our beer in the near-empty café, I felt hungry and unwrapped the *pain complet,* whole grain bread, I had bought at the famous Poilane bakery around the corner and some munster cheese I had bought at a nearby *fromagerie.* They made a perfect combination to go with the beer. My friend warned me that I would get us both thrown out: such things are not done. *Pourquoi?* Why, I asked, pointing out that there is only one other table of customers, almost out of sight at the other end of the café. Besides I said, offering him a taste, you have to try this combination. *C'est formidable!* After my second bite, he said again that the café would toss us out. After we talked a bit, I took yet another bite, which brought the waiter striding briskly toward us, his unsmiling look confirming Antoine's words of warning: Munster had struck again. *Au contraire,* in a friendly voice and with consummate courtesy, our waiter said customers on the other side of the café found the munster's odor a bit strong. Would I mind wrapping it up after I had a bite. I absolutely would not mind--and did. Antoine smiled and shook his head.

❄

The fact was, it seemed, that Touraine and I had a professional relationship, nothing more. That was why when I called his office he showed no interest in meeting me. Our relationship was not personal, as such relationships can often be in the States, but it was normal in the French professional world. Unfortunately, it often leads to a social isolation that gives many French people in that work world serious problems. As I found out, forming a network of friends or meeting members of the opposite sex was, in the France of the 1970s, hard to do if you had to move for work to a different city--or came from California. As a result, people were reluctant to leave the region where they were born even if there were no suitable jobs. When they did move, to Paris for example, they socialized--like Arnaud and his friends--with people they had known since their university days or from teaching overseas while doing alternative service to the military. Globalization and the European Union have, of course, dramatically changed this picture in the past forty years. Not for the better, I have read.

Touraine did the right thing--referring me to someone who offered me work--but without the social interaction that in the States normally is part of such relationships. It was an important cultural difference that took some getting used to.

What people said about Touraine and class woke me up to the traditional and rigid French social system that still exists but was even stronger over forty years ago. I had a lot to learn. After a few months at my job, I was invited to a weekend dinner at the elegant country home of one of my MSH colleagues. There were stables and horses and a riding ring with jumps. There was also the unmarried horse-loving older daughter of my colleague. In her late twenties, she was, my hostess told me, fresh out of a failed relationship; not the first, she added. With short black hair and an athletic body, strong jaw, and clipped movements, she seemed to have the character to keep any man in her life performing with precision whatever style of riding she fancied. As if to prove the point, she came to this family gathering in jodhpurs and riding boots.

At my colleague's invitation, I brought a guest, Sylvie, a young woman I had met through Arnaud. Like myself, she was from a lower-middle class background. She worked for a group of movie theaters that showed art films, like those of the New Wave, and wanted to be a screenwriter. After meeting my hostess and her horsewoman daughter and spending a few awkward moments at the wine bar, Sylvie wanted to take a walk. In fact, she insisted. "Why," she asked angrily "did you invite me?" She was being snubbed, it was clear, and it puzzled me, but not for long. Sylvie quickly enlightened me on the French class system. From the moment my colleague's son picked us up at the train station, I felt something was off, and that it had to do with Sylvie. When my hostess introduced us to her husband and daughter, I had the feeling that I was seen as a possible suitor for the horse-loving young woman, although her coolness at our introduction did nothing to suggest it. More importantly, however: Sylvie was not of their class. (Neither was I, but my Yale degree and my connections with Touraine and Clark Kerr misled them.) In barely speaking to her, my hostess and her family made it obnoxiously clear that, invited guest or no, Sylvie was to them a persona non grata, an unwelcome person, and maybe not even a person.

I thought afterward that I should have left *tout de suite* with my lady, but I had no idea how to extract Sylvie and me from the situation without creating a scene. As my hostess had an important position on the journal that was my employer, walking out would have made my work life complicated. I did nothing––except feel confused and ashamed––much more ashamed on the way home.

Sylvie knew all the ins and outs of the French class system and did not easily excuse my ignorance. She did not abide "*cons*," jackasses, of any class and made that forcefully clear when, back in Paris after a mostly silent train ride, we stopped to get a glass of wine and the only waiter tried to give us the worst table in his empty café. Having apparently told him exactly what he could do with his *service,* she stormed out of the place with me in her wake, impressed, even without knowing what she said. From the waiter's sputtering, red-faced response, however, I had no doubt that her words hit their mark. He definitely had entered *con* territory, which I had only narrowly escaped.

Translating caused my vocabulary to blossom. Unfortunately, it also started to undo the good effects of using the French dictionary. I fell back into the habit of mentally changing into English whatever anyone said to me in French before I figured out a French response, which slowed down my conversations quite a bit. But, as work can sometimes do, translating forced me to engage a larger world, where I discovered a Parisian generosity that took a form as far from smiling California as it could have been.

A dreary Sunday in the middle of a relentlessly gray winter in the valley of the Seine found me in need of completing a few pages of a translation in order to get paid on Tuesday. I had enough food at home, but my meager compensation paid me just enough to get by and I had run out of cash. The MSH library, home to *Le Petit Robert,* the ten-pound dictionary I needed, was closed on Sundays. I had moved from Arnaud's to a hotel in Clichy, but knowing his aunt had a *Robert,* I arranged to borrow the dictionary Sunday afternoon when Arnaud had planned to go to a movie.

All I needed was to park myself in a café for a few hours with this French version of Webster's Third Edition and I could wrap up my work. That meant buying at least one expresso, which cost two francs. *Zut!* I did not have two francs. I did not even have two centimes, and Arnaud had already left for his film. *Quoi faire?* What to do? I stood under a café awning in the cold drizzle and pondered my predicament. I also did a bit of pacing, the only signs of life the passing of an occasional taxi and the German Shepherds who glared at me with menace if I passed too close to the locked glass doors of the cafés they guarded. There were no walkers in the city this soggy afternoon. Wait a minute! I had just bought *un carnet,* a booklet of ten Metro tickets. If I could cash in three or four of the nine I had left, I would be sipping that expresso and leafing through that dictionary in a wink.

I descended into the nearest Metro station, as empty as the street except for the gentleman at the barred window or *guichet* where tickets were sold. Lugging my hefty tome and smiling my best California smile, I greeted him with my Belgian-accented *"Bonjour."* Sternly official in his tailored blue-gray uniform, he did not reply. Though a bit taken aback, I was desperate, so I launched into my story of need. He listened until I finished without the slightest movement of his full-bellied body. His round face, marked by a neat pencil-thin mustache that matched the blackness of his slicked-down hair, betrayed no hint of a smile. *Rien du tout,* nothing at all. I waited, nonplussed, then slid three Métro tickets into the smooth, shallow wooden depression under the bars. *"Non!"* he said, raising his left hand to stop me. With his right hand he reached into the pool of coins he kept for change and with the first and second fingers guided out through the well-worn dip in that smooth wooden counter two one-franc coins. *"Merci bien,"* I said––smiling of course––completely surprised at what was happening. Once more I offered the tickets. Once more he held up his left hand, and barely causing his mustache to ripple, said *"Pas de quoi,"* you're welcome.

It was a wonderful example, like Touraine's seeming aloofness, of how perplexing the French can be to Americans, often doing the right thing but without the sociability we tend to expect. I was perplexed often, pushed out of my cocoon of familiarity into different ways of engaging the world, and in the bargain changing how I felt about who I was. The process had some surprises.

The French national character, if one can say there is one in a country with such varied regional differences (which was certainly more the case in 1974 than in 2020), mixes the emotional and demonstrative temperament of peoples of the Mediterranean south, who are of Latin descent, with the more reserved disposition of people from the north, who are of Norman and Frankish descent. History, geography and family roots of course play a part, as they always do everywhere, but when you find mountainous areas like Grenoble and its Alps, a wave-sculpted peninsula like Gaelic Brittany, and the sunny warmth of the south all in a country you can drive across in 10 hours, things get a bit mixed up. The French language reflects the mix, combining the sensuous softness of the Latin south with the muscular vigor of the Frankish north. Both people and language, as a result, are endlessly interesting, with the southern character dominating at times and the northern at other times. The French sense of humor, for example, is said to be most like that of their German neighbors, though whoever said so was surely making a joke only the northern French and Germans could understand.

With its Latin-based "purity" carefully protected by the Académie Française, French does not enjoy the richer vocabulary of free-wheeling English, which, though basically an Indo-European language like French, welcomes words from many other languages into its lexicon. As a result, French speakers have had to create some wonderfully colorful expressions that in English might be expressed in a single word. Instead of saying, for example, that something is worthless, bunk, poppycock, or hogwash, some French might say, but not in polite company: *Ça ne vaut pas un pet de lapin,* it's not worth a rabbit's fart. Discovering such expressions is in part what makes translating so interesting. And maddening. From time to time, French colloquial expressions popped up in my work that had me wracking my brain for a good match in American. Was "thingamajig" a good translation of *truc?* which literally means trick but is used in a hundred ways. How about "good-for-nothing" for *propre à rien?* Or "monkey business" for *niaiseries,* which means silliness? Often when I used such words, my Swedish-born editor thought I was making them up. She spoke flawless English of the English variety, but had never heard most of my American colloquialisms. She said that her son's American girlfriend, however, knew them all. In a way, the Metro agent's formality and kindness reflected the temperaments of north and south. Though he had a reserve that did not give a hint of how he felt, his actions spoke with simple eloquence of his generosity. Thanks to him I got the expresso I needed, which, loaded with three lumps of sugar, carried me through a couple of translating hours before my energy flagged. To finish my work, unable to afford another expresso, I needed something else to give me a jolt.

I got Brazilians, who burst into the café in such a tumultuous whirl of color, laughter, and flamboyant energy that they seemed to come right out of a Fellini movie. (I know, I know, he's not Brazilian!) Their clothes as brightly colored as tropical birds, their laughter contagious, they all talked at once, waving their arms, grabbing each other for quick hugs, almost dancing when they spoke. Even the waiter caught their spirit, helping them to pull a couple of tables together, passing around menus, and laughing with them as they made a game of where they sat--though it was hard for them to stop moving. One even came over to my table to invite me to join them, then samba'd back to their group. Brown, black, white and all shades in between, they spoke a language full of rhythmic, sinuous song. As different and unexpected as the portly ticket agent's generosity, their arrival gave me enough energy to polish off that translation in no time.

After I found work, I moved from Arnaud's place to a small hotel on Rue Ganneron near Place Clichy in the northwestern part of the city, Henry Miller's old stomping ground.   A couple in their 80s owned the hotel, and to this day I regret not spending more time with them, as they were always shyly friendly when I passed their glass-walled lobby office. The one story the woman did tell me gave me an inkling of what a long-ago Paris was like. In the 1890s, she said, when she was five or six years old, she helped her father in the evening bring their small herd of cows inside the city walls before the gates––*portes* on today's maps––were closed and locked.

To get to work from my Clichy hotel to the MSH at Sèvres-Babylon in the center of Paris I had to go halfway across the city.   Mindful of those narcotizing triplets––*Métro, boulot, dodo*––I stayed as much as possible above ground, taking the bus and walking. My usual routine was to stop at the small, fancy pastry shop at the corner of my street, buy a couple of *pains au chocolat*, croissants with chocolate inside, and a Comice pear, completely new to me. The French call it *"La Reine des poires,"* the queen of pears. Deliciously deserving of the name, it is buttery in flavor and full of juice.   Then I grabbed a bus for my half-hour ride.

One morning, after a very cold night, I was awakened by unusual shouting in the street and saw from my window that several inches of snow had fallen.   To get to my bus stop I had to walk through one battlefield after another: *les pilliers*, the pillars, or regulars, of the cafés in my *quartier*, which in several cases faced each other across the street or were side by side were engaged in roisterous snowball fights. Gangs of children fought running battles on their way to school, dodging in and out between parked cars as they hurled volleys of snowballs, using their book bags as shields.

Then, as the dull apricot-colored sky slowly brightened with the pale yellow light of the rising sun, my bus took me through a Paris magically draped in whiteness, the driver moving us more slowly than usual it seemed, especially past Maillol's bronze statues near the Louvre. Their voluptuous female forms, made even more sensuous by a white blanket of new-fallen snow, enjoyed the courtship that morning of several snowmen.

With or without snow, Christmas in Paris offered many gifts. The streets are not jammed with tourists (remember this was 1974), colored lights festooned some shops and cafés, which offered special seasonal treats, and many concerts were offered free in *églises chauffées,* heated churches, which the posters announcing the events always put in boldface type. Since most of the churches are built with stone and have lofty ceilings, heat is a necessity. About half an hour into the first of the concerts I attended, however, I was bothered by a persistent chafing sound coming from the rear of the church. Its source was a group of ushers, who were trying to stay warm by rubbing their hands together. I soon joined them; even my down jacket was not enough to ward off the deepening cold. Later, I found that those concert posters, like the ones advertising joyful *vendanges,* embellished the truth *un petit peu,* a little bit. The church heat was turned off as soon as the concert began. Within half an hour the damp cold settled onto the huddling music lovers. Bach could do nothing about it.

When the sun came out for a few hours in late January, after a solid month of depressing gray weather, cafés immediately put their terrace tables out for their sun-starved customers. Bundled up in heavy coats and the essential scarves, they doggedly sat sipping their expressos and smoking their English Rothman or American Winston cigarettes (No one I knew smoked the French Gitane or Gauloise--*sauf moi*--except me.)

Following their example, I bought a wonderful hand-woven scarf, which I still have, but I also needed a hat. Arnaud recommended BHV, the Bazaar de l'Hotel de Ville, the market of city hall, where I could find every kind of hat, as well as stoves, shoes, vacuum cleaners, underwear-- in short, *tout,* everything. On Arnaud's recommendation, I went to that immense emporium one rare sunny winter Saturday afternoon hoping to find a cap like the one worn by the movie star, Jean Gabin. When I reached the store, a young man and a young woman were flanking the main doors selling *L'Humanité Dimanche,* the Sunday magazine of the Communist Party. Both vendors had long hair and wore jeans and Andean capes, as many young Parisians did to express solidarity with Salvador Allende, the socialist Chilean president. (With help from the American CIA, Allende was violently overthrown on September 11, 1973--Chile's 9/11.)

Alas, BHV did not sell my Gabin cap. No doubt the gods of French cinema found unacceptable that someone wearing-- *Mon dieu!*-- a down jacket could ever wear a cap worn by the French Humphrey Bogart. I left the store and walked back to the corner, passing the two *L'Humanité* vendors, who were still hawking their magazines. As I waited in a cluster of Saturday shoppers for the light to change, screams and shouts erupted behind me. I turned to see the crowd at the main entrance scattering in all directions and the female *L'Humanité* vendor huddled against the wall of the store, magazines scattered about her on the sidewalk. Facing her a short-haired young man in a crew-neck sweater and khaki pants (my prep school and college "uniform") stood in the karate "ready" pose: left leg thrust forward, rigid left arm and hand stretched out in front of him, right arm bent and close to his body. The young woman's male comrade on the other side of the entrance was still fending off kicks by another young man in "uniform." The sudden violence of the assault, which lasted only a few seconds, allowed the attackers enough time to give the Nazi salute and race off through the shocked, package-toting shoppers, knocking a few to the sidewalk as they fled. I pointed out to one of the half-dozen nearby Paris *flics,* gendarmes, where the assailants had gone. He stared at me for a second and turned away, not showing the slightest interest in any pursuit. One young *flic* did give chase, but tripped and fell as he tried to wend his way through the alarmed shoppers. The vendors, though shaken up, were not hurt, and with the help of some pedestrians collected most of their scattered magazines.

A few months later newspapers reported on a police investigation that revealed a large number of Parisian *flics* were sympathetic to neofascist views; some were members of neofascist associations. Most of these gendarmes, the story said, were moved to administrative duty; a few were forced to resign.

❊

I learned from French friends that school kids are taught rigorously about rights, though they no doubt had even fewer than were granted by my parochial school nuns. That no doubt explained their explosive energy when liberated at day's end. When that school experience is reinforced by a history marked by violent struggles––usually between the Left and the Right––for individual liberty, it is no wonder that French citizens demonstrate often to defend their "rights." It could be *priorité à droite,* the unquestioned "yield to the right" of country byways and city streets, or the right of students and immigrants living in the Marais to stage a *manifestation,* demonstration, to defend their low-cost housing that gentrification was beginning to sweep away. (Over forty years later, that gentrification is complete.)   Passing through the 20th Arrondissement one afternoon at rush hour on the way to have dinner with a friend, I joined some curbside spectators to admire the work of a driver who had left his car to clean up a horn-tooting, curse-laced traffic jam caused by drivers insistent on their "rights." In this case it was the right to cross six lanes of boulevard traffic before cars on that boulevard, exercising *le droit* given them by the now green light, surged into the intersection, though they had nowhere to go. Tati's Monsieur Hulot would have loved it.

Our hero, white shirt and tie pulled loose, stood fearlessly in the center of this automotive pandemonium and with a lion-tamer's flourish gained control of the rights-drunk drivers. Left hand went up: You--Stop! Right hand did a low sweeping motion: You--Pass behind me! Both hands went up: You--Don't even think about trying to cross! Right arm extended, hand palm down--*Ce n'est pas* Le Mans *ici, Monsieur,* as he blocked a sports car trying to zip around him like a driver at that major racing event. Pivoting and spinning, glowering and grinning, his tie and shirt tails finally flying free, this master of willful drivers slowly but surely brought smooth-flowing order to the intersection. The horns fell silent, some drivers even smiled. Tucking in his shirt as he walked to his car, this artist of order waved to my group of appreciative spectators as we broke into applause, which he acknowledged with a bow before sliding behind the wheel. Then with the green light giving him the absolute right to go, off he went, giving us a final toot on his horn. *Formidable! Incroyable!*

As I chatted and laughed with my little group about this miraculous event, the lights, of course, continued to change--and, of course, *le droit* to go when the light was green again asserted its absolute power: A cacophony of blaring horns told us that the intersection was once more completely jammed.

❄

Because the Metro system had many *contrôleurs,* or inspectors, cheating was difficult. It was easier on a bus, but if you did--and I did so regularly--you also ran the risk of being caught. Leather-coated and ready for action, the *contrôleurs* could appear anywhere at any time to check tickets, which had to be punched by machines at either the front or the back door. My bare-bones budget could ill afford a fine, which you had to pay on the spot. I also could not afford the full bus fare--two tickets when the bus passed through several zones on its route--so, since my rides always traveled through two zones, I kept using one used ticket, punched by a machine when you mounted the bus, and a second unpunched and so valid. It was a common ploy.

One drizzly winter day, doing a noontime errand, I was seated at a window near the rear door of a jam-packed bus, confident that *contrôleurs* would never want to deal with such a crowd. In fact, that was exactly the kind of bus they targeted, knowing that scofflaws like me would find the crowd a good place to hide. I had hardly gone half a dozen stops when two inspectors got on at the front door. Dressed as usual in black leather overcoats, black leather boots, and even--*Quel sacrilège!*--black leather Gabin caps, they started moving down the aisle, checking tickets as they went. I panicked and got up, hoping to give them the slip before they got to me. Alas, my luck had run out. A *contrôleur* was right there in front of me.   "*Papiers d'identité,*" he said, having quickly sized me up. Then I pulled a trick out of the sleeve of my down jacket and pretended I did not speak French, though I almost blew it by saying "*Je ne parle pas français, Monsieur.*" When I looked befuddled, I was saved by the intercession, surely divine, of a young woman standing next to me. She noticed my incomprehension--which I think she knew was feigned--and explained my situation to the inspector, then continued to act as my translator. "They want to see your passport," she said. That was worse than having an invalid ticket for I had exceeded the three months I could legally stay in France --by half a year! I passed it to the agent then waited for the fateful trip to the police station. My luck returned. The *contrôleur,* noticing a woman with two children trying to sneak out the rear door behind me, flipped past the page with the date of my entry into France. "*Merci,*" he said, and abruptly returned my passport before quickly following the woman with her children to the sidewalk, where his colleague was also approaching them. "*Merci bien,*" I said to my attractive translator. "*De rien,*" you're welcome," she said, smiling divinely.

❋

My hotel near Place Clichy, recommended by some Berkeley friends, was simple, inexpensive, clean, and located in the middle of a working-class neighborhood of four-and five-story apartment buildings of no particular distinction. Aside from morning traffic it was quiet enough, no doubt because it was very close to the Montmartre Cemetery.   When I think of my first room in that old hotel, pea soup comes to mind: everything was pea green — green linoleum, a few green throw rugs on the floor, green drapes on the windows, green wallpaper, and a green spread on the old, iron-framed bed, which, *grâce a dieu,* was actually firm. The room was spacious--probably 15 by 20 feet—with French doors opening onto a small balcony that overlooked the hotel courtyard. Furnished with *un lit matrimonial,* a double bed, a bureau, a small wooden desk painted green of course, several easy chairs with green upholstery, a sink with hot water, and a bidet--not part of California accommodations--it gave me plenty of room to do my morning yoga. A shared VC and shower were down the hall.

At least once every few weeks, around eight in the morning, a glazier, or *vitrier,* entered the courtyard and let us all know he was there by sending his drawn out cry, *"vee-tree-aay,"* caroming off the courtyard walls. (*Un vitre* is a pane of glass.) Strapped to his back was a wooden frame in which he carried sheets of different kinds of glass he could cut to replace broken panes in windows and doors. His way of making a living as an artisan, like those closed *portes* of Paris, was soon part of history.

When Christmas approached, the owners of my Clichy hotel told me that I'd have to move to another room: mine was reserved every holiday season by a family from Normandy. The elderly owners apologized for the inconvenience but assured me that my new room was very suitable. It was that, barely, but the bed was far from suitable, its thin, drooping mattress quickly restoring to my back its London B and B curve. Because it was less than half the size of the green room, it was half the price — $3.50 a night instead of $7 — and it was clean and airy, with a small sink, its one window facing the narrow street four stories below. My morning wake-up call several days a week was no longer the *vitrier's* courtyard cries, but the grinding compactor of a garbage truck and the shouts of frustrated commuters backed up behind it in the narrow street. Like most urban jammed intersections, the congestion occurred with the kind of insane regularity common to all large cities. From my window I could watch the sanitation workers deliberately move with an unhurried pace, intended no doubt to further exasperate the bottled-up drivers. It succeeded, as the drivers always fired off volleys of expletives to accompany their tooting horns.

Almost as intriguing, though, were the late-night entries of my next-door neighbor. The sound of his door opening and closing and his chronic cough never failed to wake me up and the cardboard-thin walls were no buffer to the sounds he made as he prepared for bed--the removal of shoes, the brushing of teeth, and the click of the light switch. Finally, he settled onto his creaking bed, no doubt as low-slung as mine, his hacking cough subsided, and he fell asleep.   Several times, I caught glimpses of him as he preceded me down the stairs, never wearing a hat but always wearing a trench coat.   I never saw his face. Perhaps, he drove one of those "taxis" waiting outside Le Crazy or was involved in activities of interest to Simenon's Inspector Maigret.

❄

After over a month in this tiny room, I moved into a four-bedroom apartment near the Marais that I found thanks to a friend, sharing it with two women and a man, all in their thirties. When I was introduced to the man, whom I never saw again, though I lived there for five months, he told me he had initially come to France with Algeria's national theater troupe and now was teaching at the University of Paris at Nanterre, a new campus, where a French-German student, Daniel Cohn-Bendit helped ignite the demonstrations of May, 1968.   The women worked in the education system but I do not remember what they did exactly; they were also going to school.

Within a week of sleeping on my new firm bed, my back straightened out and I learned, as I moved about the room, how to adopt a rhythmic bobbing walk to avoid conking my head on the heavy ceiling beams. A century and a half earlier, when the building was constructed, the French were much shorter than in the 1970s and even in the 1970s, at just over six feet, I was usually the tallest person in a Metro car. That certainly is no longer the case.   Moreover, when the building was constructed, no showers or bathtubs were built in; our shower was a jury-rigged arrangement in the kitchen to take advantage of the apartment's only source of hot water, a blue butane canister, which, thanks to a two-burner stove, also provided the apartment's only source of heat. The shower, with its opaque green curtain, served its purpose but its location created some interesting towel dancing and "*pardons*" at breakfast time, since the two roommates I saw most often were the young women.

The stove allowed me to prepare one of my favorite Berkeley cold-weather breakfasts, pre-cooked brown rice with raisins and cashews warmed in milk, sweetened with honey, and spiced with cinnamon and nutmeg. To one of the female roommates who occasionally would come into the kitchen as I was preparing this concoction, it was too exotic even to taste, though she did say she liked the spicy aromas. For a *petit déjeuner, comme il faut,* a proper breakfast, she said with an authority that left no room for argument, you had to have croissants and coffee.

Like that traditional *petit déjeuner,* the winter weather in Paris of 1974 has not changed much. It is still damp and gray with occasional snow, to the delight of school children and the café, regulars. Also, since the City of Light is close to the latitude of Vancouver, Canada, the sun in winter, when it deigns to appear through the Seine's veil of gray, sets around four and rises after nine. I went to work at eight, so the streetlights were still burning bright; they were also on when I left the MSH library at four thirty. On those rare clear days, the low-angled winter *lumière rasante,* raking light, sent streaks of brilliance into the outdoor morning market on Boulevard Raspail, where the MSH was located. If I arrived early enough to grab a window seat in the library, I could enjoy a glimpse of the Spanish clementines (tangerines) and Israeli grapefruit, orange and yellow jewels whose brilliance and suggestion of warmth drew me away from *Le Petit Robert* and into a daydream of bodysurfing on my favorite beach north of San Francisco on warm Autumn days.

Parisian winter weather usually comes sweeping up the Seine valley from the English Channel, gray, wet, and cold. Those turtlenecks and scarves Parisians wear in movies are not just props: they ward off a raw dampness that can chill you to the bone. More importantly, along with the weather came Sundays, which always put me in danger of getting mired in ruminations about my life--what I was doing so far from home, what exactly home meant, and, more broadly, what the hell I was doing at the age of 38 working at a job that I knew had no future. It did not help that in deepest winter the Parisian sun comes up after nine and sets just after four.

To escape the doldrums of *dimanche* – the subject of many poems-- as soon as the sun started to brighten the slate-colored morning sky, I got out of bed, dipsy-doodled out of my room to the kitchen and took a quick shower before my roommates were up. As I left my building, I passed a doorway plaque that said it was once the residence of Honoré de Balzac, one of many places in Paris where he lived for a short time, always on the move to elude creditors.

After wandering the narrow quiet streets of the Marais, its many wholesale clothing outlets closed, its small Arab and Jewish cafés full of men and smoke, I would usually choose a café near the market street of St. Antoine and read *L'Humanite Dimanche* and now, happily, *Le Monde.* The more French I had learned and the more understanding I had of French culture, the more I felt both at home and, ironically, more aware of the fact that I could never "be French," though I was still unwilling to admit that to myself. France became for me a bit like a woman I am strongly attracted to but feel is not a good match (I fail miserably keeping the two separate.). I keep enjoying her company, in and out of bed, but the more time I spend with her, the more I realize how shaky the relationship is, that the slight tremors of occasional conflict hint at a widening and unbridgeable gap. Maybe that's why I did not want to acknowledge how well I knew French. Once fluent in the language and beginning to understand what living in France might be like, I would lose the romance and, like anywhere--or any woman--I would have to deal with daily life. Even though I mentioned in the opening pages that I came to France to become more *"bien dans ma peau,"* more at home in my own skin, and that seemed to be happening in France, actually making the decision to live there would give me the kind of apprehension I felt about taking this trip in the first place. It might have been otherwise if I had not been near forty years old, which was true for many things in my life at that time. I doubt it. It was my koan, my cross to bear, my curse, my fate. Take your pick.

Fueled by a couple of expressos, I headed for the Place des Vosges, a magnificent square of restored 17th century buildings, which on sunny days, even in winter, always offered the possibility of impromptu theatrical events. On gray winter Sundays that is usually not the case, but a rabbi and a gang of unbridled pre-teenage boys, some wearing yarmulkes, changed all that in a flash. Like colts, they galloped into the Place near where I was sitting, and immediately started a rousing soccer game, unbothered by the large elegant but dry fountain in the middle of their gravel pitch. The rabbi acted as referee, trying to quiet them when their screams began to ricochet off the buildings of the Place and recovering any ball that violated the *pelouse interdite.* (Luckily no *gardiens* were present.) The shouting players swirled this way and that around the fountain, on the edge of which, oblivious to the bedlam, three other boys huddled together, deep into a *bande dessinée*, a comic book. Their cries of *"Gaston est dingue!"* told me the book's hero was Gaston La Gaffe, or Gaston, the screw-up, the office-boy star of a series that had a fanatic following. *Pas vrai!"* That can't be true! One shouted. *"Comme il est génial!"* What a genius said another at Gaston's cockeyed strategies and Rube Goldberg inventions, all designed to help him evade work. When the soccer ball caromed off one of the absorbed trio, they howled in protest before straightening out their yarmulkes and plunging back into their hero's wacky world. They could have been sitting on the floor in a bookstore's *bandes desinées* section, where, if a new Gaston had come out, his young fans could always be found. That's where I first discovered him, drawn by both the children and adults who eagerly snapped up the latest volume of their hero's adventures. No wonder. The rigorous conventions that governed the worlds of both school children and office workers cried out for a hero who would flout them and drive their enforcers to distraction. Gaston was the man for the job.

Like its markets, everyday life was more exposed in Paris––and all of France––than the life I knew in the States, richer in texture and the unexpected. In a way, the entire city was an outdoor theater, with comedy and tragedy likely to occur at any time, sometimes in the same incident. Whether it involved many people, like a major traffic jam, or a small group like a snowball fight between the *piliers* of neighboring cafés, it all nourished me. I relished never knowing when I would suddenly find myself a participant in such an event, as when I shared the wonderful aroma of my munster cheese with other passengers on a Metro car, or found my Sunday morning in the Place des Vosges animated by an impromptu game of *football* refereed by a rabbi.

In addition to scarves and turtlenecks, and croissants and coffee, another Parisian invariable I discovered was commercial sex, which in one form or another seemed to be deeply woven into the fabric of the city's life. It often disoriented me, starting with my experience in the "office" of the working girl at Gare Montparnasse when I first arrived. You might think that my woeful Crazy Horse experience would have put an end to my curiosity about that world, that I would not find the world of *putes* at all enticing, whether it offered statuesque "dancers," a streetwalking trollop or more discreet *poules de luxe,* luxurious chickens, often stylishly dressed. *Pas du tout,* not at all.

I was both drawn to this world and repelled by it––an ambivalence familiar to many who, at the age of seven, knelt in semi-darkness and tried to figure out what a sin was and if they had committed one––except being born that is. Having been raised in an Irish-American world that considered the body shameful and something to be hidden, I was often naïvely perplexed by how powerfully a woman's body affected me, forgetting that the forbidden stimulates the greatest excitement. Attending an all-male high school and university––and without sisters or close female cousins––not only turned women into mysterious and inaccessible beings but intensified my conflicted lust for their bodies, though for years I was not even very clear about what that lust was all

about. Some Irish-American Catholic guilt enriched the mixture, even though one of my parish priests
--a childhood schoolmate of my mother's--assured me that such curiosity and excitement was normal and not to worry about it. Alas, the damage was already done, as Neil Young said of another emotional pitfall. That mixture of the forbidden and the desirable is tough to beat, as any teenager knows.

Two things in particular about the Parisian world of sex for sale surprised me: how ravishingly beautiful some of the *putes* were and how integrated it was into the rest of Parisian life. Though sex was for sale almost everywhere, my friends assured me, no one seemed to care most of the time. For example, on the way home to my Clichy hotel in the evening, I usually passed a smartly dressed black woman standing under the pastry shop awning on the corner of Rue Ganneron, "my" street, and Avenue de Clichy. It took me a while to realize that she was a *pute*, the only one in my immediate neighborhood. I walked past her every night but she never said a word to me, though a couple of blocks away, in Pigalle, you could not walk half a block, even with a woman on your arm, without getting a bawdy invitation to join a lady for a drink in the tiny bar that was clearly the foyer to her "office." Such bars were everywhere in that neighborhood, their interiors dimly lit by small, red-shaded lamps, their doors flanked by a hostess or two, who, with their revealing dress and saucy remarks, hinted at what games could be played if you joined them inside, "*Votre jolie amie, aussi*," they added if I had a female companion.

To add to my confusion, Arnaud and his friends warned me more than once that any woman I could successfully *drague*, pick up, at a café would either be a *pute* or *dingue*, wacky. What of the attractive women I often saw strolling *les grands boulevards* or sitting alone in a fancy café? "*Poules de luxe, sans aucun doute*," said Richard, high-class prostitutes, no doubt about it.

"With fur coats and fancy clothes?" I asked.

"*Exactement*" they said. "They're wearing their work clothes, like businessmen wear suits. The cafés are where they make their deals. And the waiters often get a cut."

Then I remembered an encounter I had on walking back to Arnaud's on a blustery, rainy late Sunday in April. The final blast of departing winter got to me, in spite of my new turtleneck and scarf and, of course, my down jacket. I wanted something warm to drink and pushed open the door to a place that was more of a bar than a traditional café, with low lighting and leather-covered stools at the dark wood bar inside the door. I took a stool a few seats away from a nicely dressed blonde woman who was chatting and laughing with the barman when I entered. When I ordered "*Un chocolat chaud, s'il vous plaît,*" she turned to give me a casual once-over. The barman served me that wonderful mixture of hot chocolate syrup and hot milk, served from separate small white pitchers, and went back to his conversation with my neighbor.

A few minutes later, I had polished off my hot chocolate but still felt cold so I ordered a second one. With a look of mock surprise and an amused smile, my blonde neighbor turned toward me and said "*Ah, deux!*" Ah, two! arching her carefully fashioned eyebrows. Was she letting me know she could offer something else that would warm me up? I was not confident enough in my French to enter into the give and take necessary to find out. Moreover, I was on a hot chocolate, not a champagne budget, which put her, financially and physically, out of my reach. And what if the smartly dressed blonde was not a *poule de luxe?* So I smiled--my default reaction--said nothing and went back to sipping *numéro deux. Numéro un* was definitely better.

The saucy prostitutes in Pigalle, though never explicit, let you know without any doubt what business they were in, and their presence, which, according to a woman friend who lived in Pigalle, made that *quartier* very safe for a respectable woman. My neighborhood of Clichy, right next to Pigalle, was out of the *pute* zone so the few prostitutes there, like the one at the corner of my street, were appropriately discreet. So long as the ladies of Pigalle, or similar places, did not solicit you, they broke no laws. But how was one to know the where the boundaries were that separated respectable women from the more subtle variations of commercial sex-- my "*numéro deux*" bar neighbor, for example, or the *poules de luxe* of the *Grands Boulevards*? As I found out when I returned from France to live in San Francisco--which had experienced an explosion of massage parlors--boundaries separating the high-minded from the down and dirty are often vague and shifting in any large city, and even in nearby residential communities likeéBerkeley, though people who live in such towns often pretend otherwise.

Paris, of course, has long been famous for the many varieties of sexual services it makes available, so it should not have been a big surprise when one evening I more or less walked into the middle of one that seemed to have gone awry. As I came up to the street from the Metro on my way home from work, I heard the yapping of a dog and the sharp voice of an angry woman. On one side of the street, across from the Metro exit, there were two seafood restaurants, side by side, both fronted with displays of oysters, clams, mussels and a variety of fish laid out on beds of ice decorated with sprigs of parsley and slices of lemon. Waiters brought orders from inside to men in long white coats and black rubber boots who filled them by prying open shellfish or preparing fish selected from the display. They were always an animated group, joking and chatting as they worked, but this night they were lined up at the curb laughing at something going on behind me.

I turned and saw at another entrance to the Metro a hundred feet away from me a young woman holding a baby and shouting at a six-foot tall black-haired woman, who wore a mini-skirt and stiletto heels and had her back to me. Suddenly, the angry, yelling woman turned, shoved the baby into the arms of the startled man standing behind her, who already had his hands full trying to control a small, wildly yapping dog, then whipped around and launched an arm-flailing attack on the black-haired lady. Big mistake. Clearly experienced in such *bagarres,* or dustups, the bigger woman easily fended off her smaller attacker's windmill blows, counterattacking with well-aimed smacks from her purse and cursing in a deep bass voice as she drove her overwhelmed adversary back toward the man with the baby and the dog. Right on cue, two paddy wagons, *paniers à salade*, pulled up, half a dozen smiling Parisian *flics* got out, a couple of them quickly moving to separate the combatants. The tall transvestite straightened his stylish, form-hugging clothes, pulled out his mirror to check makeup and hair, then, joined by an equally tall, mini-skirted blonde, strolled casually from the scene and down the steps to the Metro. A policeman followed. Shortly, chatting amicably, all three came back up the stairs and walked over to the field of combat where a couple of other gendarmes were talking to the smaller woman, who once again held the baby, still wailing unhappily. As soon as the two transvestites got close, however, back the baby went into the arms of the flummoxed man, still restraining the yapping dog, and the short woman moved in for another attack on her tall adversary. The gendarmes swiftly intervened before more blows were struck and this time walked the combatants away from each other. The white-coated, rubber-booted spectators from the fish restaurants, still laughing, went back to their shucking and filleting. Whatever triggered the disruption, the boundary between my respectable neighborhood and Pigalle was back in place.

I had lived in bra-less Berkeley for twelve years, where free sex, if not free love, was almost an imperative and AIDS, herpes, and other STDs had not yet derailed the rock-and-roll express. There was no reason to pay for sex when a woman you met at a movie or checking melons at an organic food store would hop into bed with you. In most cases, they were no more nutty than you, and might have been seeing the same therapist. The Berkeley air was as redolent of pheromones as it was of cannabis and tear gas.

❄

Pigalle had long been known as having a pheromone index to rival Berkeley's so the drama that I witnessed nearby was not a complete surprise. I knew nothing, however, of another area of Paris I decided to explore except that it was one of the city's oldest quarters. Walking from the Gare du Nord toward the Centre Pompidou as a *flâneur* one sunny morning, I found myself in St. Denis, named for a saint whose name derives from the Greek Dionysius, the god of wine and ecstasy, among other things. It seemed appropriate for a *quartier* that I later found out was famous for the prostitutes who worked from its many small hotels as well as from its streets. It was also home to cafés with wooden facades and elaborately painted or etched windows that dated back to the 19th century or earlier and were slowly being "modernized" out of existence.

Wandering about, my camera at the ready, and using my guidebook as something of a cover, I passed one hotel after another, most having entry halls fifteen feet or so deep with glass doors at each end. The outside door offered protection during foul weather; the inside one was the "display window" for the hotel's ladies, dressed in revealing lingerie and often strikingly beautiful. How did they end up in those hotels, I wondered.

I stood on a corner, under a shop awning, taking in the scene when a middle-aged man wearing a smartly tailored suit and carrying a briefcase briskly crossed the street near me and headed toward one of the hotels.

Out of it to meet him came a very attractive young woman in a form-fitting stylish suit of her own, her brown hair conservatively styled. As they neared each other, the man smiled broadly. She, on the other hand, made a show of looking at her wristwatch and shaking her head in a scolding manner: He was late! Then, laughing, she took his arm and they crossed the sun-filled cobblestone street to her hotel.

The gleaming golden wood facade of an old café in the full sunlight then caught my eye. Standing in front of it, leaning back against the facade while reading his newspaper, was a silver-haired man in a white shirt and long blue apron. It was a quintessential Parisian photograph. As I was framing the shot and adjusting the focus a man in a business suit came down my side of the street and shaking his head said, "*Casse-gueule*," very risky (the term literally means "smash-face"). Well, thought I, naïvely stubborn, I'll just step into the shadows of a nearby pedestrian passageway and get the shot from there. A briefcase-toting man came along the passageway behind me and, as I stepped aside to let him pass, shook his finger at me and said: "*Casse-gueule*." I took no photo. That second warning made even me realize that the man in that "perfect Paris photograph" might well have been a pimp or brothel owner whose whistle could have summoned some thugs to make that *casse-gueule* a painful reality.

I was lucky. Not so the women in those hotels, who no doubt were painfully familiar with *casse-gueules*. Any prostitute, beautiful or otherwise, who tried to escape her hotel "office," if addiction to drugs even made that thought possible, risked a bone-breaking beating or a brutal death, a fate undoubtedly shared with the women in my post-Crazy Horse brothel visits. Visitors to those St. Denis hotels at least knew what they were getting. What did I think I was getting when I slid into that taxi outside Le Crazy? One of those titillating dancers––a version of the "hot" girls from this pudgy boy's eighth-grade class? If I could "have" her, as the phrase charmingly puts it, I would be transformed, *n'est-ce pas*? Maybe into Jean Gabin. I had no clear idea then and I am still not sure, except it had nothing to do with being the man I wanted to be. I still felt secretive about seeking sexual pleasure, a feeling that was at once thrilling and made me feel like a child. Neither feeling, I imagined, burdened the briefcase-toting businessman late for his mid-morning "coffee" with his honey. The somewhat covert character of the commercial sex world, whether of St. Denis or of the *poules de luxe* on the Grands Boulevards, had to be part of its appeal to many men, though an empty feeling usually follows a *rendez-vous* with a *pute* of any kind.

*

My Parisian life, or at least the amorous part, became eventually like the Berkeley life I naïvely thought I had left behind: I had another girlfriend, *une petite amie,* who wanted from me more than I was willing to give--marriage, in fact--but I could not break it off. My job was going to end in a few months because the journal where I worked was, for lack of funding, going out of business. When it ended, then what? Could I find more work through my contacts at the MSH? Did I want to remain in France? I was now using the subjunctive every day--the tense that leaves the door open, a French teacher once said--but appropriately I still was not sure. What if I did stay? Could I find work translating fiction, or at least something less tedious than automobile manuals or math books, work that, I was told, always seemed to be available. Maybe if I had been 25, but at 38? Teaching "American" in the business world was a possibility, but the people I met who did that seemed to be living in limbo. Required to speak English all day and socializing mostly with other American teachers, the ones I met never fully entered the French world. What was worse, when they went home for a visit, they said, few people showed any interest in their French life and they were completely out of touch with the American one. Would I miss California and my friends? Also my parents were in their 70s. And what of my *petite amie?*

Many of these questions passed through my mind as I stood in my window late one Sunday afternoon, something Balzac might have done 150 years earlier as he mulled over a scene from *La Comédie Humaine.* I was able to see down into the room of four Algerian workers who lived on the top floor of the building across our narrow street, one of many buildings in the Marais used as dormitories for immigrant laborers — especially Algerians — who, like their student neighbors were attracted to the area's inexpensive lodging and restaurants. Their room was just big enough for two bunk beds. In the space between they had placed a cardboard carton that they could use as a table for playing cards by sitting on the lower bunk.

Taking a break from their game, which was punctuated by shouts of mock outrage and laughter, one of the men came to the window and looking up at the pale band of peach-colored sky over our narrow street, began to sing in Arabic. He sang softly at first, then, full of sensuous longing, his voice became stronger and he closed his eyes. The other card players fell silent, moved as I was by the evocative rhythms of the Arabic language and the rich, throaty timbre of the singer's voice. As the song, like the fading light, softened and came to an end, I felt a heart-piercing longing for a home, for a place where I was accepted for who I was––fears, indecisiveness and all. His song over, the singer looked up at the sky, then at me. With a smile, he nodded a greeting, which I returned, then he rejoined his friends and their card game. Life was pushing me out of a place in France that had become familiar but that could not last, like my stay at Arnaud's, whose hospitality, in the end, I abused, though he was too kind to say so. What did I want? Even my girlfriend could not get me to answer that question and, believe me, she really wanted to know. To sort things out, in addition to smoking a pack of Gitanes every day for a week (the only time in my life I did that), I went several times to see Dr. Ourgoulian, a psychiatrist at the American Hospital. (Those Berkeley habits die hard.) When I told him stories about my troubles with the maddening French, especially the women, he did not respond with the serious concern I expected. *Au contraire,* he roared with such hearty laughter that I was soon laughing along with him. Whatever my childhood issues were, he said, we all have them: they are part of being human. But I was no longer a child, nor were the people in my life. Certainly, my Parisian girlfriend agreed with him, and I owed her an answer: "*Il faut être brutal,*" the doctor said of that relationship. (*Brutal* in French here meaning brutally frank.) *A la fin, c'est plus gentil.* In the end, it is kinder.

❄

Since my early twenties, I have been a swimmer, originally to deal with muscle spasms caused by a slight case of scoliosis, or curvature of the spine, which the swimming completely relieved. For the past 30 of my 85 years, I have regularly swum in San Francisco Bay with the Dolphin Club. Once in a while I feel so comfortable with the cadence of my stroke and the sensuous feel of the water that I imagine I can swim forever. I am in the "zone," as top athletes sometimes say when every one of their tennis shots hits the line, or every baseball they hit makes it through the infield or over the fence. Of swimming, Oliver Sacks has said: "Swimming gives me a sort of joy, a sense of well-being so extreme that it becomes at times a sort of ecstasy... I have never known anything so powerfully, so healthily euphoriant." Though I have never been a Murray Rose or Michael Phelps, it does not matter: what matters is the profound, almost spiritual pleasure these experiences give me. But I cannot make them happen.

Half a dozen times in my life, I have entered a similar zone on dry land, times when I have clearly known what I wanted and felt completely at ease in saying so. I remember them vividly, though none lasted more than a few hours, some only a few minutes. During those times, I was surprised both by how I felt and how I acted. If I were with people I knew, they also were surprised (as they were surprised by the integrity of my ceramic creations and later in my life by my photographs). My voice became deeper and I was completely calm, free of the usual nagging need to explain myself, to justify my wants and needs, defensive, in the end, about who I am. I have never understood where that "me" goes when I come back to being the person I feel I am most of the time.

The good Doctor Ourgoulian responded to that will-o-the-wisp "me," ignoring my normal *tombeur*, playboy, persona. When I joined him in laughter, I let the cat out of the bag, revealing that I no more believed my melodramatic tales of woe than he did. They were a ruse to hide any number of things, perhaps most of all the desire never to make decisions that would limit me in any way-- and its siamese twin, the desire to pursue my sexual fantasies. I had hoped that being in a different culture would make it impossible for me to maintain that duplicitous posture. *J'avais tort.* I was wrong. No wonder Fellini's *8½* is one of my favorite films, Guido's crisis of indecision at the film's end ringing all kinds of bells for me. As for the doctor's advice about my *petite amie*, in the end I was not *gentil* at all. I made an indecisive mess of that relationship-- irresponsibly hurting someone I cared about. The truth is I did make significant decisions around this trip to France, starting, of course with the decision to make it at all. Then I decided to stay in France, forgoing a trip to Lapland--or Ireland. I also decided to take a pottery workshop in the country's southwest; to pick grapes in Macon; and then, after returning to San Francisco for ten wretched floundering months, going back to France--to make pottery in Grenoble, the next chapter in this tale. For the first few weeks of my return to California, I was totally conflicted, not wanting to hear or speak English or see it on street signs. Part of it was my brain trying to readjust to my mother tongue, but much of it had to do with trying to deal with my conflicted desire to return to France. I house-sat and couch-surfed, abusing the hospitality of a number of friends. Finally, in March of 1976, I did go back to France, to Grenoble to make pottery, stopping for a couple of nights in Paris before going south. I carried the same orange backpack but I had less money and even shakier expectations of being able to make a living than I did on my first visit. Rose Faubert had invited me to join her and two French women in their pottery *atelier*, or workshop, and said another friend would help me find free-lance translation work with the University of Grenoble. She also said that someone she knew had an extra room available that was near the center of the city and the *atelier*. Unfortunately, these enticements were based more on wishful thinking, among other things, than reality. Though the University of Grenoble Press needed translation help, the oil embargo crisis had wiped out their budget. The room had already been rented so I ended up staying with the Fauberts.

Chapter 8

Grenoble and the Atelier

I arrived in Paris on a sunny April morning in 1976 and headed to a hotel near Gare Montparnasse that Berkeley friends had recommended. I had ignored the economic crash caused by the oil embargo when I made my first trip to France in 1974 and not one to change an approach that had been so successful, I repeated the oversight for this second trip, ignoring the importance of the day I arrived in Paris: Easter Sunday. As it is a long weekend holiday, if the weather is springtime fair, many Parisians leave the city, replaced by thousands of tourists, who, of course, fill every decent hotel. I found the street where my hotel was supposed to be but disoriented from jet lag could not locate it among a dozen similar small hotels on that street.

I stopped an older woman in a conservative suit and a hat bedecked with flowers who looked as if she had just come from Easter service, and asked her if she knew of the hotel. She was Italian, visiting Paris to attend mass at Notre Dame, and was a bit lost herself. A couple pushing a stroller came by and we asked the young parents. They were from Argentina, they said, and were also having trouble finding their hotel. *Pas possible!* Parisians had completely vanished. We then tried another older woman who also seemed dressed for Easter service with a dress and light coat in springtime yellow and light green. She was French, even Parisian, but though she had lived in the neighborhood her entire life, she could not help any of us. She knew that all our hotels were close by, but where exactly, she could not say. *Pas possible, encore!* We laughed at our absurd situation. Jacques Tati's Monsieur Hulot could surely have been able to help us. Finally, an older man straightened us all out, sending the Italian signora in one direction, the young Argentinian parents in another, and yours truly a couple of hundred feet down the street. My hotel was filled, of course, but they had a free room for that night and the next, though it would not be available until 5 pm. They agreed, however, to store my backpack until I checked in, so I paid for two nights, and still in jet lag stupor, went back into the bright springtime and made a beeline for a café across the street, which was beginning to fill up with lunchtime customers.

I had two double expressos and set off on foot to ramble around Paris for six hours, planning to end up at *Le Jardin des Plantes,* the principal botanical garden in France and a place I had come to like.   Surprisingly, my jet lag did not keep me from the somewhat surprising feeling that I had come home, even if I had trouble finding my hotel. Although some of this feeling had to be colored by fantasy, it was not really surprising that I felt comfortable in a city I had lived and worked in for most of a year. What was surprising to me was that after an absence of ten months, I could still speak French so well that in spite of my telltale orange backpack, no one in that group of lost strangers thought I was American--or even Belgian. The key to my feeling at home seemed to be French itself, which emotionally, felt like my own language in a way different from the English of my mother tongue.

In Alfred Kazin's book about New York, *A Walker in the City,* a Kazin neighbor, Mrs. Salovey, comes upon the teenage Alfred studying a French grammar book at the kitchen table.   From Europe herself, and a speaker of French, she says you cannot learn to speak French from a book. This lovely and somewhat exotic woman then invites the completely charmed Alfred to have a conversation in French. When he manages to negotiate a few exchanges, Mrs. Salovey encourages him to continue, so he can discover the magic of speaking another language. "To speak a foreign language," she says, "is to depart from yourself," a discovery I made that Easter Sunday morning. It was like putting on one of those velour suits I saw in shop windows when I first arrived in France and discovering not only that I looked *formidable et chic!* but also felt completely comfortable in it, as if it were made for me. I left Berkeley in the Spring of 1974 to find an improved if not a completely different Sid and I did, though how different I could ever be from the Berkeley Sid time would tell. Whatever being at home means, how I felt that Springtime Sunday morning near Montparnasse is surely a part of it.

My attraction to the French language probably started when, as a child, I first heard my French-Canadian neighbors speaking Québécois, which some French people might not call French at all. It also came from that single hour of French Three at my prep school when Joseph Savoie Stookins, by his passion for his native tongue, startled me into an awareness of French's musical beauties and supple strength. Paradoxically, as I felt more at ease speaking French, I also began to feel more ambivalent about it. Did this new linguistic intimacy mean I had to abandon my family, my friends, *tout,* everything I had known until then?

At times, how I felt about France seemed like a betrayal.

Of course, as the young Alfred Kazin's neighbor knew well, I would not be losing anything. *Au contraire,* I would be gaining not only a new language--which increased my appreciation for English--but learning how that language changed my experience of the world. For example, the expression "I miss you" in English with its emphasis on the "I" does not carry the same feeling as *"Tu me manques," you* are missing to me, which, of course, emphasizes the person who is missed.

People seem to be made to live in certain places where the rhythms and texture of life are natural to them, where they feel most free to be themselves. For me, France in the mid-70's was the one place where I felt that way: I felt accepted there, a rare feeling for me. I knew that I would always be an outsider there, but on that beautiful Easter Sunday morning, it did not matter: I felt at home--with the language and the people. Maybe I'll understand this better by the time I finish this book.

Learning to Dance with French

In spite of all your preparations, you will blunder
at first as you move from rough cloth to smooth skin,
feeling your way with clumsy eagerness
toward entrancing complications.

She will expect you to listen, to shape new sounds
with lip and tongue, to handle unfamiliar forms
of past, future, and present, to accept her conditions
and remember all her exceptions. (There are many.)

When the frustration of learning what goes where
drives you to outbursts of anger, she will offer you
a quick sinuous movement
revealing hidden curves, subtle meanings.

Delighting in these endless enticements, you will slide
from the properly formal to the spontaneously informal,
from classroom *plus-que-parfait* to always changing argot.
Her richness — your ignorance — will continually surprise you.

She will exhaust you, and even when with you
will exclude you, especially from her laughter.
You will ask yourself how to get closer?
You will ask yourself why bother?

Naturally, you will miss your mother tongue.
Ready to call it quits, you will agree to a last dance,
and suddenly will know the quick delight
of when to glide and pause and deftly turn.

Enchanted, you will not want the dance to end:
you will want many more. There will, of course,
be dull conversations, heated arguments, daily transactions.
It will not matter: having gone this far,
you will know there will always be music.

✳

As I slowly wended my way to the *Jardin des Plantes*, I almost yielded to my desperate desire for sleep and stretched out on the inviting green of a *pelouse interdite* for a rest, but a guardian could well be lurking nearby, even if I could not spot him, so I walked on, stopping only for another expresso. By mid-afternoon I reached the *Jardin*, with its wide gravel pathways and flower beds in full springtime glory. There, I could enjoy the fragrant air of a warm Spring day, watch passersby, and lounge on a bench, though these *bancs publics* were as off limits to snoozing as the manicured lawns. No matter, by this time my nervous system was so cranked up by caffeine that I could not sit still for very long, let alone nap.

As I passed one of the byways off the garden's major walkways, I was drawn to a group of serious-looking people gathered around a few tables where chess games were in progress. The city provided the stone tables and the dark green folding chairs available to the public in most Parisian parks in the 70s. The games underway were all being played with timers, which is a clock with two faces. The players decide on the length of the game and often the number of moves within that time period. After a player moves he hits a plunger on his clock, which stops it and starts his opponent's. A time limit could be twenty minutes or two hours, but the game must end at that time. If a player does not push the button as soon as he moves, he is reminded by his opponent's sharp *"Appuyez le bouton!"* press the button. The competition was intense, drawing quiet comments from the spectators, including the man next to me, who, as soon as I arrived, started talking to me about the game we were watching. *Pas possible!* He was the same chatty chess player I sat next to at Polly Magoo's two years earlier. I thought I was imagining it. *Mais non! Sans aucun doute!* No doubt about it! He was the friendly Frenchman with the long curly red hair who had enlisted my support at Polly's against his American rule-breaking opponent.

Once again, he assumed I knew French––which this time was true––and, encouraged by my nods and occasional *"C'est vrai,"* that's true, commented to me quietly about almost every move. He only stopped his kibitzing when a long-haired, head-banded, sandal-wearing countryman joined the group on the other side of the table.   *"Salut, chef des peaux rouges"* or Indian chief, my talkative neighbor called out to him. A bit insulting, I thought. *Le chef,* though, took no offense. Instead, he came to our side of the table, where he shook hands with my neighbor. "Why not come over for dinner tonight?" my neighbor said. "My wife has been wondering about you. She'll be happy to see you. Around eight o'clock." "*D'accord. Merci,*" said *Monsieur Peau Rouge,* who shaking hands again with my neighbor, said "*A plus tard,*" see you later.

I was still wondering how the timer worked when my neighbor said to me, "Why not play a game?" Why not, I thought, still bobbing along on my stream of expresso energy. I took my place across from a black-haired gentleman in a nicely tailored blue suit, agreed to the time limits, and moved first, then waited for my opponent to make his countermove. Instead, he said, "*Appuyez le bouton, monsieur.*" I forgot to hit the timer. Several more times, I heard the blue-suited monsieur say with growing impatience: "*Appuyez le bouton.*" Only several times because it only took him a few moves to checkmate me. He was bored but gracious, and thanked me as we shook hands and another player took my place. I continued to watch the games, waiting for the approach of five o'clock.

The afternoon light was fading as an older, elegantly dressed, white-haired woman approached us and warmly greeted the man who had just trounced me, then exchanged *grosses bises* with my long-haired Polly Magoo friend and shook hands with the others she knew. She had been a player there for a number of years, my neighbor told me, but had not come by for a while. Visiting the chess games again reminded her, she said, of the time right after the end of World War II when she was a military attache in Berlin. There was a lot of tension between the Russians and Allied forces, and diehard Nazis occasionally fired at people or set off bombs, she said. She had an affair with a Russian officer from Belarus, who not only protected her in that terrible time but taught her to play chess. As she finished her tale, a man her age, wearing a beautifully tailored topcoat, approached us, greeted her with *grosses bises,* and tipped his hat to us. Taking his arm, she introduced her new husband, smiling warmly as the group applauded. Then they bid us *bonsoir,* and arm in arm, walked off through the twilit garden, abloom with new flowers.

This cluster of interlaced events made me aware again of why I came back to France, illustrating that in Europe the personal and universal were intertwined in endlessly surprising ways. Some of the surprises, like the fascist violence at the BHV in Paris, the anti-semitic graffiti, and the rigid class system were abhorrent to me, but I did not want just the France of picnics in a sun-splashed countryside, though they, too, were part of the mix. I wanted the real France. I returned that Easter Sunday to get just that, and for the language that gave these experiences their unique color and life.

It was approaching five o'clock. I shook hands with my neighbor, said, "A *la prochaine, alors,*" until next time, then took the Metro back to my hotel in Montparnasse.   After paying for two nights, I climbed to my room and, without sleep for twenty-four hours, flopped into bed without unpacking. You cannot, however, turn off the power of expressos that easily. I could not even close my eyes. Luckily, I had one of my mother's sleeping pills, whose effect I knew would be intensified by a *un demi sans faux col*, a draft beer without foam, which called, of course, for a *"sandwich jambon."* I crossed to the bar across the street, and enjoyed, once again, that appetizing combination, then took the sleeping pill with a second beer. How I made it back across the busy street to the hotel and to my second-floor room I can't remember. All I remember is hearing the clatter of new hotel residents arriving, then nothing. When I awoke, my watch said 7, time for breakfast, but something did not feel right. My window looked out on a wall so not until I went downstairs, did I see the streetlights and shop lights coming on, not going off. *Pas possible!* I had slept 24 hours straight! The next morning, I left for Grenoble and my life as a potter.

✳

Unfortunately, as I said, the long-distance optimism of Rose Faubert was based more on wish than reality, which I had sensed back in San Francisco, but chose to ignore. She told me when I arrived at the Grenoble train station that the room in a friend's house where she thought I could stay had been taken by someone else, but there was an extra room at their place. She did, however, have a contact at the University of Grenoble Press who told her the director of the press would be happy to meet with me. One out of two, not bad, it seemed. But first things first. Before we went to the Faubert apartment in the Olympic Village, we participated in that old French tradition, *une manifestation*––a demonstration. Serious and comradely, complete with banners and bullhorns, it was a protest against the planned replacement with upscale apartment buildings of older city apartments crowded up against an escarpment along the Isère River and inhabited mostly by students, artists, and Algerian workers.

Within a few days, I met with the director of the University of Grenoble Press, who told me that the continuing recession had dramatically reduced his budget for such help. *Les Trente Glorieuses,* the French term for the thirty years of prosperity after World War II, were definitely over. The Press could use someone with my skills, the director said, as it published a number of French translations of American works, especially those of Jack London, whom the French liked as much as they liked Jerry Lewis. But that did not mean they understood London's colloquial American and the result was embarrassing. For example, the director said, on the first page of a recent press translation of a London novel, the author describes some cowboys having dinner around a campfire, a typical cowpoke scene. Naturally, the word "pardner" is freely tossed about over the crackling logs and bubbling beans. At its first appearance in the phrase "pass me them beans, pard'ner," it is marked with an asterisk referring the reader to a note at the bottom of the page. "Pardner," the footnote explains, is a business associate. *Mon dieu!*

No place of my own to stay and no editing or translating work. Both, it seemed, had existed, at least partly, in Rose's imagination. That was not at all what I thought would be waiting for me. After ten months of house-sitting and couch surfing as I tried to figure out if I were coming or going––to France and more generally in my life––I was back in no-man's land, having made another one of my head-down assaults on life. What that eccentric decision-making process did bring me, however, was work in the pottery *atelier,* or workshop, with Rose and her two French partners, Suzanne and Valérie, who were busy turning out an order for 300 wheel-thrown butter dishes with lids. They were also getting under Rose's skin by chattering away in French so rapidly she could neither clearly understand them nor join them in their banter. She needed an ally: I was it. The ladies immediately became annoyed when Rose and I imitated their behavior in English. Our ploy worked, however, and they abandoned their slangy chatter. Neither *les potières* nor I wanted to throw the same piece over and over, but our dreams of making *pièces uniques,* one-of-a-kind pieces, would have to wait. Those pieces, for me, were hand-built in the Japanese Tamba tradition, of which I made just a few. For what or for how long that wait would be we had no idea. They would attract few buyers, as the dominant commercial ceramic styles in France at that time were exquisitely decorated porcelain or colorful regional pottery from areas like Brittany or Provence, though there were an increasing number of ceramists working in their own unique styles.

Then came dealing with the complexities of my living situation with the Fauberts, in particular Emma's pouting resentment of my intrusion into her world with *papa et maman*. In the evening, she tolerated me--barely. At breakfast, however, her glower told me that I made her very unhappy. After a few days, I made it a point to be up and out the door before *la famille* Faubert fully awakened, taking the bus downtown to get my morning coffee and croissants. Emma actually gave me a gift in disguise--time alone, which I relished the longer I stayed in that small room, in spite of the Fauberts' generous hospitality. It puzzled Rose and Marius, but it took them a while to ask where I went so early. Emma, the ruler of the roost, showed not the slightest interest.

✳

Once downtown, I needed to find a café where I could have my coffee and *pains au chocolat* and quietly read my paper, French or English. Cafés generally don't mind if you bring in pastries they don't serve, so long as you ask first. For the first few days I picked up my pastries at what became my favorite bakery shop, called *Patisserie Viennoise*. It was on a narrow pedestrian passageway lined with fashionable boutiques and one or two cafés. I tried the one between a couple of the boutiques and realized after I found a seat that all the other customers were *minettes*, young women in their teens or early twenties--most of them quite attractive--who worked in the boutiques. Dressed in the latest fashion and perfectly made up, they clustered around the café tables in chatty groups, passing around a newly discovered lipstick or eye shadow and discussing why they liked one or the other. After all, shop talk about the newest styles and the proper cosmetics to wear with which outfit was an essential part of their world of fashion. I ordered my *café au lait*, though the waitress, who I quickly realized was *la patronne*, did not even wish me the customary *Bonjour*. Something was off. Perhaps it was my *International Herald Tribune*? Being surrounded by attractive young women, however, was definitely appealing so I went back for another try. As I walked in the next day, *la patronne* and some of the *minettes* tossed my way the kinds of looks that I got the first time my backpack and I rode the Metro in Paris. I got the message, but, like pursuing a woman who has given me nothing but discouragement I persisted. Once, however, was enough for *la patronne*, who never brought me the café I ordered, ignoring my calls of "Madame," and finally giving me a look that would have made the four-year-old Emma proud. I left. I still needed a coffee and a café that made me feel welcome. I wandered toward Place St. André, where I knew from my visit to Grenoble several years earlier there were a couple of cafés as well as many imposing regional administrative and judicial buildings. I took a seat on the terrace of Café Tribunal. When other customers nodded *bonjour* and the *garçon* was warm and welcoming I felt that I had found my café.

The boutique-lined street, however, remained my regular path to the Tribunal from my bus stop, not only because I really liked the *pain au chocolat* from the Viennese *pâtisserie* but because it gave me a chance to watch a bit of street theater that co-starred *les minettes*. When they emerged from the café that shunned me and another similar café almost next door and headed to their jobs at the street's boutiques, they became players in an endless vaudevillian farce that starred the villainous *balayeurs,* or streetsweepers.

In the narrow streets of most French cities these *balayeurs* skillfully wield large hoses to spray streams of cleansing water back and forth across a street, then, like hydraulic engineers, use large stiff, red-bristled brooms and small carefully positioned sandbags to guide the runoff this way and that until it sluices down a drain. In this particular farce, however, their most important, if unofficial, task was to menace the *minettes*. Several times a week, the *balayeurs* washed down the street and every time, they artfully guided the snaking stream of water closer and closer to sidewalks crowded with the young ladies, who, crying out in mock alarm, skittered to the safety of their shops as fast as their three-inch platform shoes could carry them. Every time, the *balayeurs*, dressed in the ubiquitous French blues, and often with a *maïze* cigarette in place, yelled *"Pardon, mademoiselles,"* chuckling at their role in a comedy that none of the players seem to tire of playing. These little dramas, like a driver dramatically clearing an intersection in Paris, or a *maître fromager* inquiring about my cheese research, or even a woman's *"Ah, deux!"* when I ordered a second hot chocolate on a cold Parisian Sunday afternoon, offered me a more animated life than I had in California, and sometimes a role to play, even if I did not know what it was. They took me back to my life in the multiethnic south end of Hartford and also to my suburban street in West Hartford with a mix of people that almost matched Hartford's south end and was a unique aberration in that suburban town.

Café Tribunal was where two years earlier I had met Julien and Sandrine, but on my Grenoble visits then I did not go there on a regular basis. On this trip, it became "my café," a critical step in feeling at home in a French city, where each café has its particular clientele, its *piliers,* the regular customers that keep the café in business and give it its unique character. I was not a good fit for the *minettes'* café, but I was made to feel at home right from my first day in Café Tribunal. Once I made it my regular morning stop, the owner and his son would hang onto a book or coat I had left behind, or advance me some money for a couple of days, or tell me someone had stopped by looking for me. Every morning, at the same hour, the same group of students, professors, office workers, lawyers, and artists filled the tables in front of the café. Eventually, as happens in the San Francisco where I have lived for thirty years, people came to know each other, sometimes just to exchange a nod of recognition or a *Bonjour,* sometimes as *copains,* sometimes as *amis,* friends. It was a refuge from the city's hustle and bustle, a social center where you met people, read the paper, or even did some business.

On the café terrace, I talked often with graduate students and teachers at the University of Grenoble who were in one area of the arts or another. We became friendly enough that they invited me to go to a party one of their colleagues was giving Saturday night at a house outside of Grenoble. They would pick me up near the Tribunal, which we called simply *"le café."* For us, there was no other. Getting a ride back to town would be easy they said.

At the party, most of the people I met were from the university, dressed in the sport coats and corduroy trousers or more colorful shirts and bell-bottoms common to such gatherings in Berkeley. Although no one sported a headband or wore Birkenstocks, the women were casually dressed in the longer skirts and blouses also common in California in the 70s. Several of the men smoked pipes and many men and women smoked cigarettes. One young woman, however, fulfilled the need for oral pleasure in a way that made me look twice: she sucked her thumb. When I caught myself and stopped staring, I discreetly looked around to see if others were paying her particular attention. No one--except *moi.* Everyone else ignored her digital dependency as she engaged in animated conversation with one group or another.

After I had chatted with a few people for a couple of hours without connecting with anyone, my café *copains* said a friend of theirs was going back to Grenoble and would be happy to give me a ride if I wanted to go. I gratefully accepted the offer, until, with some trepidation, I discovered that the driver of my ride was to be the black-haired, thumb-sucking woman. As we walked to the car, exchanging questions in a friendly way about what we were doing in Grenoble--she was a graduate student in French literature--she was thumb free. Surely she would remain so when she got behind the wheel. Not a chance! Once she started the car, in went a thumb. All the way back to town she switched like a virtuoso from left thumb to right as deftly as she shifted gears and handled sharp curves. In spite of her considerable skills, I was relieved when she dropped me off in town where I could easily grab a bus back to the Fauberts in *Village Olympic,* built when Jean-Claude Killy was winning medals at the 1968 Olympics in Grenoble.

An adult woman sucking her thumb so openly in public was no more common in France than in the States, but after noticing how many people in the room were using the usual thumb and nipple substitutes--cigarettes and pipes--her habit seemed like a healthier choice. That she was comfortable with people she knew I might have expected; that she was at ease in my company, a stranger, I found remarkable.

❊

Did I return to France to make another try at transforming myself into "a new and improved" Sid Hollister, Gabin cap included? One who would feel as comfortable in my own skin as that thumb-sucking graduate student? As Alfred Kazin's neighbor says to him about learning to speak another language: "To speak a foreign language is to depart from yourself" and I had done that so successfully on my first trip to France that I profoundly, almost painfully, missed both the country and its language during my ten-month purgatory of indecision in San Francisco. Nonetheless, though my first stay in France had failed to move me one millimeter (Sorry, .039 of an inch) toward any change in my fundamental character, I still had a fading hope that another visit would do the trick.

Most French people I knew were impressed with how hard I worked to improve speaking their language; trying to change my personality, however, they felt was *dingue,* crazy--and, of course, impossible. I think they are right, most of the time. Changing how I act--abusing a friend's hospitality, for example--is certainly possible; changing what impels me to do it, could well be impossible. In fact, most French people have an intense respect for every human being's individuality. Generalities are always riddled with exceptions, but if a French person accepts you as friend, *un ami* or *une amie,* they may get mad at you for something you do, but rarely for who you are, whether you wear a headband like a *peau rouge* or suck your thumb at cocktail parties. Maybe that's why their *amis* are often people they have known since they were young. To the French, living my life as I saw fit was not only my absolute right, it was a duty more sacred than *priorité à droite,* yield to the right.

In one unforgettably disturbing instance, a girlfriend I broke up with in Paris laid into me for failing to honor that responsibility. As always in relationships, the reasons for her anger were complicated, but she made her main point with brutal frankness (*Elle était brutale.*): I was failing myself, she said. I had the sensibility, memory, and intelligence to be a writer, but I was just diddling around, wasting my abilities––and my life. In other words, she gave me a good kick in the ass. Only by following her anger-fueled counsel could I feel *bien dans ma peau*, at home with myself, which I thought going to France would make more possible. I resisted fully hearing or heeding her words for many years––using my trips to France, work, and marriage as excuses––until I finally made up my mind to finish writing this memoir, which has helped me understand what she meant.

At the *Tribunal,* one of the university-affiliated people was a young woman who worked with the large number of Spanish and Portuguese immigrants who had made their way to Grenoble and to other southern French cities during the Franco and Salazar dictatorships. Long established in France, they were concerned that their children were losing touch with their Iberian cultures. To support them in keeping those cultures alive, the city and regional governments helped them organize workshops to pass on the culture and artistry of Spanish flamenco and Portuguese fado, a version of our blues. My Tribunal friend, who had lived for several years in Spain, worked in that program and invited me to go with her one night to a presentation by both older immigrants and their children and grandchildren. We were early, so she took time to introduce me to a colleague in the program who was from Sénégal, the one black African among the fifty or so spectators. I was struck by his warmth and gentle manner, but puzzled by his almost limp handshake.

When the program ended, we gave him a lift back to the University of Grenoble and he, in return, invited us to a *boum*, or party, in a cinderblock building that served as a social center for sub-Saharan African students from Francophone countries attending the international university. As soon as we entered the building, filled with joyful and strongly rhythmic African-based music and dancing students, our host was transformed. He instantly became a gracious and animated host, getting us cold juice drinks, finding us places to sit, and introducing us to several of his friends, some even while they were dancing. They all shook hands, as our host had done, not with the Western manly "vigor," but with gentle warmth, continuing to hold on as we exchanged a few words––and they kept dancing. I felt awkward, as when I first met our host, but I also liked the feeling of connection these extended handshakes gave me, encouraging me to look the other person in the eye, to really see them: An African version of *grosses bises*.

Years later, I had an exhibition of my photographs in the library of the botanical gardens in San Francisco's Golden Gate Park. When I stopped by one day during the exhibition, I was introduced to an older African-American woman who for years had worked there as a volunteer. We shook hands and for several minutes she told me how much she enjoyed my images, pausing as she worked to look carefully at one print or another. As with the Africans at that *boum* in Grenoble, she held my hand warmly in hers until, after several minutes, she decided our conversation was over.

At that Grenoble *boum*, I was the only white male among the black Africans, but there was one brown man there, an African American. Our host, gracious as he was, told me that the man was from Los Angeles and found him among the dancers to introduce us. We shook hands in the American manner, firmly and very briefly––but long enough for me to feel his hostility. The jarring discord between that flash of anger and the welcoming warmth from my host and his African friends unnerved me. Nothing seemed to fit with my past experience. In the States, if I saw a black man walking toward me in my largely white neighborhood, I loaded him with all the stereotypical characteristics of my imagination––none of them positive. During the short time I spent at that *boum* in Grenoble, I began to see each person I met as unique, a black person to be sure, but an individual. It happened again many years later when I boarded the Paris Metro near Gare du Nord and after a few moments became aware that most of the passengers were black. Then I realized why I did not notice that from the start. My fellow passengers came from the many different ethnic groups in the francophone countries of that continent: they all looked very different from each other. They became individuals. What would happen to my prejudiced feelings, my racist feelings, if my life gave me a chance to mingle with African Americans in my daily activities the way I did with the French-Canadians and Sicilians on my West Hartford street?

Though we may be a tribal species in our particular lives, American life is less so than when I was growing up in the 1940s. Clustering then with other people like yourself was vigorously and often hatefully defended. The association at the beach where my father built a cottage he rented out to help put my brother and I through college, would not let my parents rent to childhood friends because the woman was Italian-American. Yet the Irish Americans of that association would go to the same priest for confession and communion as the Italians and Sicilians from the beach next door, their common church being on the border between the two beaches. As a child, I never understood what was being defended by these separations, as I was not told why I was no longer supposed to play with a particular girl my age (I later found out that she was Jewish). What parochial or tribal fear drove those guardians at the gates, those establishers of covenants and exclusive associations, and of imagined differences? God forbid that they discover we are all much the same?

I went to San Francisco to avoid all that. The barriers existed there, too, of course and still do, though weaker and different from the Northeastern variety. I simply had to live in the Bay Area long enough to become aware of how they worked--which schools and what ethnic background would get you a job or into a club. In France, as a foreigner completely ignorant of the rules that governed class and social behavior, I had a wonderful freedom--up to a point. Once I started working, however, those rules distinguishing one class from another began popping up--in social settings, in casual comments, and in everyday interactions in my office. Just as in Connecticut, my professional colleagues made certain assumptions about me as soon as they discovered I went to Yale and knew Clark Kerr. Upper class for sure, and WASP, they naturally assumed. Though they could not know it, I never fit that identity, ethnically nor emotionally. Instead, I remained in a no-man's land between the multi-ethnic world of my childhood and the Wasp-dominated world of Yale, struggling to find my own path between them. Why I did not simply play whichever role was suitable for the world I happened to be in at the moment, I don't know. I think it had--and still has--something to do with not having a stronger sense of the director of the show. *Moi.*

❄

Grenoble, like many cities in France, offers a variety of outdoor musical and dance events in the summer months. Such outdoor events did not always go smoothly, especially when temperatures soared into the 90s and the air was heavy and still. Free concerts by a chamber orchestra, for example, were held every other week in the modest courtyard of the *Externat* of Notre Dame, a residence for older parishioners of the church. One wall of the courtyard was formed by the residence, the windows of which on hot and humid nights were wide open to whatever breeze came along.

That was the case the night I decided to go. As spectators milled about finding their seats, we were treated via those open windows to a full sampling of what TV and radio were offering at that hour. When the conductor mounted the podium and tapped his baton on his music stand, the orchestra came to attention and all the radios and TVs fell silent-- except one. From an open window came the back-and-forth dialogue of a TV *policier*, or detective story. The young conductor smiled with forbearance at this disturbance as he said a few words about the night's first piece, a concerto for strings by Corelli. Then, after a quick glance at the open window that was disgorging its gun shots, sirens and angry voices into the now quiet courtyard, he brought his arms down to lead the orchestra into the concerto's first movement. The TV blared on. When the movement ended, we expected that our TV watcher, having asserted his or her sacred rights, would no doubt relent and turn the TV down. *Mais non!* It stayed on right through the concerto's last two movements, which the conductor and the orchestra played with exemplary aplomb. When it ended, many spectators joined in sending a volley of shouts at our unseen antagonist. Even I shouted a plea that the sound be turned down. In response, the rasping voice of an older woman, who remained out of sight, said she had the right--the sacred *droit*--to play the TV as loud as she damn well pleased. It's the orchestra that should be quiet, she said, so she could listen to her favorite program in peace. To make her point, as the orchestra started the concert's second short selection, she turned up the TV's volume.

Ça, c'était trop! That was too much. When the short piece ended, a broad-shouldered, black-haired young woman, dressed in white, leapt from her front row seat and with a "take no prisoners" charge rushed up the stairway. The yipping and yapping of what seemed at that point like an entire pack of small dogs let us know that the battle of *droits* had been joined. The first voice--our heroine's--was strong, sharp, and protesting. The second voice, reedy and strident, out-shouted her. Attack met counterattack over the berserk yip-yapping of the dogs. A door slam ended the engagement and, in seconds, brought the evening's nemesis to the window, from which, still unseen, she unloaded on us her rich vocabulary of curses, ending with *"Quant à la musique, je m'en fous,"* As for the music, I don't give a fuck. Our valiant white-dressed protestor, having vented her wrath, descended to settle into her seat just in time for a needed intermission. When the second half of the concert started, the TV was silent though our critic's window was still open. Apparently the *policier* had ended. The music's feisty foe, however, still riled up from the recent skirmish, slammed her window shut, heat or no heat. *Un droit c'est un droit.*

❋

Within a month, it became clear that whatever the four of us earned on lamp bases and butter dishes was not going to make us a living as potters, free to make individual pieces. We met one day with a potter who had an *atelier* on his farm in the Alpine foothills outside Grenoble. He was *brutal.* To do what we wanted to do, he said, we would have to hire immigrant workers to fill the bulk orders. He had been in our situation a few years earlier and though he did not want to do it, he had to hire some Vietnamese immigrants to fill his large orders. He saw no other way to keep his *atelier* open so he could make the individual pieces all of us wanted to make. We left in a gloomy mood, me most of all, though his advice was not a surprise. Over the next couple of months, we fantasized about other possibilities, but the reality described by that more experienced potter made it clear that our *atelier* could not continue as it was and that the other potter's option of using immigrant labor was not a realistic possibility for us, economically or politically. More importantly, it was clear to me that I would have to leave Grenoble and most likely return to San Francisco.

We all liked working with clay, however, so we kept the wheels spinning and put off making the inevitable decision. With the beginning of summer, a few tourists wandered into our *atelier* in the city's old section on the banks of the Isère River. A few even few bought a piece or two. But it was a trickle; we needed a steady stream. Several students also signed up for Rose's throwing class, coming by after their workdays ended. One, Ghislaine, an attractive young blonde with lovely broad shoulders and almost my height, would change into her pottery clothes inside the second-floor work area where, after spending most of the day at the wheel,

I would fashion hand-built pieces, my favorite way of working with clay. She said *"Bonjour"* coyly and for the first few visits, in an age-old play of feminine modesty, half-turned away from me as she took off her daytime clothes and put on her pottery work clothes. Her movements, however, told me that she knew I was doing exactly what she wanted me to do: watching her every gesture as, in bra and panties––white as I remember––her heavy blonde hair half-concealing a smile, she bent forward to pull on her work trousers and gave me a view of her voluptuous body. Occasionally, I was still working when she finished her lesson and as we cleaned up, we talked about the difference between throwing on a wheel and hand building, the one requiring concentration and following the wheel's pace, the other allowing the potter to work more with the clay's responsive softness free of the wheel's spinning demands.

After several of these conversations, we made a date for lunch. Foolishly thinking I was hiding my lustful desires, I said that we could talk more about ceramics. I hid nothing from her, of course. Nonetheless, as attractive as she was, she was 21 she had told me and I had just turned 40. She would pick me up, she said, around noon. The *potières* had already left for lunch when she pulled up to the *atelier* and suggested we do something simple for lunch. *D'accord,* OK, I said. An omelet at your place, she asked, smiling again through her heavy blonde hair. *D'accord,* I said again. Clearly ravenous, she got us to the Fauberts in no time. I started to show her the kitchen, but happily discovered her appetite was of a different sort, as was mine, and we were quickly in my bedroom satisfying a hunger that did not require any cooking. Afterward, I enjoyed watching her put on her clothes as much as I had enjoyed watching her take them off. It was the first of our many omelets.

On weekends and holidays, whenever family obligations did not take her away from Grenoble, we took trips. We went to the town of Beaufort where the exquisite, buttery cheese is made that bears the town's name. Slow to get going in the morning, we missed the cheese-making but from a visitors' balcony, we watched the workers in long white coats, white caps, and black boots hose down the large red-tiled cheese-making room and wash shining copper pots as large as a Citroën *deux chevaux*. We bought some Beaufort and had a swim in a local pool. On the way back to Grenoble, we stopped in Chignin, looking for its *vin de Savoie*. We were directed to a vintner who, a passerby said, definitely had the best. Halfway up a dirt road toward his house on top of a small rise, we stopped at the open doors of a barn surrounded by vineyards where a gray-haired man was at work. Sitting on a low, three-legged stool, a beret on his head and a *maïs* in his mouth, he was using a brush and a pot of paste to put labels on bottles of the preceding year's vintage. It was the vintner himself and those very bottles were going to Paris tomorrow, he said, smiling. But you can still get a few bottles from Madame up at the house. We did just that, for the Franc equivalent of two dollars each, a price that was ridiculously low even then. Back in Grenoble, we drank the Chignin and ate some Beaufort and fresh baked bread we got at Ghislaine's local baker. The centerpiece of our evening meal was, of course, an omelet, which were getting better all the time.

Ghislaine took me into the mountains to watch hang-gliders launch themselves into the void and glide over small Alpine villages below. We went to Chartreuse, nestled into a small valley in the Alps, and had a picnic under an enormous oak tree. We went to a folk music festival in a foothill town outside of Grenoble, where I discovered from an accordion player in what seemed to be an Irish group that the Celts had long before settled the part of the rugged Auvergne region the group called home.

We even went to Grenoble's spanking new *supermarché,* where, with some misgivings, I ordered at their caféteria-style restaurant one of my favorite ice cream treats: a *café liégeois,* a concoction of slightly sweetened, chilled coffee and a scoop or two of coffee ice cream, topped with whipped cream and crushed coffee beans.

A busload of American tourists crowded into line behind us. A very young teenage girl took our orders and served us, then turned to the older woman next to me and waited for her to order. "Peach Melba," the short, stout American woman said firmly. The blank stare of the teen-age server did not change. "Peach Melba," the woman said more loudly, as if shouting would inspire comprehension, a common tourist misconception. The stare of the young woman did not waver. "It's right up there," said my American neighbor pointing to the menu on the wall above the server, adding under her breath, "What the hell is wrong with you?" Then she bellowed: "Peach Melba!" I sighed and, bending over slightly to address my frustrated neighbor––who did not need a Pêche Melba, a Café Liégeois or any other ice cream dessert––and said: "She does not speak English." The lady was stunned. "She does not understand you." More bafflement. Then I ordered a Pêche Melba for her, yet another victim of tour companies who seem to tell their clients: "All the French know English, but you have to shout at them to make them understand you." In fact, many French could indeed understand English then, English English, as it was commonly taught in school. Speaking it was another matter. That was why Rose had warned me not to assume people at a bus stop or in a café did not understand me if I spoke English. They often did, so I would be wise to mind what I said about the French and their ways.

Another bit of information that would have helped my exasperated compatriot is the importance of civility in France, and in Europe generally. If she had taken the time to learn to say just *Bonjour* and *S'il vous plaît,* the response of the young woman behind the counter might have been very different.

It was time to join Ghislaine at our formica table and dig into my Café liégeois to see how it compared with ones I had enjoyed at Berthillon's in Paris, which for years set at least the Parisian standard for ice cream and the many concoctions made with it. She said her *sorbet de citron,* lemon sherbert, was *pas mal,* not bad. My more exotic dish certainly looked inviting, but the canned whipped cream that topped it off should have been a warning. As soon as a I dug my spoon into the ice cream, it was apparent that this was not even a distant relative of its Berthillon counterpart. Buried under the tasteless whipped cream was a chunk of ice the size of a golf ball. It was all downhill from there. *Supermarchés* were novel in France in the mid-70s, but they were soon offering all over France packaged foods and all kinds of other food products. As the quality of foods they offered––cheese and wine for example––improved, many smaller shops, like *fromageries, charcuteries,* and wine shops started to go out of business. Sadly, as I discovered when my ice cream dessert turned out to be mostly ice, some of the products available in such large *supermarchés* were pale imitations of the original gustatory delights whose names they bore.

※

Ghislaine, however, was the real thing. I spent a lot of time watching her take off her clothes, and often helped. Eventually she told her parents how old I was. Her mother asked only if I made her happy. *Mon dieu!*

Rose understood right away what was going on, not only because I frequently did not spend the night at their place and did not go to Beptenoud with them on weekends, but also because I was a lot happier. Ghislaine, was, too, Rose said. Neither Marius nor Rose said a thing about the age gap between this 40-year-old American and the beautiful 21-year-old Grenobloise, though they must have had some thoughts about it. I know I did, but Ghislaine's voluptuous warmth and calm openness dispelled them. She was too present, too real for such worrisome notions. I had been without the pleasures of a woman's affectionate and sensual companionship for many months, so when she became part of my life, the unpleasant aspects of reality, which I kept only dimly in focus, disappeared from view. Almost.

Our shared pleasures––in bed and out––suggested the possibility of something more, but the reality of our lives, our ages, and who we were, told both of us that this relationship would not last. Ghislaine was, I think, more realistic about that than I. After all, she had her family and friends in Grenoble, where she had grown up; I primarily had her. It was not enough, we both knew. Of course, the fate of the *atelier*––and mine––was always in the background. Without a steady stream of large orders, which none of us wanted but would have to get to pay the bills, the *atelier* would soon have to close.

I have never accepted very well that any pleasure I am enjoying cannot go on, and on, and on, that most of the time, every pleasure ends sooner than we like. When I was a kid, I raised holy hell if my parents tried to pull me away from any ocean beach we were visiting before the sun went down, which I thought might not happen if I watched it with all the strength I had in me. Time has chastened me, though not entirely. Swimming in San Francisco Bay on a sunny day when I feel one with the water and ageless, the feeling as euphoriant at 80 as it was at 50, I cannot imagine not being able to enjoy that magical experience for ever. That such pleasures will end someday as surely as the sun set on the beaches of my childhood, I find, as director Francesco Rosi once said, asked if he was afraid of death: Not at all. I just find it completely unacceptable.

At the *atelier*, the wheels kept spinning and I kept hand-building pots, which, I was told, the French would never buy, though one or two actually did, far from enough. One day, Suzanne told us with great excitement that Franklin was visiting. He promised, she said, to make his famous fried chicken that night and we were invited. As we closed up for the day, Franklin came to the *atelier*. He was a tall, bespectacled, slender African American, fluent in French. We shook hands and he left with Suzanne, who lived with her husband right below the Fauberts, to prepare his special chicken.

It was an indoor picnic, with all of us sitting on the floor around a blanket hungrily devouring Franklin's succulent chicken and licking our fingers. Rolled in crushed *flacons de maïs*, corn flakes, the chicken was crispy on the outside and tender and juicy on the inside. Delicious, as Suzanne predicted. When Rose and Marius heard that Suzanne and her husband were leaving early the next afternoon for the country, they invited Franklin to have dinner with us the next night and offered to take him to the station for his overnight trip to Paris.   (No high-speed TGVs until 1977.)

At dinner that night, we talked of the civilizing benefits of train travel--primarily seeing more of a country at ground level and meeting other travelers.   I said how much I enjoyed it in Europe but not so much on the New York, New Haven and Hartford train I frequently took from my home to Yale in New Haven. Franklin was quiet for a moment then held out his hand so I could see clearly his Yale class ring. We were both astonished.   There were three African Americans in my class. I had scholarship jobs with two of them. The third was Franklin, who dropped out for a year, graduating in 1959 and missing participation in an early version of an "encounter group" we both had been invited to join our senior year.   He was living in Paris and working for a large French technology company, he said. We did not say much about our Yale experiences, which had some things in common, as I found out, but were of course basically different. "Come visit me when you get back to Paris," he said. I did, but between his Grenoble visit and a memorable, drunken, and painful Parisian dinner with him, I left Grenoble and Ghislaine, and changed occupations.

Saying goodby to Ghislaine was painfully difficult but major shifts in our lives played a role in separating us. Her parents returned from a summer in the mountains and my room at the Fauberts was not a place for us to hang out. Our summer romance had come to an expected end, though my feelings about it--being 40 and with no career plan to speak of--had to be far from those of the 21-year-old Ghislaine, whose life was largely in front of her.   To earn the price of my plane ticket back to the States, I had to switch from making pots at the *atelier* to scrubbing them as a dishwasher at *Les Produits*. I took some comfort in knowing that the restaurant was not that far from Grenoble and so could kid myself that my parting with Ghislaine was not final.

Chapter 9

Team Faubert — and Sam

"Plus d'assiettes!" More plates!

"Elles sont dans la machine. Pas de panique! They're in the dishwasher. Don't panic!"

Then, a minute later.

"Plus des petites! Mais pas chaudes. Pour le Baked Alaska*!"* More small ones. But not hot. For the Baked Alaska.

"Dans le congélateur." In the freezer!

"Très astucieux!" Very clever!

So went my introduction on May Day weekend, 1976, to the world of dishwashing at *Produits de la Campagne* (Foods of the Countryside), the Faubert family's restaurant situated in a hamlet near Lyon. Three months later, my Grenoble ceramic career at an end, that weekend dishwashing job became my full-time employment. During a long, hot August, I was the restaurant's *plongeur,* or dishwasher, low man on whatever passes for a totem pole in the world of French restaurants. In this case, lower even than Ivan, the older White Russian who, among other jobs––some certainly odd––helped the gardener, fed slop to the chickens, and more or less looked after Sam, mongrel "watchdog" for the family's farmhouse down the road from the restaurant. An American *plongeur,* however, does not go unnoticed in a French country restaurant, especially if he is well educated, 40 years old––and tall.

As a friend of Marius, one of the owners' sons, and also a potter in his wife, Rose's *atelier* in Grenoble, I had, as I have mentioned, already helped out a bit in the *plonge* on earlier weekend visits. When the year moved into the warm months of late spring and summer, Marius, Rose, their daughter, Emma, and I escaped Grenoble's stifling humidity and polluted air (at the time, the worst air in France) and drove 70 miles or so to the cooler countryside where *Produits de la Campagne* was located. It was built into the first floor of the 19th century house where Marius and his six brothers and sisters were raised.

Surrounded by corn fields, vegetable gardens, pastureland and a scattering of woodlands and family homes, the restaurant drew customers from the entire region, even from Lyon, called by the famous gastronome, Curnonsky, *le capital de la gastronomie*. They came for the dishes prepared by Bernadette, Marius's mother, whose artistry had drawn high praise from the finest chefs in Paris. Its small glass-walled pavilion and spacious shaded courtyard were invitingly cool in the warm months, so *Produits* was a popular choice for wedding rehearsal dinners and wedding receptions from late April to early October. Rose told me, when we were halfway to the restaurant on my first visit, that we––including *moi*––were expected to work the entire weekend at *Produits,* though doing what, exactly, depended on how busy it was.

I had no idea what lay ahead during that first hectic weekend. I certainly did not imagine that I was auditioning to be the vacation replacement for Albert, the regular *plongeur*, who for the first time during the several decades he had worked there was going to take off the entire month of August. Only once before had he taken more than a day or two off, planning a two-week break one August. He came back after a few days, having gone to his home village and exhausted in a long weekend all subjects of conversation with his sisters, who still lived there. During most of my subsequent weekend stints in the *plonge,* Albert did the bulk of the work, but the first weekend in May signaled the start of the wedding season and did not follow the normal pattern. A big luncheon was scheduled for Saturday noon and another after-wedding dinner for the evening. Then, as Sunday was May Day, a true "labor day" and an important holiday in France, the entire restaurant was reserved for a festive lunch and dinner. More than 400 reservations were on the books for those two days. Nonetheless, when Madame Faubert's regulars showed up as usual for Sunday lunch––with no reservation, of course–– she brought them right in and gave them their usual tables. *"Pourquoi pas?,* she said. "They always have lunch here on Sunday." Proust would have smiled.

Saturday morning, after an expresso or two, everyone was assigned a task. Rose was a waitress. Marius was the *maître d'*, though for dramatic family reasons he no longer worked in the restaurant. Instead, he usually worked weekends restoring the family farmhouse where we all lived, a few hundred yards down the road. I took over Albert's job on the hot and steaming dishwashing machine while he handled scrubbing the large pots and pans. His habit was to take most of the normal late Sunday afternoons off, and he was definitely a creature of habit. This weekend was an exception.   Frédéric, the Faubert son who was an engineer in the

Auvergne, also came, and his wife, too, to help out the two regular waitresses. On most balmy weekends, Emma and her two *cousines* wandered in and out of the house gorging on *fraises*, strawberries, one basket after another until from nose to chin their faces were red from the fruit's sweet juice. Not this weekend. The restaurant was jammed with hungry people, so Madame Faubert set aside her role as the indulgent *mémé*, or granny, and sent the girls to do their dance of the *fraises* at the farmhouse. My work at the dishwashing machine Sunday was, as I mentioned, just a foretaste of what my August tenure at that steamy beast would be like, though no day during my dishwashing stint was ever as frantic as that weekend. Thankfully. Sunday's May Day celebration was a trial by fire that went well into the evening.

Albert left me on my own late in the afternoon: his day was done, as usual, no matter the work. Luckily Madame Martel filled in for him. She was a long time neighbor of the Fauberts whose husband was the local postman. Around 9 on weekday mornings, Monsieur Martel, stopped by *les Produits* for a glass of white wine with Monsieur Faubert and Jean-Pierre, the Faubert son who most days accompanied his father to the markets in Lyon at 5 a.m. The cheerful Madame was not only a big help to me, having done occasional spot dishwashing duty in the past, but her warmth made my job a lot easier and got me thinking about the solitary way I made my living.

❄

Some members of that weekend *équipe* could not believe that at my age I was working as a *plongeur*. *Incroyable,* unbelievable, they said. It was to me, too, but even more *incroyable* was that I enjoyed it--not the dishwashing itself, but being part of *l'Equipe Faubert*. I have earned my living most of my life as an editor, a solitary occupation, though close relationships with some authors--especially photographer Eliot Porter and the French Sociologist Alain Touraine, whom I mentioned earlier--have been deeply rewarding. Rarely have I worked with a group on anything, the one exception being a film-making project as a graduate school student with three fellow students. Working in the Faubert restaurant gave me surprising pleasure for surprising reasons.

Every member of the family team had been summoned by Madame Faubert, who used guilt like the experienced mother she was. All but the two youngest, who were too far away, came home to pitch in. And why shouldn't they come if she needed them? Madame often asked. With her as the Chef, the restaurant had given the large family a comfortable living. To many of its regulars, in fact, it was known as "Madame Faubert's," though Monsieur played a key, if largely backstage, role. First and foremost Monsieur Faubert alone held the secret to the popular terrine that he rose at three every morning to make, dotting its creamy texture with bits of dark *morille* mushrooms. The terrine made, he and Jean-Pierre, went at dawn several days a week to buy in Lyon the produce, cheese, fish, meat, wine and other items Madame had ordered. It was Madame's creativity with the ingredients they bought and her strong and sociable presence as a hostess that earned *Produits* its reputation.

Time and the constant pressure of restaurant work, however, had taken their toll on the talented Madame. Her curly hair was now gray, glasses were now perched on the end of her nose, and her back and legs constantly reminded her of the many hours she had spent at the black iron stoves. The family also felt the strain.

Marius, for example, would no longer work in the restaurant. Lean, quick with sharp energy and a stubborn streak he inherited from his mother, he had done just about every job at *Produits* during his school years. He still remembers helping his father bring in the few cows they owned then, wading in the soft Spring sunlight through fields of those poppies loved by Impressionist painters, their scarlet blooms seemingly afloat above their light green stems. By 1976, those years were far in the past. A university student in the late 60s, he now taught Physics at the University of Grenoble and was more comfortable with that city's cosmopolitan world than the provincial life of the restaurant and its nearby towns.

No one was surprised then when Marius 's new world and his mother's old world collided. Everyone who was there remembers the dramatic explosion in the *plonge* on a windless, muggy August day. Marius was in the *plonge* doing prep work with his mother, when Madame made one of her casual racist remarks about the Algerians living in a nearby historically preserved town––*"Bien construite, mais mal habitée,"* well-constructed but badly inhabited. As he continued to unpack a crate of cantaloupe-like *melons de cavaillon,* a quietly simmering Marius reminded her that she nonetheless constantly relied on some of those "undesirable" inhabitants to work at the restaurant. The good madame, though, was not about to let go of a subject that she knew had gotten under Marius' skin, and tossed off another insulting remark or two. That was all it took. Shouting at his mother that he would never work in the restaurant again, Marius took the ripe melons from their crate one by one and hurled them against the walls of the *plonge,* first one wall, then another, where they exploded like juicy blossoms, leaving orange trails of seeds and juice running down the walls and putting his mother to screaming flight.

Until this weekend of more than 400 lunches and dinners, that was the last time Marius had set a working foot in the kitchen.

Even as the *maitre d'* that crazy weekend, he stayed out in the courtyard. As for his usual filial duties, he fulfilled them by restoring that rambling old farmhouse down the road from *Produits.* Even during the infrequent lulls on that busy weekend, he only came back to the kitchen to get something cool to drink. Wearing a smile that, viewed from my steamy post, seemed a bit too self-satisfied, he stood in the backdoor of the *plonge*, sipping his drink and watching the rest of us, especially *moi,* busy at the restaurant tasks he would no longer do. The rest of the time he used his charm to guide guests to their courtyard seats and make sure wine and something tasty to eat quickly arrived to dull their edgy hunger. Unquestionably, he had his mother's gift for sociability and was a remarkably creative and engaging conversationalist, an artist really, with a skill the French value highly.

The farmhouse still needed lots of work, especially on the ground floor, but Marius had finished enough rooms so the sprawling building could provide comfortable if simple accommodations for Guy, the young chef Madame Faubert had recently hired to succeed her; the sixty-year-old Albert; yours truly; and also occasional weekend guests. Most of the finished rooms were upstairs, mine included. Made of gray fieldstone, the interior was plastered over and whitewashed, its ceilings supported by dark-stained wooden beams, its floors covered with brick-red tiling. The fieldstone walls kept the building cool in the summer, thankfully. The rear outside wall was draped with vines in which grape-snacking rats habitually scurried.

❅

A bachelor in his sixties, Albert, who came from the Jura Mountains in eastern France, had been the dishwasher at *Produits* so long he had forgotten when he had taken over the job or even how he came to be there in the first place. Square shouldered and of medium height, Albert's red, big-boned hands spoke of both his strength and his life of hard physical work. Apart from those hands and occasionally his mostly bald head, his broad, ruddy face was the only part of his body that ever felt the air's touch—or the water's. In the retirement home where he happily lived in his later years, he took, I was told, the first shower of his life. Word was that he enjoyed it.

Whether in the hot and steamy *plonge* or the shaded courtyard––even on the hottest days––he always wore sturdy work pants, tough leather boots, and a plaid wool shirt buttoned tight at the wrists and right up to his large Adam's apple.   A soft cap was usually pulled snugly onto his large head. Several of his teeth were stained to a dark brown and from his years as a *plongeur,* the thumb of his right hand was bent back at the last joint, had almost no nail, and was as black as the stub of a charred stick.

When I first saw that thumb, I asked him if he had injured it in an accident.

"Mais non, pas du tout" he said, not without pride, *"C'est le travail qui l'a fait."*   Not at all, it's the work that did it––years of scrubbing beer-keg sized pots with a stiff-bristled brush. In spite of that disfigured thumb, or maybe because of it, I thought Albert might have learned some tricks of the job and would give me a few tips. I liked my thumbs just the way they were.

"What's the best way to wash those?" I asked him, pointing to the pots that were too large to fit into the dishwashing machine and so had to be wrestled into the sink.

"Well," he said, "you just use the brush like this," and, tipping and turning the large pot, he gave me a demonstration, too quick for me to see exactly what he did. *"C'est tout,"* that's all, he said, and with a thin, sly smile, turned back to the steaming dishwasher. No tips for me. This clangorous, steamy domain was his and he intended to keep it that way. Thanks to his lifetime connection with the Fauberts he had a comfortable bed with clean sheets, three meals a day, and no worries––a simplicity of life that no doubt enabled him to live several more decades, dying at 92. That's not to say Albert was unfriendly. Apart from his desire to protect his "turf," he was, in a way, like anyone who has done a job for years, not really aware of exactly how he did what he did. His tight-lipped response to my questions also was characteristic of the legendary, and often wily, reserve of the French peasant, especially when it came to a tall "city slicker," who was a foreigner to boot. I gave him a hand for a few days before he left on vacation and kept a sharp eye on his movements, but never could spot a single trick he used in his thumb-blackening chores.

What he repeatedly did certainly wasn't complicated, but every job, even shoveling dirt, has tricks that make the work easier. Some older Italian immigrants in Connecticut taught me the right way to handle a shovel when I worked with them shoveling dirt one hot summer college vacation. They spoke little English, but made it clear on my first day that my graceless shoveling was bad for my back, generously showing me the right way to do it. You might think grace has nothing to do with such simple manual tasks, but it does. My back immediately felt better. I had hoped Albert would do me the same favor, showing me some *plongeur's* tricks he picked up along the way. Not a chance.

❇

Marius first met Albert when he spent summers working in the bakery of his aunt's village near Albert's home. Aside from bits of sociable chit chat, Marius said, what Albert had to say about his life at *Produits,* and maybe life in general, could be summed up in what everyone there called Albert's song: "*Jamais fini. Le travail ici n'est jamais fini.*" Never finished. The work here is never finished. As it was French, the "song" had some existential overtones, but it undoubtedly referred more concretely to Madame's habit of never turning away a paying customer, even on Tuesdays, when *Produits* was closed. She welcomed the company of friends and neighbors every day of the week, and was often invited to join them at their table. If someone called out at the closed wrought-iron gate and Madame was within hearing distance, she would come into the courtyard to see who it was. Then, saying, "Ah, since it's you," or "Ah, since so-and-so said to come by," she would open the gate and invite them in, even if there were no waitresses, the new cook and the apprentice were off, and she had to do everything herself––with Albert's help, of course. "*Jamais fini*" in a nutshell.

Albert, of course, had all day off on Tuesdays as did the rest of the staff, but with no family in the area and nothing he cared about in the nearby town, he often puttered around the restaurant, doing this or that. On hot afternoons, he relaxed in the shade of the courtyard's enormous plane tree, removing his hat to enjoy whatever breeze caressed his large, bald head, but always keeping his flannel shirt buttoned tight at the neck and wrists. Anyone entering the courtyard received Albert's amiable greeting and a few words about the weather in his singsong voice. The afternoon's languor and a lunchtime glass of white *vin de Savoie* would often tip him into sleep in his seat near the front door.

Albert's second-floor room, which he proudly showed me one day, had two windows, one faced the farmhouse backyard, a cornfield, the other looked out on the small cinder-block house where Ivan the handyman lived. Sam the watchdog, chained to a stake near Ivan's small home spent most days languorously sprawled in the dust. Albert's room was small, like my own, but its two windows let in ample light and air. A chair of unfinished pine, a small dresser, also of unfinished wood, and a bed covered with an eiderdown comforter filled most of the room. Next to the chair, placed in front of the window that overlooked the backyard cornfield was a neat stack of almost unwrinkled newspapers from Albert's home-town area. Until a few years earlier, when Madame and Monsieur Faubert persuaded him to move his savings to a bank, Albert had hidden wads of Franc notes among those papers and under his mattress. Many older French people who had lived their lives in the country had a similar habit.

Albert's lack of confidence in banks and other "new" ways of doing things was rooted in the life of the French farmer. Until the late 1950s, those who worked the land made up a quarter of the French population. But France had been changing for years and *Produits* and the people of its world did not escape the effects of new ways of doing things. The construction of Satolas, the new Lyon airport (now called St. Exupéry-Lyon Airport) was about an hour away, and several new houses were going up across from the restaurant. The pressure of coming development was palpable.

In the mid-1970s, however, much of the old way of life persisted at *Les Produits,* so when the weather warmed up in June we left open to the cool night air the glass-paned double doors of the ground-floor living room in the renovated farmhouse. No rooster worth his name could pass up such a good stage, so, on the first hot Saturday morning of June, as dawn light began to drift through the poplars on the horizon, the courtyard's high-plumed fellow strutted right in and announced to all hens, roosters and humans within earshot exactly how splendid he was. His first round of *coo-coo-ri-coos* bounced about the house like Emma's cries for more *fraises*, yanking everyone awake. Another round or two brought Marius and I rushing to the living room to drive the foppish fowl outside to his hens. One of those early morning serenades was enough. After that night, the doors stayed shut.

On my first few weekend visits to the restaurant, my room, small like Albert's, was on the second floor, its one window facing the cornfield on the eastern unshaded side of the house. I kept that window open all night to catch May's springtime breezes, which carried with them, as the dawn light filled my room, music that had been played in this land for centuries. A rhythmic clumping and jangling teased me from sleep; soft "Yo-hos" and "Yo-hays" got me up and to the window: Monsieur Didier, the restaurant gardner, was at his spring task in the field below. Slowly and steadily, hands on a plow, he followed an enormous gray horse as it pulled the plow's blade through the reddish earth, encouraging the head-bobbing animal with soft calls and an occasional switch-tap to its rump. Pulling lightly on a rope from the front, a boy helped guide the snorting horse into its turns as, row by row, the field was readied for planting the corn. An accompanying dawn chorus of birdsong came from the field's bordering poplars. The scene brought back to me childhood memories of my French-Canadian neighbors, whose main workman, also named Albert, let my brother and I watch him chop the heads off chickens and help him chase yellow cat-sized rats that he flushed, pitchfork held high, from cornfields he tended across the street.

The Albert of *Produits* was determined to visit his family in the mountains for an entire month the summer I worked there, planning to stay mostly with one of his sisters. Hence, the restaurant's need for *moi, plongeur extraordinaire.* Long vacations, however, did not fit the rhythm of Albert's life, so to leave *Produits* for a few weeks, as both he and the Fauberts were planning to do, made him nervous. What would he do there for four weeks, he wondered out loud to me, shaking his head.

"You have your sisters," I said, "and nephews and nieces?"

"Yes," he said. "It will be good to see them. But a month!" and he removed his hat to run his black-thumbed hand over his bald head.

After less than a week, he was back at *Produits.* The restaurant was the center of his life: he worked there, he lived there, his social life was there. On vacation, he did not know what to do with himself. My Irish immigrant grandfather was cut from the same cloth. Coming to the States from Ireland's Cork City when he was a young teenager, he earned his living almost from the start in a steel foundry in New Britain, Connecticut, a few miles from where he lived. Most years, he took only a week of his two-week annual vacation, returning early out of boredom. After more than 50 years of labor in the foundry, he collapsed there one day from the heart attack that killed him. He was 75. Albert's life had an easier ending, in a retirement home where he was everyone's friend.

Back at *Produits,* the still vacationing Albert turned in languorous circles––from the *plonge,* to the courtyard, to his farmhouse room. He spent hours just sitting outside, or, if it were raining, in a window of the small dining room across from the kitchen. From either location, he could keep tabs on the comings and goings at *Produits.* Someone had to do it and Madame was away. He seemed content and though he regularly came to the *plonge* with his dirty dishes, he never, except for a few moments on busy weekends, offered to help me out. A vacation is a vacation.

✻

When I first started going to *Produits,* I assumed Albert and Ivan were probably *copains.* Not only were they close in age, but they both had the habit of wearing the same clothing combinations, day after day, whether it was blazing hot or cloudy and mild. Their tasks certainly gave them no reason to change. Even so, Ivan's customary woolen turtleneck, heavy work shirt and trousers, dark blue apron, work boots, and a soft cap similar to Albert's, seemed even less comfortable than Albert's buttoned-up woolen shirt, though both clothing choices were not exactly suited to the summer heat. These sartorial similarities, however, had no effect on their relationship: they rarely exchanged a word.

Near seventy, Ivan actually spoke more to himself in Russian than in French to Albert or anyone else, carrying on animated conversations in his native tongue when working alone in the fields or doing odd jobs around the property. His erect distinctive bearing, strong, sharp features, and an aloofness that spoke of his earlier more refined life, combined with his formidable taciturnity to establish an almost palpable distance between him and the rest of the restaurant *équipe.* Albert's antipathy to Ivan came from something basic: the Russian was just that, Russian; not French. He did not even speak French fluently. Albert had similar feelings toward anyone—I was no exception—who was not French. Or was not from the Alps. Or, drawing the circle tighter, was not from Albert's Alpine region. The two are closer now, buried side-by-side in a nearby cemetery.

The lanky old Russian, it was said, had been a brilliant university student in mathematics and music in Moscow when the 1917 Revolution erupted. He joined the cavalry of the White Russian army when he was sixteen or seventeen, was gassed fighting the Reds, and had not been quite right since. He ended up at *Produits the* same way Sam, the farmhouse watchdog did: someone dropped him off at the courtyard gate. As he had done elsewhere for forty years, apparently, he made his living at *Produits* doing this and that. He helped Monsieur Didier tend the restaurant's large vegetable plots, watched after the chickens, and took care of Sam, which meant feeding him restaurant leftovers.

Not surprisingly, Ivan had bad teeth––Albert did as well––which led to his unappetizing habit of piling on the table next to his plate bits of meat he couldn't chew before slipping them under the table to the other dog in the restaurant family, a cosseted Springer spaniel. Though he had repeatedly been asked not to continue this unappetizing habit, he persisted. Unused to taking orders, his only concession was to move to another table when the complaint was made, muttering as he did so a few words in Russian followed, in descending dismissive tones, by "*Ça va, ça va, ça va.*" His favorite French saying, it can loosely be translated as, well, a number of things that all mean "Everything's OK, take it easy." Alone at his new table, he stiffened even more his ramrod posture and continued to share his tidbits with the tail-wagging spaniel.

Every day, when lunch was over and we all sat about under the courtyard's magnificent plane tree, Ivan would ask in a quiet but peremptory tone for someone to bring him from the hallway a pack of Gauloise cigarettes and an expresso, both of which he could easily have gotten for himself. He did not ask for a favor; he simply expected someone to do his bidding. It was a reminder for both him, and for us, of his life in czarist Russia where making such requests had no doubt been as normal to him as playing the violin or working on mathematical problems. As if in deference to that past, someone always fulfilled his request.

One weekday in August, I returned to the farmhouse for a nap after my lunchtime shift and had another glimpse of Ivan's past life. His small cinder-block house just inside the farmhouse gate had no windows, so in order to catch whatever breeze was stirring, he left the door open on hot days; this day was no exception. Guy had gone to Lyon on an errand and Ivan had left the restaurant when I did, going in the opposite direction to work in *Produits'* storage buildings. The courtyard was empty, except for Sam, who, in the heaviness of the mid-afternoon heat, bestirred himself only to roll from his side onto his back so I could give him the obligatory belly scratch. I walked to the door of Ivan's house and tried to see inside, but standing in the bright sunlight I could make nothing out, so I took a few steps into the small building's cavelike darkness to let my eyes adjust. I was stunned. Papers covered every surface––the bureau, two or three chairs, a single table, part of his bed, and most of the wooden floor. Sheet after sheet was filled with scrawled equations and other mathematical calculations that seemed to leap from one page to another. Punctuated with plus and minus signs, equal marks, and other mystifying mathematical symbols, the lines came apart to go off in all directions like split and frayed twigs. None of what I saw made any sense to me, but all of it apparently made some kind of sense to Ivan, who clearly had worked over them for hours in that dark, windowless room. I stood in silence for a minute, then, feeling like an intruder, left the house and a part of Ivan's life that seemed to be as alive for him now as fifty years earlier.

To nourish another part of his Russian past, Ivan needed a wonderful French invention––a moped, a motor scooter started by peddling until its small engine buzzed to life. In this case it was a shiny black Solex, a gift from Madame and Monsieur Faubert. Every Sunday, winter or summer, Ivan took his weekly sponge bath at the outdoor farmhouse faucet, carefully watched by Sam, who could have used a bit of a wash himself, but never got it. Attired in a black suit, white shirt, and black tie, a black Sunday cap pulled down snuggly against the wind, he put-put-putted the few kilometers from his monk-like house to a Russian Orthodox church nearby to get together meet his Russian pals. When he buzzed past the restaurant on these Sunday trips, he always sat straight and focused, his strong-featured face a mask of concentration that gave not the slightest hint he heard the shouted hellos from Guy, myself, and the rest of the crew gathered in the courtyard for breakfast.

Equal to me in height, but above my bottom rung on the staff ladder, Ivan was spared all attempt to get him to do anything beyond his usual duties. His innate aristocratic aloofness, I think, discouraged such requests. He was also granted, as was Albert, a respect older people usually receive in France.

✳

My defense against such exploitation was Albert's: "*Il faut dire 'Non!' Il y a des limites à tout!*" You have to say no, there are limits to everything, he said, slapping his hand on the pot he was scraping. I needed that advice, especially with Anne, Guy's assistant, a short, wiry young woman with curly red hair, a slight mustache, and a charming smile. No one plied me with more special requests: one minute she wanted an expresso; an hour later a mineral water; then there was her favorite: "*Comme tu es grand...*"

As you are tall... "Would I reach up there to get this? Up there to get that?" Each request gave Anne a chance to flaunt, flirtatiously of course, her superior standing in the kitchen hierarchy.

Before ever scrubbing a pot at *Produits,* I had developed a craving for a French dessert called, *Poire Belle Hélène,* created by the famous chef, Escoffier, and named after an opéra bouffe by Offenbach, none of which really matters when you take your first bite of this delicious concoction. It is made with a poached pear, usually Bosc, topped with vanilla ice cream, and a sauce of dark chocolate melted in the pear's poaching juice. The cupboards on the restaurant's first floor under the staircase were always cool, no matter how sweltering it was outdoors, making it the perfect place to keep not only a few bottles of the best wine for special occasions, but more importantly to me, jars of preserved pears, peaches, and apricots. After moppimg and scrubbing my way through a few days as a *plongeur,* I decided to end my noontime shift with a *Poire Belle Hélène.* I knew where everything was except the chocolate. To find it, I had to pay my respects to Anne.

"Why do you need that?" she asked with the slightly haughty air her position gave her over a *plongeur.*

I told her, then asked if she and Guy would also like *Poires.* But she did not like pears that much, nor did Guy, who had come back to the *plonge* to stand in the doorway to the *potager,* the small garden outside, and smoke his after-lunch cigarette.

"Ok. How about banana splits? I'll make one for each of you."

"*C'est quoi, ça?*" What's that, Anne asked? They had never heard of such a concoction, but as professionals they were more open than many of their compatriots to try something new.

"*Vas-y!*" Go to it, Guy said.

"Wait in the courtyard," I said, "and I'll bring everything out."

A few minutes later, I triumphantly emerged bearing the three treats. For a moment we looked with silent admiration at the chocolate swathcd creations, then bite by delectable bite made it clear that the enjoyment of these sweet concoctions was as good a way as any to establish a bond between *les Français* and *les Américains.* For me, the setting, the company and the concoctions created a unique combination of what I liked in France—-with a traditional American treat as part of the mix. I was not alone.

"*Trés bon!*" Guy exclaimed.

"*Très, très bon!*" Anne agreed.

"*Chapeau!*" Guy said, toasting my scrumptious *Poires belle Hélène* and "*Splits de banana* as we clinked our empty dishes. My performance was repeated, by popular demand, several times during that month.

❄

One request, however, did cross the line: the waitresses, Sonja and Françoise, asked me to set aside the choicest bones and scraps of meat for their own family dogs. Sonja, an immigrant from Greece who lived nearby, worked mostly in the summer and on busy weekends. She was paid, as I was, in cash, leaving no record that would require the Fauberts to pay taxes and make it difficult for foreign workers such as Sonja and I to get work. Black haired and a bit over five-feet tall, she fought a continual battle with the *gratin dauphinois,* what we would call scalloped potatoes. This dish, however, was far from any scalloped potatoes I had ever tasted. In fact, Madame Faubert made it a *Produits* specialty. Rich with butter, *crème fraîche* and milk, it emerged from the oven a bubbling, golden-crusted treat worth every kilometer of a drive from Lyon and guaranteed, as Sonja well knew, to add a couple of pounds to your waistline or some other place you did not want them. Once or twice, Sonja lamented to me in the *plonge,* smiling all the while, about her lack of will power as she scraped the delicious cheese-like crust off another half-full platter of leftover *pommes,* a dish diners rarely finished. I often joined her.

Françoise, not long out of high school, lived with her parents, who wanted her to get a factory job that offered good pay and union security. A bit taller than Sonja and Anne, with brown curly hair and a walk that said "watch out," she had different ideas. The way Guy looked at it, her career plan was to get him into bed, get pregnant, and then get him to the altar. If that really was her strategy, it failed. She never even made it to the passenger's seat in Guy's prized car, which he kept in a garage away from the restaurant, though he never revealed exactly where.

Even when Ginette joined Sonja and Françoise in their demands for the bones that were Sam's, I was unyielding, firmly asserting whatever authority is granted a *plongeur.*

"*Non!*" I said to the trio's demand. "*Absolument pas! Il y a des limites.*" Absolutely not. There are limits, quoting Albert.

Leftovers went to Sam, who was Ivan's dog if he was anyone's. The waitresses knew that, Albert knew that, and even I, *plongeur,* knew that. A shorthaired, floppy-eared Labrador-sized mongrel with tan fur, Sam was broad-chested, muscular, and covered with a matting of dust and bits of food. No one, so far as I could tell, had ever given him a bath, though with his living situation it might not have made much difference.

Abandoned at *Produits* front gate by parties unknown, Sam was never fully welcomed into the restaurant "family." Chasing chickens and sheep when he first arrived did not endear him to the Fauberts. With such a predatory disposition and a rather undistinguished appearance, Sam was banished to the farmhouse and put on a stout chain. It was hoped that he would at least behave like a useful watchdog and act threatening to anyone unfamiliar who approached the farmhouse gate. It was not, however, in Sam's easygoing nature to scare anyone. If a stranger did approach the gate, Sam dolefully gazed at him from the shade of the courtyard oak tree wondering if he should get up and give a woof or two. If the stranger took this silent greeting as a welcome and entered the grounds in a relaxed manner, Sam, instead of growling with stiff-necked menace, started wagging his loopy tail. If the stranger came nearer, Sam bared not a single canine tooth, but instead leapt and spun about, shaking a cloud of dust from his matted fur before flopping to the ground for a belly rub.

Of course, Sam liked a chase as much as the next dog, but living a chained-up life, he no longer could enjoy, if he ever had, the pleasure of running after a ball or stick. Moreover, he never lost the bad habit of chasing whatever he could eat. No matter how hot the day nor how deep the torpor, if that high-stepping farmhouse rooster and his hens scratched and pecked too close, which they often did, Sam exploded into action, scattering the clucking fowl and running his chain out until it snapped him back in mid-lunge to sit frustrated in a cloud of dust and feathers.

Naturally, Sam and I became *copains*. Consequently, my "*Non!*" to Sonja, Françoise, and Ginette was final. One looks out for a *copain*, especially if, in France, he does not correct your grammar and never asks why you are there. To this dusty rug of a dog with soft but alert retriever eyes, it never mattered what language I spoke, knowing I was there just to give him belly rubs.

❈

Ghislaine, of course, was not at *Les Produits* and I missed her, in bed and out. She had a full-time job in Grenoble so it was difficult for her to come to the restaurant during the week. Plus she often spent weekends with her parents at their place in the mountains above Grenoble. Calling her, which I did a couple of times, was complicated, as the only phone I could use was in the busy restaurant hallway. She did come to *Produits* one day for lunch but could not stay the night. And I had to work.

My other, less common, struggle was against the feeling that I was a failure in my life. Working as a dishwasher in France at the age of 22 can be an adventure that could lead anywhere; at 40 it was something else entirely. When I was busy, I did not think about it too much, but during afternoon breaks my *plongeur's* life and anxiety about my future enveloped me like steam from the dishwashing machine. The lovely Ghislaine could not help me with this problem. In fact, I had no answer: my future held only the prospect of returning to San Francisco with no job, little money, and no place to stay. So I lived as much as I could in the present, which is, after all, the only thing anyone can ever do. When that present offers such memorable experiences as enjoying *splits bananes* and *poires belle Hélène* with my colleagues, complaining seems petty. Such moments buoyed my spirits: I felt fully present in my French world without a thought of either my uncertain future or the past I came to France to escape. The most dramatic of these moments involved Sam and discombobulated the entire *Produits* staff one afternoon.

I was swishing a mop around the red tile floor of the *plonge,* my final chore before taking an afternoon break, when I heard rapid panting behind me and a volley of shouts: *"Sam! Sam! Viens ici!"* Sam in the *plonge*? *Pas possible*! Yet there he was at the slop buckets, exploring everything that might be edible, completely oblivious to my friendly greeting. Right behind him came Sonja, Françoise and Ginette, the Fauberts' daughter-in-law and the restaurant's manager in their absence, all three laughing nervously until Sam turned toward the doorway. Alarmed, the trio pulled back, tottering on their platform shoes, as Sam, on a mission, brushed by them and trotted down the dark hallway and out the front door of the house. He seemed to know where he was going, though none of us had any idea.

"Who let Sam off the chain?" Ginette asked.

"He's very dangerous!" Sonja said.

"He's savage," said Françoise. "Ivan said so."

Ivan, I knew, would never say such a thing, except perhaps to tease the waitresses. But when the entire staff had assembled for this emergency outside the restaurant's front door, Ivan did say, in French, that Sam was used to being on a chain: free, he would probably do what got him chained up years ago––go after the sheep. Ivan took off his cap, ran his hand over his thick head of white hair, and, for emphasis, said a few words to himself in Russian. He was worried. Ginette had found out that friends of Christian, the youngest Faubert son, on leave from the Navy for a week, had released the amiable Sam and were taken by surprise when the freed dog bolted out the farmhouse gate. What would Madame Faubert think, Ginette worried. Sam had to be chained up again.

"Maybe he went back to the farmhouse," Sonja said.

"I don't think so," said Ivan. "I'll check the sheep."

We returned to work: the waitresses and Ginette chattering nervously, began again to set the courtyard tables for dinner and I went back to my mopping. Not for long. Within moments, the high-pitched, alarmed voices of Ginette, Sonja, and Françoise rolled again down the hallway. "Another day, another French drama," I thought. If it's important, it will get back to the *plonge* sooner or later.

Within seconds, it did, in the breathless form of Françoise.

"*Vite! Vite!*" she shouted. "*Viens tout de suite! Et apportez un balai.*" Quickly! Quickly! Come right away! And bring a broom!

A broom? *Qu'est-ce qui se passe?* What's going on?

"*Vite!*" Françoise shouted over her shoulder as she ran back down the hallway.

I followed her, *sans* broom, past Guy, who cheered me on by waving his latest issue of the daily *Journal de Football*. I ran faster, through the courtyard and out the gate, passing Françoise and Sonja, who had stopped in the road and now were shouting something about Sam being near the storage sheds.

When I turned into the dirt driveway alongside the sheds, I spotted Ivan at the edge of the field beyond the rabbit hutches and the clothesline full of billowing white tablecloths. He yelled at me to follow him and in spite of his age, weighty clothes, and heavy boots, galloped with clumping strides and surprising speed across the rough field, waving a stick high above his head as if leading a full-out saber-flashing assault on the Reds and shouting Russian and French commands that all ended with the word "Sam!" At that moment, no language had any meaning for Sam. He had downed a full-grown sheep and with his teeth buried in the thick wool of its neck was shaking the terrified animal back and forth, whipping its shock-stiff legs this way and that like sticks and growling all the while.

Reaching Sam first, Ivan whacked him several times on the snout with his stick. Sam held on. Ivan grabbed him with both hands by the thick scruff of his neck and yelled at me to grab him, too, so I hooked an arm around the growling dog's chest. Ivan and I dug our heels in and leaned back with all our weight. Sam held on. Finally, as I continued to pull, Ivan worked the end of his stick between Sam's jaws and leaned on it with all his wiry weight. That did it. Sam let go and abruptly sat down between Ivan and me, all three of us breathing heavily. With bits of wool hanging from his lips, Sam never took his eyes off the downed sheep. Still rigid with shock, it lay motionless for a few seconds a short lunge away before exploding into life and racing in a crazed zigzag toward the other sheep at the far end of the pasture. Then, as one, they turned their black-masked faces, wide-eyed with fear, toward the panting dog, which Ivan and I still held tightly. Sam stared back, his breathing slowly returning to normal.

Rubbing the wiry hair of the dog's chest, I could feel his heart racing––and my own. How strange that I felt no fear of this dog and that Sam never made so much as a low growl of protest as Ivan and I deprived him of his prey.

Ivan went to the storage shed and brought back a long heavy chain to put around Sam's neck. "I'll take him back," I said, and walked the dog past the shed and out to the road toward the restaurant. When I passed *Produit's* closed gate, Françoise, Sonja, and Ginette, standing just inside, gave chorus again to their unshakeable belief that Sam was savage.

"*Pas du tout,*" I said. "*Regardez! Il est très gentil.*" Look. He's very sweet, I said, and led the tail-wagging Sam toward them so they could see for themselves.

"*Non! Non!*" they shouted, and pulled hard on the gate to make sure it was shut tight.

"Just chain him up," Ginette said.

Continuing down the easy curve of the blacktop road, I could feel Sam pull forward with all his panting strength, tightening the muscles in my arm and shoulder. The texture of the stones in the fieldstone wall, the sheen of the green, tasseled corn behind it, and the spinning silver leaves of the distant poplar trees all seemed alive with the force that shaped them, as did I.

I have felt that way at times, body surfing at Stinson Beach north of San Francisco, coursing down a steep hill on my ten-speed bicycle, and especially swimming in San Francisco Bay's cold, restorative waters. They all awakened in me a sense of being fully in my body, *bien dans ma peau,* keenly alert to the life around me. But this episode with Sam was different:

the dog's intense animal presence, his strength, made me fully aware of myself as a creature of flesh, blood, bone, and muscle, an animal, long chained up and still trying to get free.

I also felt a longing for something beyond physical exhilaration. What that might be I did not know, though I had gone to France in part to find out. By the time I ended up at *Les Produits,* I had at least learned that becoming fluent in French or, more absurdly, becoming French, was not the answer. Little time was left to me in France to find it.

✳

Since I was a friend of Marius and Rose, they invited me to make myself at home in the second-floor living room of the Faubert home when it was not being used. Right over the *plonge* and doubling as Madame's office, it was carpeted, paneled in dark wood, and offered views of the cornfields on one side and the home's small landscaped backyard on the other. It was furnished with comfortable easy chairs, antique wooden cases of family crystal, and built-in shelves filled with school textbooks, Simenon novels, and the leather-bound works of French classics. The room's long, dark walnut table that had been in the Faubert family for generations was the center of any festive occasion--birthdays, special visits, the end of vacations, all celebrated with cake and champagne, usually on Sunday afternoons, as few customers came to the restaurant for dinner. I could imagine the Faubert children bent to their homework on that same table, wistfully daydreaming--which I also did there--as they looked out the window past the yard and cornfield, to the distant poplars, which the French appropriately call *les trembles*. To Madame Faubert, the room was most important for its large desk, abloom with wads of bills, recipes, and other papers; for its ironing board where she would smooth the wrinkles from the blouses of her youngest child, near to finishing high school; and for a place of refuge from the stressful world of the restaurant downstairs. Sometimes she would enjoy dozing for a few minutes in one of the easy chairs.

For me, the most important piece of furniture in that room was the stereo with its collection of record albums. As the Fauberts were away for the month and Marius and Rose were only visiting on weekends, I often had this upstairs room to myself and sometimes took my afternoon break there instead of going back to the farmhouse for a siesta. That's how I discovered Jacques Brel. I would watch the poplar leaves shimmer in the wind like flakes of mica and listen to Brel sing *Amsterdam, Le Plat pays* (his native Belgium), and *Ne me quitte pas,* a plea to a departing lover not to leave. He sang other songs as well, full of satirical humor about different types of people in French society––especially the upper classes. Those of longing and loss, however, struck the strongest chord in me, often bringing me close to tears. Thanks to Monsieur Brel, I already felt a longing for France, though I was still there. What had I discovered there that I would miss once back in California, as I expected soon to be? It was more than the friends I had made, or the light, or the language. Was I living in a fantasy world? What if I could have made a living doing translation work I liked? Would I have stayed?

❉

In May of 1975, when I left France the first time, having lived there for 15 months, I flew out of Luxembourg after taking the 200-mile train trip from Paris. To my surprise and considerable embarrassment, I cried the entire trip. The young woman who shared my compartment watched me with puzzlement, and some concern. I assured her I was just sad. Even when I went out into the corridor and stood in an open window I could not stop crying.

Fundamentally, how I felt had something to do with that French notion of *bien dans ma peau,* comfortable in my own skin, but it was more than that. Several times in my life, I have experienced that feeling for a few moments or a few hours, always unexpectedly and always affecting me in the same ways: my voice dropped and I felt calm and self-assured. Rather than my familiar playboy persona with its boyish indecisiveness and the fearfulness my girlfriends mocked, I felt clear about my feelings and accepting of who I was. My way of relating to others also changed, to their surprise as well as to my own. When I noticed their reaction, even if it were positive––or maybe because it was positive––I retreated to being "nice," betraying the "me" that had momentarily come out of hiding. It was as if feeling that way was somehow hurtful to others. I abandoned myself, and felt a loneliness that became a trap.

I hoped when I went to France to make that feeling of being *"bien dans ma peau"* a more integral part of me, not to run away from it. On that train to Luxembourg I felt as if I were in part giving up that hope, cutting forever my emotional bonds to a country––and a language––I had come to love, and to a part of me that came fully alive only when I spoke French. All of this is hindsight, of course. During those afternoon hours with Monsieur Brel I felt mainly a pained befuddlement about how, at my advanced age, I ended up working as a *plongeur* in the French sticks yet still did not want to leave this country where, as odd as it seemed, I felt at home.

Madame Faubert wondered about that, too, at least as far as Rose was concerned, as I found out one afternoon early in August. Albert had already left for his month in the Alps, but the Fauberts were not going to leave for a few days. Though I almost never saw Monsieur Faubert, Rose had told me that both he and Madame were anxious about spending that much time away from *Produits*. What made them even more anxious was the prospect of spending that much time together, as the normal ups and downs of a long relationship and a houseful of children had given them few ups in recent years. Going to the family room to listen to some music one Sunday afternoon, I was surprised to find there not only Rose, engrossed in a book, but Madame as well. I took a Simenon novel off the shelf, sought out my favorite chair near the window, and watched the shimmering poplars across the fields, the book unopened in my lap.

Bent over papers at her desk, Madame was working worriedly on the final arrangements for the vacation that, in fact, would mark the beginning of her semi-official retirement, "semi-official" because neither she nor anyone she knew could imagine her letting go of the reins no matter how her back and legs complained. The more she fiddled with details about turning over her kitchen to the much younger Guy and the plans for her upcoming vacation, the more she sighed and took off her glasses to clean them on the hem of her cotton print apron. The more often, too, she looked at Rose, absorbed in her book. Finally, she put the glasses down on the papers in front of her and walked to the ironing board and the chair of still to be ironed clothes. When Rose offered to lend her a hand, Madame Faubert nodded her head of gray curly hair toward the laundry. *"Tu peux ranger les serviettes,"* you can put away those towels, she said, then bowed to her daughter's yellow blouse and the meditative glides of the iron, the only sound to break the silence of a room that suddenly seemed full of sadness.

To me, Madame Faubert did not seem *sympa*, short for *sympathique,* which might translate as amiable and open. She was quite the opposite, in fact, judging from the ritual she required of me during my first two paydays as Albert's replacement. We had arranged that to collect my pay I would meet her every Friday after lunch at the cash register in the ground-floor hallway. Each time, without looking at me, she asked me exactly what weekly wage she had agreed to pay, though as cagey as can be about money matters she clearly knew the amount. *"Vous êtes certain?"* she asked, each time. *"Absolument,"* I replied. Then, glasses pushed down to the end of her nose, she counted out the franc notes, handed them to me, and without saying another word, and still without looking at me, turned and walked toward the kitchen. Not only was this arrangement Madame's way of avoiding the legalities of declaring me as an employee, it was also her not so subtle way of letting me know exactly what my place was in her French world. The slightly demeaning ritual also expressed her disapproval of my being far away from my family, as was her daughter-in-law, Rose, something she could not understand.

She had asked Rose more than once how she could do that––live so far from home? Something must be very wrong for her to put an ocean between herself and her family, Madame said. Yet here she was, coming with Marius and Emma most weekends and helping out when things got really busy. It puzzled her. "I have to plead with my own children to come when I need them. They act like they don't want to see me or this place that helped support us all."

Putting down the iron, she moved to help Rose with her folding, then stopped and suddenly asked her American *belle-fille:* *"Pourquoi?,"* the words leaping out before she could stop them, *"Pourquoi est-ce que mes enfants ne m'aiment pas?"* Why don't my children love me? Then, before Rose could answer, this strong and resourceful woman let go of the restaurant, her husband, the shape-shifting memories held by that room, let go for a moment even of her own children, and against all her characteristic kitchen-tempered toughness, held Rose tightly to her with large red hands, and wept.

Family relationships, naturally, are almost impossible to understand, all of them being tangles of emotional attachment and fierce competition, of affectionate bonds and bitter resentments, and of secrets the family cannot even admit to itself. Like Madame, I did not understand the emotional tangle of my own family nor what it had to do with my feelings about France. My father, though, had recently written to me that my mother, near 80 and suffering from some form of dementia, had in her confusion fallen downstairs one night and was now in a convalescent home with a broken hip. The news roiled my conflicted emotions even more.

Whether Madame ever found a way through the troubling professional and personal rapids of her later years, I don't know. Restaurants are never easy to run, even with the owner as head chef; the successful *Produits* was no exception. Its staff of professionals and amateurs, French and foreign, young and old, was, however, a *bouillabaisse* of unique ingredients that blended beautifully––most of the time.

✽

"Somewhat bizarre," is how a critic in the travel section of the esteemed *Le Monde* described it. The critic, however, also praised the high quality of its food and its friendly and efficient service. Gathered together in the courtyard one morning over the spread-out newspaper, Guy, Anne, Françoise and I had no idea what the critic meant. A restaurant's inner workings are unquestionably as mysterious and finely balanced as those of a family, especially to an outsider. Nonetheless, we all agreed that anyone who stopped on a sunny day for lunch or dinner in the courtyard of *Produits* would not have had even a whiff of the bizarre. *Au contraire,* that lucky diner would have been seated at a table in the sun-dappled shade of the courtyard's plane tree and enjoyed from the restaurant's gardens a rich variety of flavorful vegetables, often picked minutes before by yours truly, *plongeur extraordinaire.* They could have chosen from among a number of hearty fish and meat dishes––from roasted *pintade* (guinea hen) to boar (during hunting season) to spicy Louisiana crayfish––all served to please the eye as well as the palate. With them came fine Beaujolais, red Burgundies, and light, dry slightly sparkling wines from the Alpine Savoie. These pairings had put *Produits* on the culinary map, carrying Madame's reputation all the way to Paris. The local customers knew that; the staff and the family knew that. So what exactly did that "big city" reviewer mean by saying that there was something a bit peculiar about *Produits*?

Perhaps his dinner had been momentarily disturbed by the twittering sparrows that, though routed again and again by sharp raps of a knife handle on one of the metal tables, found the courtyard plane tree an irresistible place for their family gatherings. Or perhaps the staff of Poles, Algerians, Russians, Americans, and French had struck him as being at odds with the pastureland, gardens and fields in which the restaurant was serenely set.

Nothing bizarre in any of that. *Absolument pas!* For me the small world of *Produits* was an amicable concoction of strong-minded individuals that the great French film director, Jean Renoir, would have envied. Some members of this rich cast of characters were, like myself, only there for a short time. Others, like Sonja, Albert and Ivan had been there for years. Of course, there were the usual little dramas--people rubbing each other the wrong way at times, a dish not turning out as the chef or a diner had expected, and owners not always respecting the people they hired--*moi,* for example. Certainly none of us had marched to the same drummer, or marched at all, for that matter. Skipped, jumped, ran, maybe, but no one marched. In fact, the international staff gave *Produits* an atmosphere as piquant as those spicy Louisiana crayfish that the new chef, Guy, had added to the menu and that quickly became a favorite.

❅

"*Ott!*" Guy shouted as he rushed into the *plonge* and on the large metal table behind me dumped from his gloved hands a clattering stack of metal platters. "*Ott!*" he said again, without a hint of the aspirated English "h" that almost does not exist in French. To make up for its absence, Guy said the word louder and with explosive force. Good thing for me, as those platters of all sizes came straight from the oven and could burn at the touch. Madame Faubert hired Guy several months before departing for the mountains so he could become familiar with *Produits'* menu and she could sample some new dishes he wanted to introduce. Guy, I later found out, did not have a long stay at *Produits,* but that August, once Madame and Monsieur Faubert had left, the kitchen became his, as he soon made dramatically clear.

Every morning the click, click, click, of the young chef's metallic heels on the hallway's tiled floor announced his arrival. "*Bonjour. Ca va?* We both grunted.   His workday mornings began, as did everyone's, at the expresso machine, which was located under the stairs near the cash register, the critical midpoint of the hallway. My preferred wake-up drink was a mocha, a shot or two of expresso in a cup of hot chocolate. It was not a common way in France to get your caffeine wake-up jolt.

Guy made his daily double expresso, dropped into it a couple of sugar cubes, then, with our drinks in hand we walked into the courtyard and stood quietly, listening to the sparrows making their usual racket overhead as the chef smoked his morning *Gitane,* a French cigarette. Only one, because he had a limit of just three a day. Sometimes, as the caffeine kicked in, he would curse the sparrows; sometimes he would shout a greeting in his incomprehensible Alsatian dialect to the local farm girls guiding their cows past the gate to the pasture down the road; sometimes, he would abruptly sit, pull out his rolled up copy of *Journal de Football*, devoted to soccer, of course--the real football--and read about the last match played by his team, Strasbourg. Most mornings, though, he would stand tensely silent. Short and trim with straight jet-black hair, he was a lightweight boxer waiting to enter the ring. Once he click-clicked into the kitchen and tied on his apron, he became all purposeful movement, sidestepping from one stove to another, grabbing this pot or that pan, adjusting a burner or oven. As he demanded this or that of his apprentice, Anne, he flicked off sparks of dissatisfaction about the quality of the *haricots verts,* thin French green beans, or the crayfish for his special dish, or the play of Strasbourg.

One Tuesday, our day off, I arrived at the shining machine later than usual and found Ginette and Olivier, the Faubert son who had just returned from working in a Geneva hotel restaurant as part of his management training. As we chatted, I prepared my mocha, carefully watched by Ginette. *"Qu'est ce que c'est ça?"* what's that, she asked, wrinkling her nose. *"Un mocha,"* I said. Jacques described the mixture, his training having given him a more cosmopolitan view of the food world and, as a result, more authority in such matters. *"C'est bon,"* he said encouragingly to Ginette. I offered her a taste. Though fundamentally wary of what this American *plongeur* was up to, she took a sip. The wrinkle in her nose vanished. *"Pas mal,"* she said. But she turned down my offer to make her one. *"Demain, peut-être,"* tomorrow, maybe, she said.

For Monsieur Faubert, his son Jean-Pierre, and the postman, Monsieur Martel, the expresso machine and courtyard became, around nine o'clock or so, the setting for a different daily gathering. All three had been up for hours, so it was time--especially on a warm summer day--for a glass of white *vin de Savoie,* a coffee, and some bantering about politics and the price of cheese or shrimp. Then, having already made his exquisite *terrine de la maison* and gone with Jean-Pierre to the markets of Lyon, Monsieur Faubert went to bed on the third floor and was rarely seen the rest of the day. In fact, I cannot remember ever meeting him during my time at *Produits*.

❄

From the time I met Guy, I was struck by his knotted energy. One warm evening, his work almost done, he came back from the kitchen to enjoy his third and final smoke of the day. I asked him if he had always been so edgy.

He was sitting on the back step of the *plonge,* staring at the restaurant's small green garden outside the door, his mind's eye roaming far beyond it. Without turning around, he said:

"No. Before I started cooking I wasn't like this at all. Nothing bothered me." He paused to inhale. "Now... Now every year I get more tense and want to smoke more of these," and he stubbed out his cigarette on the stone step.

"Do you like the work, being a chef?" I asked.

"*Il le faut,*" he said, I have to like it. Then he jumped up, tossed his cigarette butt into the garbage can, and click-clicked back down the darkening hallway to finish his work in the kitchen. *Il le faut* applied to me as well: I, too, had to do work of some kind. My life, though, did not seem to reflect very consistently the hard reality of those words. Perhaps it had something to do with hanging on to that *tombeur* role, though I certainly did not think of myself as a playboy. I was fat as a young adolescent and that self-image, like those developed by many adolescents, was hard to erase. (My father's undermining criticisms of my genital deficiency did not help.) That image was also part of my denial of who I was––an almost forty-year-old man––allowing me to refuse to believe that I had a strong visual sense of the world that gave me skill as a potter and, later, as a film writer and photographer. Most importantly, it kept me from accepting that I could speak French fluently (even if I had a Belgian accent), write well, and was an excellent editor, three skills that spoke to my love of language, which I discovered when I was a senior in college. All these creative interests gave me energy instead of sapping it. I just had to find a way to use them to *gagner ma croûte,* literally, to earn my crust of bread. The French encouraged me to say *adieu* to that distorted notion of who I was, whether by laughing at it, as the psychoanalyst did at the American Hospital, or by taking me to task for not rejecting it, as my Parisian girlfriend did. As I stood in the cloud of vapor from the dishwasher, waiting for its hissing, clunking cycle to end, I realized that only by ridding myself of that distorted self-image could I be at ease with myself, *être bien dans ma peau,* and lessen the grip of that deep sense of longing that often was with me––as it was on that train to Luxembourg.

Guy usually snapped me out of my vaporous musings by a warning shout of *Ott! Ott!* as he dumped another clanging jumble of metal platters on the worktable behind me. In a way, Guy was lucky. Like anyone entering a trade or craft in France, he started his training to be a chef when he was sixteen. Now only 22, he had done his two-year apprenticeship, passed his certification exam, spent several years as a sous-chef in Lyon, and had been chosen by Madame Faubert to be her successor in a restaurant mentioned in *Le Monde*. *Pas mal!* Not bad as a start to a culinary career. Especially since family enterprises like *Produits* don't usually embrace outsiders. Madame Faubert had ruled her kitchen for a long time and in spite of how much it had taken depleted her robust energy, she still loved what she did, taking special pride in the fact that people came there for *Madame's* cooking.

Giving all that up to Guy, or to anyone, provided lots of reasons to worry, and not just because, like Albert, she had never been away from *Produits* for more than a few days at a time. She and Guy both knew that the young man's biggest challenge would be holding on to the restaurant's loyal customers while trying to expand and even change *Produits'* menu of traditional butter-rich dishes. Guy was determined to put some things on the menu that not only tasted different but--*Mon dieu!*--looked different as well, since presentation is essential to the serving of fine French food. He was not above using sleight of hand to bring about these near miraculous conversions, as I discovered a few months later.

Guy also had another indisputable advantage in the chef's world: he was male. That fact surely added a dash of bitterness to Madame's frustration at not being fully admitted into the exclusively male world of top French chefs, even though those chefs had long acknowledged her enviable abilities. The sight of this young man, talented, energetic, and free of varicose veins, standing at the stoves--her stoves--must have rankled her.

❄

For the 20-year-old Anne, who just a few years earlier had been tending the family cows in mountain pastures, the culinary road from apprentice to chef would be almost as hard as Madame Faubert's, no matter how talented she might be--just because she was a woman. Knowing what was in store for the young woman, Madame Faubert showed a motherly interest in Anne's welfare, occasionally taking her to Lyon on a Tuesday for lunch and some shopping, perhaps buying her a dress or a sweater. Anne worked the apprentice's customary exhausting 12-hour day, six-day week. When it came to the customary chef's criticism, however, Madame's harshest chastisements--at worst a quick tug of

Anne's curly hair but usually only a few sharp words—were much milder than what a male chef would have doled out.

With Madame away and Guy in charge, Anne had to deal with a dramatic change. His guidance, like Madame Faubert's, was somewhat parental, but his criticisms tended toward a more physical masculine style, a modulated version of what he had to put up with during his two years as an apprentice. For Anne that meant unquestioned acceptance of his autocratic rule, including pokes, hair-pulling, and occasional backhanded cuffs or slaps. Though, as with Madame, a few quick words of annoyance were the norm, the possibility of something worse put Anne on edge. To make matters worse, she had to take her certification examinations just as Guy became ruler of the *Produits'* culinary domain.

The exam was in Dijon, so when she returned, Marius, Rose and I picked her up at the local train station. As soon as we saw her, we knew that things did not go well. The ride was funereal: Anne failed to pass by just two points. "*Deux points! Deux points!,*" she repeated, shaking her head of curly blonde hair, I failed by just two points. "I don't know what I'll do now," she sighed. To retake the test, she would have to do another two years as an apprentice, an idea that was more than she could bear. During the following days, dispirited and fretful, Anne plodded through her chores with dulled attention: she wasn't fully there. It was a situation sure to get "*Ott!*"

When he was an apprentice, Guy told me, you never knew when you might get a sharp slap or a punch in the back or arm, or even to the side of the head. "*N'importe où.*" Wherever. Such treatment had been as much a part of his day as the usual apprentice chores of chopping and dicing vegetables, scrubbing stoves with stiff-bristled brushes, or the late-night mopping of floors on the weekends. "It's the life of an apprentice," he said. "I did not like a lot of it, and some of the chefs I worked for were "*vrais salauds,*" real bastards, but all you can do is put up with it. Once again: "*Il le faut.*"

At the end of the first week of Madame and Monsieur's vacation, a week of intermittent drizzle, humidity, and gray skies, everyone at *Produits* was snappish. Inevitably, Guy's "*il le faut*" ran into Anne's "*Deux pointes! Deux pointes!*" After a Sunday lunch that drew only a handful of customers, I was in the *plonge* waiting for the dishwasher to finish its last whooshing cycle when a clattering racket followed by a scream filled the entire building. I rushed into the hallway as the door of the bathroom near the *plonge* slammed shut and its bolt shot into place. "I will never work with that devil again," Anne shrieked from behind the locked door. "*Jamais! Jamais! Jamais!*" Never! Never! Never! Ginette raced downstairs from the second-floor. "He's a brute," Anne shouted from her redoubt. With an authority as unconvincing to the assembled staff as it was unfamiliar to her, Ginette strode into the kitchen to put Guy in his place. After a few seconds of silence, she ran out again, routed by a barrage of curses. "*Il est fou! Sauvage!*" she shouted, her voice trembling with alarm. "This is my kitchen," Guy shouted. "No one tells me what to do in my kitchen." Then, standing in the doorway, carving knife in hand, he growled: "I'll do everything myself if I have to." Which is exactly what he did the rest of that dreary day.

Anne stayed behind her locked door, crying some more and insulting Guy every possible way without completely abandoning all measure of feminine civility. "*Non! Non!*" she said to Ginette's pleas to come out. Eventually, of course, she did come out and went upstairs with Ginette to talk things over, all the while insisting that she would never work with Guy again, "*Jamais! Jamais!*"

What set Guy off, the rest of the staff wondered as we huddled in the hallway? Apparently, Anne, "*qui n'était pas grande,*" using the small stool in the kitchen as usual, but without her customary care, stacked haphazardly dozens of those oval metal trays—some dinner-plate size, some large enough to hold a Thanksgiving turkey—that were used to finish off dishes in the oven so they could be served "*Ott!*" Guy could not easily add another platter to one of the slapdash piles or grab the one he wanted without risking the collapse of the entire stack. This, of course, was dangerous to both Anne and Guy, an uncharacteristic lapse and as unacceptable to Guy as it would have been to Madame Faubert. That he yelled and cursed, Anne expected. What she did not expect was a sharp slap and Guy's wild swing that sent the several stacks of pewter-colored trays in a clanging, bonging, caroming avalanche to the tile floor. The racket not only sent the sparrows exploding in alarm from the courtyard plane tree it roused the distant Sam, who rolled a few mildly alarmed woofs our way from the farmhouse.

This was not a personal matter for Guy. He liked Anne, but what she did was unprofessional putting both of them at risk. When he reacted, he was just doing as he had been taught about running a kitchen. If it made him abusively dictatorial at times, it also gave him a strong conviction that things had to be done in a professional way. (He surprised and delighted me one day by telling me that's why he liked working with me: I worked like a professional.)

On the other hand, he did not have much respect for Ginette and Françoise, who, he said, were completely unprofessional. Moreover, they did not do right by Anne. Having a good idea of where they stood in their class-bound French world, they made it clear to Anne that however low they might be, she was definitely lower. At least, that's what they thought. To make their point, they invited her to join them one Monday night on a jaunt to the nightlife of Lyon, then drove off before the appointed hour, leaving Anne in the courtyard, all dressed up with no place to go. Just a misunderstanding, they said later. Guy did not think so.

No more of a misunderstanding than the "exotic" fare Ginette served the staff for lunch one day. Anne, who often prepared these midday meals, as well as what she called her *entremets,*" her desserts, brought to our courtyard table the usual bowl of green salad, a metal platter of green beans, and a *gratin dauphinois.* The main course, which Anne placed in the center of the table with unusual wary hesitation, was a platter of glistening dark brown meat. Ivan and I had already moved a piece to our plates when Guy's indignant cry stopped our tines in midair. *"Pas vrai!"* This can't be true, he exclaimed. *"Impossible! Incroyable!* Unbelievable! We had been served horsemeat. Guy slammed his knife on the table--routing the sparrows overhead--leapt to his feet, and click-clicked into the kitchen. In seconds, skillet in hand, he appeared in the window. "If this ever happens again," he said with simmering anger, "you can look for another chef." Ginette shrugged and sat down to lunch. I returned to the platter the piece of roasted meat I had taken, but had a bite first--*pas mal,* not bad--then settled for a lunch of salad, potatoes, and beans. Horsemeat is not uncommon in France, but, like corned beef and some other cuts of meat that are not considered choice, it is regarded as the food of the lower classes. It certainly is not food for the chef and staff of a restaurant that had been recommended in the pages of *Le Monde.*

That platter of glistening horsemeat revealed Ginette's tangle of feelings about Guy, the rest of the staff, and herself. Managing the lives of three small children was one thing. Dealing with this "bizarre" restaurant and its crew called for a special set of skills, though maybe not all that different. After Guy's dustup with Anne, Ginette knew she could not control the young chef. She also seemed to resent *moi,* the American friend of the family who would soon return to his "real" life (something, in fact, I was dreading); and she was trying to find the confidence to measure up to replacing the formidable Madame, whose shadow seemed to reach all the way from her alpine vacation retreat. By serving inexpensive horsemeat, which would save the restaurant money, Ginette undoubtedly thought she would impress Madame. As Guy reminded her, she was in a bit over her head.

❄

The following Tuesday night, with *Produits* closed as usual, Ginette and Françoise, *sans* Anne, had once again gone to Lyon. Marius and Rose, there for a long weekend with some friends, decided to treat the visiting couple from the States to a *boum*. It was a beautiful night, pleasantly balmy for August, so when Guy said not only that he could put something delicious together for dinner but — *Mon dieu!* — could also put his speakers in his window facing the yard behind the farmhouse so the party could be outside.

In the late afternoon, I helped Guy load some of the food onto the restaurant courtyard cart and wheel it to the farmhouse. On the way, we talked about Anne. She was really looking forward to the evening, he said, and had gotten over her snub by the other women. More importantly, Guy had finally patched things up with her after a couple of rough days when Anne related to him only with scowls and the silent treatment. When she finally yielded a bit, Guy told her that the depressing weather and Ginette's attitude had finally gotten to him––*Il y en a marre*––he had had it up to here. That did not excuse Anne's slipshod platter stacking, which, he emphasized, was dangerous for them both and not at all like her. On her part, Anne said that failing the examination and her uncertain future had put her on edge. As professionals, they agreed to forget that miserable afternoon and work again as a team in the kitchen––at least until Madame returned and Anne figured out what she was going to do. The storm of that Sunday had passed, even if Anne said she still preferred working with Madame, which got from Guy a "*Bof*" a Gallic shrug––and a smile.

Once we had tamped down the loose dirt of the back yard, I tried, with Marius, who should have known better, to roust the tree rats from the grape vines covering the back of the house. First we bombarded them with clods of dirt, which they completely ignored. Then we tried the technique Marius often used, swinging rakes and poles at the dark-green tangle of leaves and vines the rats called home, but that only drove them higher. Unfazed, these rodent versions of the courtyard sparrows resumed their usual grape snacking as soon as we eased our attack. Our efforts were, we could almost hear Albert say, *jamais finis.*

We pulled up a few weeds, did some raking and tamping of dirt for an hour or two, and *voilà:* we had a passable dance floor, so long as no one tried any fancy disco moves. From the unfinished downstairs living room we hauled out some tables and chairs. By late afternoon, we were almost ready to go. As the shade cast by the house moved to cover the entire dining and dancing area, Guy came from the restaurant and went upstairs to test the speakers in his bedroom window. "Far out!" the longhaired American guest said, adjusting his headband as the sound blasted out of Guy's window. When Guy returned from another trip to the restaurant, Anne and a cart loaded with platters, utensils, and casseroles came with him: the *boum* commenced booming. From Guy's speakers came the greatest hits of the Beatles and the Rolling Stones, rendered in slangy French by Johnny Hallyday, known to his adoring public simply as "Johnny." Dylan was in the mix, too, and some French groups I had never heard, all carefully selected by DJ Guy from his extensive tape collection.

It all put us in the mood to share a Gruyère-crusted onion soup, "The best I've ever made," Guy proclaimed. It was followed by slightly sparkling white wine from the Savoie; fruity, fresh Beaujolais that went well with everything; garlic sausages brown to bursting with fatty juices; several dishes of the irresistible *gratin dauphinois*, with its cheesy, chewy topping; and greens and tomatoes I had plucked from the *potage* a few minutes earlier. To end it all came, of course, an array of cheeses: Crottins de Chavignol, tart, hard goat cheeses the size of flattened golf balls; the local mild-tasting Saint-Marcellin; Beaufort, so buttery and sweet you could taste the Alpine grass that gave it its prized flavor; and *fromage blanc*, a fresh cheese a bit thicker than yogurt that you can eat with chives and minced garlic or, as we did, with fresh fruit for dessert.

Marius and his wife, Rose, toasted their friends, and we all toasted Guy and Anne and danced on the floor of packed dirt, some of us inspired by the Beatles and Stones, some of us by Johnny, and all of us by the lovely Summer evening. Anne braved differences in both culture and height—I was more than a foot taller—and asked me to do a 'slow,' a languorous ballad. We shuffled and scuffed around the dance "floor," her head of blonde curls against my chest as I looked around at my friends, the farmhouse where I was living, and the French countryside that for this short time was my home. When it ended, I bowed, Anne smiled coyly and then, laughing, said *"Enfin, alors, tu n'es pas trop grand pour moi,"* after all, you are not too tall for me.

By 11 or so, our *boum* had stopped booming, though Johnny was still serenading us--as well as others in the neighborhood, we found out the next morning. Some of us started to move chairs and tables inside the farmhouse and began loading up the cart to take things back to the restaurant. Rachida, a young Algerian-born woman who was my helper once or twice a week, had joined us that night to help out on the *boum*, but her father had laid down the law: Be home by midnight. The night was soft, the moon was full, so this eldest of ten children was ready to walk the two kilometers home. "Not without us," we chorused. For the occasion, Guy said he would roll out the car he often talked about but that we had never seen. Go on ahead, he said *"Je me vous rejoindrai."* I'll catch up with you.

We had only been walking for a few minutes along the narrow two-lane road when we heard behind us a melodious tune on a cornet-like car horn and the smooth low purring of a finely tuned engine: Guy had arrived. Though he often talked about how much he had spent on his prize possession and how much work he had done on it himself, nothing could have prepared us for the gleaming, bright yellow sport coupe that eased up next to us. It was a beauty, fully equipped with leather-covered steering wheel, sheepskin seat-covers, oversized felt dice dangling from the interior rearview mirror, and a multi-toned-- and illegal--Italian horn, which, Guy said, he used only on special occasions. This was one. Guy looked as serious as a Formula One driver ready for the endurance race at Le Mans--until our ooohs and aaahs broke through his pose and he beamed with pride, revving the engine gently as if to tell us that the car also acknowledged our admiration.

Gleaming in the moonlight as it slowly rolled along next to us, a symbol of automotive splendor, it offered an irresistible temptation to the long-haired American guest. Before you could say "Far out!", he eased his cutoff-clad posterior onto one of its fenders and, smiling, with beer in hand, was sitting pretty for a nighttime ride. The car jolted to a halt, the surprised American slid off, and Guy leaped out to confront the startled rider, who had no notion of the gravity of his offense. Guy called him *"ippie"* and *"idiot"*--and a few other insulting French names--then turned to me and said to tell him that if he ever did that again, he would not get a warning. " Tell him," he said, "that no idiot can treat my car like that." Then, still *"ott,"* he slid behind the leather-covered steering wheel and rumbled off down the road, leaving Rose to explain to her chagrined friend how inviolate such cars were to their French owners. With Rachida safely home and Guy off to Lyon in his yellow beauty, our return walk to the farmhouse was reduced to quiet conversation and the inevitable barking of watchdogs. The pleasures of the *boum* were forgotten.

Not by everyone. The neighbors had not shared a moment of our midsummer night's pleasure—not even at Johnny's warblings. All the next day, word came from as far as a half mile away across the flat countryside that our wingding was definitely not *comme il faut. Pas du tout!* The messages were not irate phone calls or fist-shaking personal visits, perhaps because Monsieur and Madame were away, common knowledge, apparently, in the neighborhood. Instead they came indirectly — through the postman as he took his midmorning glass of white wine in the restaurant's hallway; through the *laitier* who delivered fresh *fromage blanc,* milk, and butter; and even through the girls who passed the courtyard gate the next morning with their cows as we were drinking *boum*-recovery double expessos. "*Eh oh,*" they shouted in a teasing tone, "*Quel boum hier soir! Johnny était chouette.*" Quite a party you had last night! Johnny was great! All the other messages, unfortunately, concluded with the same indignant sentiment: never before had such a party been held at Monsieur and Madame Faubert's! They were right about that, Marius agreed, and once his parents had gotten an earful from the neighbors, no such *boum,* he said, would ever happen again.

✳

Another event that would never be repeated occurred on a lazy, hot Friday afternoon. Guy, we now knew, was quick to flare up about things that he considered important, professional or otherwise. Fortunately for Anne and the rest of the staff, he was also quick to get over what set him off, except that in his book, once an "idiot," always an idiot. Certain behavior--abusing his car or being served horsemeat--left no room for redemption.

One Friday afternoon during Madame's vacation, the staff had the task of making gallons of sangria for the next day's wedding reception. It would be held in the courtyard with its small glass-walled pavilion. Ginette was busy with her children, so it was up to Guy, Anne, Sonja, Françoise and I to peel the boxes of oranges and succulent peaches and rinse and cut the stems off the strawberries. The next day was predicted to be a hot one, so Guy knew we would need to make enough sangria to fill many pitchers. We had hardly started our tedious task, sampling the peaches as we went, when squadrons of hornets arrived to buzz around us and drown themselves in the sweet liquid they liked as much as we did. Since they had been pests for weeks, as they always were in the late-Summer heat, we had already tracked them to the nest they had built high on the eastern wall of the house. We could fight off a few at a time with occasional swats but their all-out attack on the sangria was too much for Guy.

"*J'en ai marre de ces guêpes!*" I've had it with these hornets, he said, and click-clicked into the kitchen. A few moments later, he emerged ready for battle. He had put on a long-sleeved chef's coat, wrapped a heavy towel around his neck, and fashioned what we would call a "do-rag" on his head. All he needed, he said, was a small rag and a stick as long as his arm. Anne found the rag, I found a stick in the garden outside the *plonge,* and we followed Chef Guy as he bounded up the stairs to the landing between the second and third floors.

The nest was attached to the house underneath the sill of an unused third-floor window. Guy said he could smoke them out if he could get the towel close enough to their nest. Leaning out the window, he held the stick up toward the paper nest: "*Ç'est à ma portée,*" I can reach it, he said smiling, but Anne and I would have to hang onto him. Would he set fire to the house, Anne worriedly asked? Then, more worried: Will the angry hornets attack us? Not if I do this the right way, Guy said. He told Anne to dampen the towel, then dribbled onto it some of his lighter fluid. He was ready. Sitting on the windowsill, with Anne grasping one leg and I holding the other, as well as his belt, he leaned out and held his flaming lighter under the towel tightly knotted around the end of the stick. In seconds, it started to smoke. Quickly, with one hand clasping the window frame, he reached up and out as far as he could until the smoking rag was right under the hornet's nest. We waited; he cursed. We waited some more; he cursed some more. We could smell the smoke. "*Un peu plus longtemps,*" a little longer, he shouted. "*Tenez-moi bien*" hold onto me tightly. Then, victoriously, "*Ça y est!*" That's it! The nest was smoldering and the hornets were buzzing frantically away from it or falling dead to the ground. We quickly hauled Guy back inside, closed the window against hornets trying to escape the smoke, and, after the nest broke free and fell to the ground, went downstairs to see how successful we had been. The house showed no signs of damage and the hornets littered the ground around their smoldering nest. Guy took off his coat, unwound his scarf and do-rag, and triumphantly led Anne and I--a trio of hornet-busters--back to our task in the courtyard's heavy late-afternoon heat.

An hour or more of peeling and, Guy, without a word, abruptly disappeared into the house. A couple of moments passed. Then, splat, an overripe peach hit right in the middle of the table, lobbed from the second-floor staircase window by the devilishly smiling chef, who ducked out of sight just in time to avoid a peach flung his way by *moi, plongeur*. He bounded downstairs, then, click-click-click, sprinted through the corridor toward the *plonge*. I followed in hot pursuit, throwing and missing as he ducked out the door into the vegetable garden and around to the courtyard. Inside and out, from kitchen to *plonge* and back, ripe, juicy peaches flew and splattered, smaller versions of Marius's melons. The women were dismayed at our boyish shenanigans, though Anne did toss a few peaches at both of us.

In minutes it was over, a short and definitely sweet rumpus that ended with Guy and I cleaning up the sticky skins and juice with rags from the *plonge*. To make sure I knew who won, Guy gave me a couple of stinging snaps with a wet towel. "*Assez! Assez!* " I said. But it was not enough for him and he delivered a couple of more whips. I grabbed a towel, wet with dirty water and threatened to use it, saying loudly and close up, that this time he was the "idiot." We glared at each other for a tense moment then he clicked off back to the courtyard.

Our impasse lasted through the next day's wedding reception--the sangria was a smashing success--and a big lunch on Sunday. By late Sunday afternoon, later than usual because of the crowd, we were all exhausted. Pushing a final rack of dishes into the dishwasher, I heard behind me the clatter of trays being dumped on the *plonge* table and, for the first time that weekend, the warning: "*Ott! Ott!*" Turning, I saw Guy smiling broadly. I shouted "Hot!," emphasizing the "h," then reached for a wet towel in a mock threat as he ducked into the hallway and went back to the kitchen. We were *copains* again.

✳

At times, as I've said, I felt depressingly trapped in that restaurant, but I was never so disheartened as when I had to take several days off because my right forearm and hand ached so badly I could not sleep, and several fingers on my right hand went numb. Marius 's older brother called a doctor friend of his working in Grenoble and Marius took the day off to drive me to the hospital from the restaurant one Monday to see her. As the French were known then for taking lots of pills, I expected to receive several medications. *Pas du tout!* Not at all! After poking my fingers and arm with a pin, the doctor said I had irritated nerves in my wrist and had carpal tunnel syndrome. She gave me a bottle of vitamin B. Those pills will help, she said, but rest was the only cure. The sharp ache did diminish enough after a few days so I could sleep and go back to work, but the numbness in several fingers on my right hand did not completely go away for a year. Luckily, for both me and *Produits*, Albert had, as usual, become bored staying with his sister and returned after a week of vacation. In a reversal of roles, he took over for me at the dishwasher, but made it emphatically clear, that it was just temporary: he was still on vacation. Of course, he never offered me tips that might have prevented the return of the ache in my arm and hand. They might have been useless anyway because I did not have Albert's stolid, big-boned body. Besides, his blackened right thumb told me that no matter what technique he may have used, being a *plongeur* inevitably took a physical toll.

During my short hiatus, Marius insisted that I continue to eat at the restaurant, but I turned down his invitation––except for one memorable occasion: a Sunday afternoon gathering in the second-floor living room to mark Christian's return to his navy service. During the cake and champagne party, someone suggested a cure for my arm that the good doctor in Grenoble knew nothing about: a regional liqueur made from a variety of herbs. Locals said that it could cure anything. "*Pourquoi pas?* I said, but when I was handed the small bottle of greenish yellow liquid and saw the snake floating inside, I wasn't so sure. My startled reaction got, as expected, a burst of laughter. I took a deep breath and had a shot. I doubt if it had any medicinal effects but it packed a powerful punch that certainly made me feel better. Other than that Sunday gathering, I felt that my meals were part of my pay; if I did not work, I did not feel right eating lunch and dinner there with the rest of the crew. After morning coffee and bread, I walked into the nearby town, bought what I needed for a few days, and ate in the courtyard of the farmhouse, with Sam watching my every bite. It came as no surprise that when I went back to work, using my right hand more carefully––Albert returned to dozing in the courtyard. What surprised me was my discovery that I had missed working with *éqipe Faubert,* with being a part of the *Produits* working community.

Though I could not work during those five days, I could ride a bike. I went one evening with Marius and Rose on an easy ride into the flat countryside around the restaurant as the sun slowly disappeared far, far to the west. Looking across the fields and rivers of what felt like most of France, the sun seemed much larger and farther away than it did when I watched the day's end from the shores of the Pacific. Veiled by air golden with bits of French earth, the gigantic disc's color changed slowly from yellow to deep orange-red as it slid below the horizon. We stopped and watched in silence until it had completely disappeared, then rode slowly and in silence back to the restaurant. As we coasted along the country road back to our farmhouse home, the air still full of a magical, diffused light, the hoots of unseen owls signled our passing from the dark roadside woodland.

❄

Summer's balmy weather brought to *Produits'* courtyard the expected blossoming of wedding receptions, which often went past midnight and sometimes led to mayhem, as happens everywhere with such intensely emotional family events. Fists and knives sometimes settled deep-seated hostilities between family members of the bride and groom, or, more commonly, between relatives from the same family. Hot weather and too much sangria or Champagne usually played a part in such flare-ups. The outdoor setting was so pleasant, though, that high spirits, music and laughter generally ruled the day.

Late on an August Saturday night one of the most festive of these events sent waves of laughter down the hallway to the *plonge,* rising and subsiding with provocative regularity. What the devil was going on? To find out, I joined the rest of the crew crowded at the front door.

The younger men at the party were gathered near the pavilion, each man wearing a napkin blindfold. Their wives and girlfriends, a dozen or more, sat in a row of chairs, their dresses pulled up above their knees. At the direction of an older couple who acted as judges for the event, one man at a time, sometimes on his knees, went the entire length of the row of seated women, exploring like a *voyageur* the terrain of each woman's knees, passing from one woman to the next until, according to the rules, he succeeded in identifying his partner, which, of course, never happened on the first pass. To ensure a knee was unmistakably identified as the right one, the exploring men took great care with each knee, caressing it, feeling it with their fingertips, investigating under-knee territory, and often pushing beyond the narrow limits of the knee to the softer thigh above it, which earned the adventurer a quick slap on the hand and provoked the eruptions of laughter I'd heard in the *plonge*. Of course many of the men claimed that it was impossible to identify their mates without a second pass down the row of women. Such entreaties brought hoots and laughter from the women and, except for a few men whose gift for high drama or buffoonery earned them a second chance, were imperiously dismissed by the officiating older woman. On the other hand, when the women used every ruse in the book to befuddle the men––switching seats, changing their voices, and brazenly denying correct answers––the stern female judge laughed off her judging partner's protests by using Ivan's dismissive *Ça va. Ça va*. It was a fitting end to a festive day for the bride and groom, and for this tired American *plongeur*. It was also a lighthearted ending to my month-long tour at *Produits*. Albert had returned to his post and I returned to Grenoble for a week or so to see Ghislaine and other friends and plan my trip to Paris, where I would make one last stab at finding work that would support me.

❄

Before my departure, though, there was time for one last trip to *Produits*. On my final Sunday in Grenoble, Marius, Rose, and Emma, to my surprise, took me back to the restaurant for a proper multicourse *Produits* feast, the best the restaurant had to offer. The plan was to drive back to Grenoble late the next morning, Monday being one of the many French holidays. Marius said we would all need a good night's sleep after our *ripaille*, blowout: as usual he knew what he was talking about.

The weather was still summer warm but Autumn was in the air, signaled by the cloudy sky I knew well from my *vendange* near Macon two years earlier. The restaurant generally did not serve Sunday dinner, the exception being local friends of the Fauberts, so only a few tables were occupied. Also Madame and Monsieur were off for the day visiting friends, so Guy did himself proud for his *plongeur copain*. He and Anne, sometimes with our help, brought one course after another to the table and Olivier brought out several bottles of fine wine––without labels. During handling, some labels regularly get so torn or scuffed, he explained with a knowing smile, that the bottles could not be offered to restaurant customers. As an expert sommelier, however, Olivier knew exactly what each bottle contained. They were all superb, although I cannot recall exactly what they were nor, in fact, many other details of the meal. I know we started with a platter of several varieties of sliced ham and local *saucisson* with bread and local butter; then *crudités;* then the *plat principal-* *-a brochet,* or pike, which I think came from Canada's St. Lawrence River. One of the finest dishes the restaurant offered, it was served whole with lemon wedges in a bed of vegetables chopped up and mixed together. To crown this masterpiece Guy placed around the whole fish some spicy Louisiana shrimp. A green salad followed, then local cheeses. We ended with Anne's special *entremet,* dessert, a raspberry tart with a crust that melted in your mouth, and finally a superb brandy. The meal was incomparable, but one ingredient of the *crudités* took Marius and Rose by surprise.

During my first week as *plongeur,* I had sampled most of the items on the menu available to the staff. Special items, however, like the whole fish of my final meal and fine cuts of beef, were, understandably, reserved for paying diners. After tasting the other menu dishes, many of which were rich with butter, I yearned for my old favorite, at least for lunch: bread and cheese and what everyone came to call Sidney's *salade de Californie.* Into it went vegetables that were in season--tomatoes, raw and unpeeled carrots, radishes, zucchini, also raw and unpeeled, and cooked green beans and potatoes--with a vinaigrette, *bien entendu,* of course. Many of the vegetables, which I cut into unpeeled bite-size pieces, came from the *potager,* the kitchen garden outside the door of the *plonge.* With Guy's permission, I kept the bowl in the walk-in refrigerator, adding freshly picked ingredients from the garden every day.

The first time I brought it to the table, the Faubert's youngest son, Christian, asked me if he could try it. *"Bien sûr, serve-toi!* I said, passing him the large bowl of colorful vegetables. He bit into a chunk of carrot and with surprise exclaimed, *"Mais elles sont crus!"* they're raw. *"Mais oui, comme carottes râpées,* grated carrots, which, with grated beets and celery root, made up the *crudités* that were common all over France. (Alas, you will have trouble finding that healthy side dish on a French menu in 2020.) My carrots were not *râpées.* And my green beans were crispy, not soft. And, adding sacrilege to sacrilege, my zucchini were not peeled. This salad was definitely not *comme il faut,* neither in the way I prepared it nor nor in the way the vegetables looked in their bowl.

Guy accepted my unconventional salad, but he knew only too well that most French diners, especially at *Produits,* would only eat food that not only tasted as tradition said it was supposed to taste, but also looked the way it was supposed to look. Carrots had to be peeled and shredded (*rapées*) and *haricots verts,* those slender green beans, had to be boiled and then sautéed in butter until almost mushy. I would ask Guy to let me know when he was cooking the beans so I could scoop some out of the boiling water after just a few minutes. Guy knew that cooking beans the traditional French way destroyed most of their nutritional value--he even regretted throwing out the water in which the beans were boiled--but "*Quoi faire?*" he said with resignation. What can you do? The only way people will try something new is if I can trick them, he said.

So when Anne rolled a cart across the courtyard from the kitchen carrying the first courses--bread, butter, slices of country ham and sausages, and a platter of *crudités*--we noticed something among the carrots, and beets a kind of *crudité* we had never seen before at *Produits*-- thin, translucent slices of a light green vegetable. The most likely candidate, cucumber, would never be served as a *crudité*. We each took a few slices, along with our shredded carrots and beets, and gave it a taste. *Incroyable! Comme Guy est astucieux!* Incredible! How clever Guy is! It was the raw zucchini of my *salade Californienne*! Of course it was peeled (the French still peeled then all their fruit and vegetables) and so thinly sliced that curious and tradition-bound diners might try it and discover they liked it before they knew what it was.

❇

I did not return to *Produits* for ten years. By then, Monsieur Faubert, Albert, and Ivan had died. Guy had moved on and Anne had as well, having decided not to do another two years as an apprentice. Instead, she found work near her family's French Alpine home in a restaurant not rigorous about official certificates. Madame had retired, hiring a middle-aged chef to replace her, though she was often about, visiting with longtime restaurant patrons.

Over dinner on that return visit, Marius recalled Christmas at the restaurant, when Albert and Ivan used to join the family for a holiday feast. As the meal came to an end, Ivan, much as my mother did at Christmas, took his prized violin from an old black case he carried to the restaurant from his one-room windowless house. He knew he would be expected to play, and he was ready. Focused and serious, as if riding his Solex to Sunday service, he played at first some traditional carols, warming up his fiddle and his fingers, then took everyone on a musical journey to his vast Russian homeland, his violin singing songs that leaped and dipped with Slavic rhythms, carrying underneath their passionate exuberance a deep and poignant longing.

❄

Ghislaine had visited me once at *Produits,* driving up for a late lunch one Sunday but not staying the night. During my last days in Grenoble, because her parents had returned from their summer vacation at the family home in the mountains, we no longer shared a bed or omelets. Coffee and an occasional dinner was all we could arrange. The Sunday evening my train left for Paris, I went with Marius, Rose and Emma, to have a final coffee at Café Tribunal, *mon café.* Then Emma and I strolled along the river while her parents tended to some business at the *atelier,* soon to close. This little girl and I had, it seems, fought our way to some kind of bond, though I was unaware of it until that final meeting.

After Battle

Two years after our summer in Quercy,
we meet again in Grenoble: an American
whose improved French still carries a Belgian accent
and this girl who bears a venerable English name, though
her mother's English is still fiercely rejected.
Every day she demands
entry into my small room, tucked
into her parents' small apartment.
She demands
la bouteille jaune, the yellow bottle
of lemon-scented cream for my potter's hands.
She says I don't have the right
to be in the kitchen,
the living room, wherever
she does not want me.
She says I don't have the right

to speak English.
Her battering kicks against my closed door
say she has the right
to enter whenever she pleases.
Not until my final day in Grenoble,
when circumstances put her in my charge,
does she ease her attack, knowing, perhaps,
that I am leaving.
As we stroll the river bank,
She confides in me
some secrets of her small and growing life;
she asks me to push her on a swing;
she tells me what animals she sees in the river's swirls.
Finally,
as we walk to the train station,
she takes my hand.

At the station, I say goodby to the Fauberts, but the teary, squiggly Emma will not let me give her *grosses bises,* turning away to hide on her face on her father's shoulder. The three of them then walked back along the river toward their car, leaving me and Ghislaine, who had come from home to say goodby. I remember that we both cried––she a bit, I, enough for her to comfort me. We embraced and she gave me her usual warm hug and a soft affectionate kiss. Then, she held me at arm's length and looked straight at me, a look direct and warm, a look that ignored my *tombeur* mask and reached the me that hid behind it. It made me feel acutely anxious, defenseless and vulnerable until, after what seemed like a long time, I accepted it, more or less. Like the good psychiatrist in Paris and the girlfriend who berated me for betraying my writer self, Ghislaine gave me an invaluable gift: seeing the "me" I went to France to liberate. What she also did was allow me to see her for the warm, down-to-earth, lovely woman she was, age difference be damned. Why I have always felt the need to hide I don't know, but fear and shame about who I was (and still am?) has long been a part of it, especially the fear. During those moments at the train station in Grenoble, I felt a trust in Ghislaine and myself that did not yield to my fear of being seen: I dropped my familiar playboy mask. From those brief moments, as from those scattered earlier incidents in my life when I removed that mask, I knew that not until I let myself be seen could I begin to see others and the world around me as they are, not as my fantasized versions. Only by not hiding could I be *bien dans ma peau*. I had to stay with the fear I felt when Ghislaine looked at me, not quickly flee to the protection of a *tombeur* persona. It meant looking at and understanding the fear. Laughing at it seemed to be the place to start. Doctor Ourgoulian, I think, would agree.

❄

As a child I never wanted to leave anyone or any place I loved, like many children. I did not know how to keep that person or place with me if I left, so I denied, sometimes angrily, how much the person or place meant to me, how they enriched my life. That way I would not feel the sadness of losing them. If it were a woman, I tried to blot them out completely, as if my relationship with them had never existed. Not so with Ghislaine. I said *au revoir* to her, not the more final *adieu,* before walking in the late September light to the train to Paris, no longer, perhaps, that bereft kid on the beach who never wanted the sun to set.

Chapter 10

Au Revoir—Not *Adieu*

I arrived in Paris the following morning, disheartened and tired, and called Antoine, the Berkeley neighbor I had met again at *La Maison des sciences de l'homme* two years earlier. When I called him from Grenoble, he invited me to stay with him for a few days in the 20th Arrondissement apartment in the northeastern part of Paris where he and his wife lived. I got there before he and his wife went to work and, after a nap, made some calls in search of translation work. Antoine's wife reacted to me the way Solange had in London--instant dislike--so I spent little time with them, making it easier on all of us.

Remembering Franklin's invitation to get in touch with him when I got to Paris, I gave him a call. He invited me to dinner at his house the next night and said that in the meantime he would think about how he might help me find work. He had worked in Paris for many years and might have some useful contacts. I then went out to explore a Parisian neighborhood I knew nothing about, except that it had drawn immigrants since the middle of the 19th century.

I felt as though I were in suspension those few days, already on the plane back to California and so anxious about leaving I was unable to be fully present. All I remember is my visit to the internationally known *Cimetière de la Père Lachaise* and that dinner with Franklin. Frédéric Chopin, Gioachino Rossini, Oscar Wilde, Marcel Proust, Édith Piaf, Colette and Camille Pissarro, one of the founders of Impressionism, were all buried at Père Lachaise. Jim Morrison, the idolized lead singer of the rock band, The Doors, who died in 1971, was also buried there, his gravesite drawing large crowds even today. Morrison was a follower of all kinds of mysticism, as were the many fans who left passionate letters, soulful notes and flowers at his gravesite. His burial site was unmarked by a gravestone for several years, but after some of his more fanatical followers tried several times to dig up his body in the middle of the night, a monumental gravestone was put in place to keep the earthly remains of the singer where they belonged.

What interested me more was an inconspicuously located plaque on the cemetery wall. Against that wall, the plaque read, the last hundred and forty-seven members of the Paris Commune were shot on May 28, 1871. All were defenders against the federal troops that assaulted the workers' district of Belleville. Only one other such commemorative plaque can be found in Paris, though the savage crushing of the Commune during *la semaine sanglante,* the bloody week, was a pivotal event in modern French history. Even today people have strong differing views on what happened during the Commune government's two-month control of Paris. On May 28th, every year, people of the political left gather at the cemetery to mark that final mass execution. In 1936, in the first term of the Popular Front socialist government of Léon Blum, 600,000 supporters of the left gathered there for that annual commemoration. Much of the rest of Europe had fallen under fascist control.

❄

Franklin lived in an elegant area of Paris, comparable to the Upper East Side in Manhattan. His home was spacious, modern and comfortable. His wife, who was American and white, and their two young boys ate with us then left us to our talk about France and, more importantly, about Yale. I graduated from Yale in the late 50s and Franklin was one of three African-Americans in my class of over 700. By odd coincidence, I had worked with the other two at scholarship jobs, and in my senior year would have met Franklin as a fellow member of an informal "senior society group" if he had not taken a year off.

After dinner, Franklin, a French major at Yale, said he could do little to help me but would let me know if something came up. The two of us then started drinking B&B, a blend of fine brandy and the liqueur, Benedictine, that is 40 % alcohol. B&B will give you one hell of a hangover if you drink too much; we drank too much. The more we drank, the more we talked, or rather the more Franklin talked, about his unhappy Yale experience and his bitterness toward the white Anglo-Saxon elitism that was long supported by Yale and other universities like it.

At that time (late 1950s), Yale rejected most applicants with names that were recognizably Jewish, Irish, Italian or of other non-Anglo-Saxon Protestant backgrounds—not WASPS in other words. Minorities—Black, Hispanic, Asian—were a miniscule minority. Franklin's anger became sharper and my capacity to understand it diminished as the level of B&B in its ornate bottle neared the bottom. Finally, we staggered to bed.

The next morning, after several cups of black coffee and some aspirin, Franklin and I went with his two boys to the Bois de Boulogne. We walked together for a while, Franklin telling me of the racist remarks and hassles both his boys were having at school. The boys, who were around eight and five and light brown, could deal with the verbal taunts, but sometimes those taunts turned into physical aggression. He and his wife were not sure how to handle it, especially as the schools were not willing to do anything to stop the harassment. Then his oldest boy scooted ahead on his new roller skates and Franklin trotted along after him. I walked along slowly with the younger boy, holding his hand and asking him about school and what he liked to do. He answered each question with just a few words, never looking up at me. Then, after we had been silent for a while, and still not looking at me, he said: "I wish I was like you. " "What do you mean, " I asked. "Whiter, like you." I felt as though I had been hit in the stomach. Five years old! He was five years old! Stunned and almost speechless, I mumbled a few words that could not, of course, reach the place in him that made him feel the way he did, then we walked along in silence, still holding hands, until Franklin and the older boy, happy with his roller skates, came back to join us. I never saw Franklin again, but often wonder what happened to him and his fine young boys.

I got call backs from several of the people I contacted but the only work they offered was translating automobile manuals or mathematics textbooks. Had I been 25, I might have given it a shot for a year or so. The work, I knew, would pay barely enough for me to live in Paris, but it might have led to more interesting translation work—maybe fiction or books on film or French culture. At the age of 41, however, that was a long shot. I wanted to create a life for myself and my prospects for doing that in France were not bright.

I had come to France wanting to be a "new and improved" Sid. The French feel, of course, that wanting to do that is *dingue,* loony, expressing their views of it in many ways. For example, looking up in *Le Petit Robert,* a French dictionary, exploring the uses of the word, *tel,* in French I found this example: *Acceptez-vous tel que vous êtes,* accept yourself as you are. To find that in a dictionary certainly surprised me, though undoubtedly not a French person. Did I learn to accept myself in France? Looking back at what I have written here, I think with the help of Ghislaine and others--I at least got a start. This book is another step in that direction. But why was that an issue for me in the first place?

Perfect parents, of course, don't exist. I was also a difficult teenager. The most self-destructive way I undermined myself was to try to live up to my father's expectations, impossible to satisfy, as are those of many fathers who do not actually see their sons, but rather what they want their sons to be. But way before I had to deal with those expectations, something rebellious stirred in me that I was too young to understand very well. As I mentioned already, I broke out with German measles when, in my white suit, I was about to receive my first communion to confess the wickedness every seven-year-old possesses; and chicken pox when I was about to be confirmed. My body, thank God, knew that the Church was not for me, but it took years for my mind and emotional self to catch up.

I plodded along through prep school, deviating from the khaki pants–sport coat norm only once in a while, intent on getting a scholarship that would take me away from home and West Hartford. By the time I graduated from Yale, I knew I did not want to be part of the Irish-American world of my parents nor of ethnocentric New England. (The French had *métro, boulot, dodo;* the *métro* to work or *boulot,* then home to *dodo,* sleep; New England had ethnicity, religion, and university.) I also felt deeply conflicted and confused about being a "Yalie," as generally understood then. Educationally, two classes I took at Yale forever opened my mind to a larger and richer world, no question about that. They also taught me that I only do well at whatever I do if it excites me intellectually and emotionally engages me.

My all-male prep school and Yale had prepared me to be a certain kind of person, as did my life growing up Catholic. Neither one offered a model that fit me. Of course, at seven, or ten, I could not toss off the fetters of Catholicism easily; it took years to be rid of them. I had certainly learned to act like a "Yalie," and realized that whenever I did, it opened certain doors and made me attractive to certain women. I was too naïve to understand that I could put on that "Yalie" guise when it suited me-- literally and figuratively. Instead, I felt I had to jettison it entirely.

My seemingly rudderless voyage through life, however, was a reflection of my not feeling *bien dans ma peau,* of not building a life based on a solid emotional foundation. Strangely, though--especially to me--I felt absolutely sure of myself whenever I worked with language, an assurance I also had working with clay, film, and photography--feeling confident in my judgment when involved with any of them. Working in those areas, I seemed to know things emotionally and physically. In my reluctance to make any of those fields the center of my life, especially writing, I betrayed myself, as my ex-Paris girlfriend painfully, angrily, and pointedly reminded me.

Accepting my abilities and my passion for what made me feel most alive meant accepting myself, which turned out to require a courage I lacked most of the time. Most people struggle with finding that courage all their lives, since its emotional roots are in our earliest days. Later we keep trying to get it from others, which is surely futile and often leads to poor decisions, betrayals, depression, tears, and loneliness. Especially loneliness. Only when we stop looking to others do we begin *être bien dans notre peau*, to be at home in our own skin, the fundamental French birthright.

I did not cry leaving France this time. Instead, my feelings were much like those I had years before when I went back to Connecticut from California. Then, I was twenty-four and determined to return to San Francisco in my '52 Plymouth as soon as I could. This time, in 1976, I was forty-one, and no Plymouth could whisk me across the Atlantic Ocean. Of course, going back to this country I had become so attached to was possible, but only if I said goodbye cleanly, treasuring my experiences, the people who became my friends, and the inevitable sadness at leaving. To do that, I had to realize that I was no longer the adolescent *tombeur*, the role I persisted in playing, but the Sid Ghislaine saw at the Grenoble railroad station. I then might find a life in California that would make returning possible, *n'est-ce pas?*

Usually in France, when you sneeze, people say *Salut*, an equivalent to our "God Bless You." Sometimes, however, someone will say "*A tes amours,*" to your loves. Your response is "*Que les tiens durent toujours,*" may yours last forever. Writing of my life more than 45 years ago leaves for me no doubt that France is a love that will last forever. How could I not feel that way about a country that offered me the gift of so many wonderful French people, but also such an affectionate exchange on the occasion of a common sneeze.

Epilogue

If you got this far, you might be wondering if I pulled it off, if the man Ghislaine saw at the Grenoble train station became more and more present, less and less dependent on the *tombeur* mask. The Sid who is *bien dans sa peau* began more often to get the better of Sid the *tombeur* but at times it has felt like a hopeless battle. Swimming in San Francisco Bay through the Dolphin Club--the membership a gift from my former wife, Laura, that I can never repay--continues to give a fighting chance to that me without a playboy mask.

Acknowledgements

No author writes a book without lots of help. Many friends and fellow writers were generous with their counsel and suggestions about the manuscript as I worked to give it its final form. Without their kind and perceptive words this book would have made its modest appearance on the public stage with far less grace. I am grateful most of all to friend and fellow writer, Fred Raker, who goaded and supported me through a long process, to Stephan Crawford, Tim Holt, Bill Pieper, John Gregg, Anja van Ditmarsch, Stan Teng, Lisa Carson, Richard Louis Perri, Peter Darlington, and Sharane Darlington.

Made in the USA
Middletown, DE
18 May 2022

65777868R00144